THE ECONOMICS
OF DISTRIBUTION

WITH AN
INTRODUCTORY CHAPTER FROM
The Evolution of Modern Capitalism

By

JOHN. A. HOBSON

First published in 1900

British Library Cataloguing-in-Publication Data
A catalogue record for this book is available
from the British Library

"OVER-CONSUMPTION"
CONSIDERED AS CAUSE OF DEPRESSION.

A CHAPTER FROM
The Evolution of Modern Capitalism
BY J. A. HOBSON

It is of course quite possible that a temporary over-production in one or several trades may be explained by a correspondent under-production in others—that is to say, there may be a misplacement of industrial enterprise. But this can afford no explanation of the phenomenon Depression of Trade, which consists in a general or net over-supply of capital, as evidenced by a general fall of prices.

In like manner it is possible to explain a commercial crisis in a single country, or part of a commercial community, as the reaction or collapse following an attempt to increase the quantity of fixed capital out of proportion to the growth of the current national income, by a reckless borrowing. This attempt of a single country to enlarge its business operations beyond the limits of the possible savings of its own current income, Mr. Bonamy Price and M. Yves Guyot speak of under the questionable title of Over-consumption. Since they tender this vice of over-consumption as the true and sufficient explanation of commercial crises, it is necessary to examine the position.

Professor Bonamy Price applied the following analysis to the great crisis in the United States of 1877:—

"We are now in a position to perceive the magnitude of the blunder of which the American people were guilty in constructing this most mischievous quantity of fixed capital in the form of railways. They acted precisely like a landowner who had an estate of £10,000 a year, and spent £20,000 on drainage. It could not be made out of savings, for they did not exist, and at the end of the very first year he must sell a portion of the estate to pay for the cost of his draining. In other words, his capital, his estate, his means of making income whereon to live was reduced. The drainage was an excellent operation, but for him it was ruinous. So it was with America. Few things in the long run enrich a nation like railways; but so gigantic an over-consumption, not out of savings, but out of capital, brought her poverty, commercial depression, and much misery. The new railways have been reckoned at some 30,000 miles, at an estimated cost of £10,000 a mile; they destroyed three hundred million of pounds worth, not of money, but of corn, clothing, coal, iron, and other substances. The connection between such over-production and commercial depression is here only too visibly that of parent and child. But the disastrous consequences were far from ending here. The over-consumption did not content itself with the wealth used up in working the railways and the materials of which they were composed. It sent other waves of destruction rolling over the land. The demand for coal, iron, engines, and materials kindled prodigious excitement in the factories and the shops; labourers were called for from every side; wages rose rapidly; profits shared the upward movement; luxurious spending overflowed; prices advanced all round; the recklessness of a prosperous time bubbled over; and this subsidiary over-consumption immensely enlarged the waste of the national capital set in motion by the expenditure on the railways themselves. Onward still pressed the gale; foreign nations were carried away by its force. They poured their goods into America, so over-powering was the attraction of high prices. They supplied materials for the railways, and luxuries for their constructors. Their own prices rose in turn; their business burst into unwonted activity; profits and wages were enlarged; and the vicious cycle repeated itself in many countries of Europe. Over-consumption advanced with greater strides; the tide of prosperity rose ever higher; and the destruction of wealth marched at greater speed."[172]

Now, in the first place, our analysis of saving and the confinement of the term consumption to direct embodiments of utility and convenience forbid us to acknowledge that the action of the United States or the analogy of the improving landowner is a case of over-consumption at all. If the landowner borrowed money on his estates in order to live in luxury for a season beyond his income, or similarly, if a State raised loans in order to consume powder and shot, the term over-consumption rightly applies. But where the landowner borrows so much money to improve his land that he is unable to hold out till the improvements bear fruit, and must sell his land to pay the interest, he is not rightly accused of over-consumption. His reduced consumption later on while practising retrenchment is simply a process of "saving" which, when complete, is to take the place of an amount of "saving" previously made by some one else and borrowed by him. What happened was simply this. A, wishing to drain his land, had not "saved" enough to do it; B has saved, and A, borrowing his "saving," holds it for a time in his shape of drainage. If he can continue to pay interest and gradually "save" to pay off the capital, he will do so; if not, as in the case supposed, B, the mortgagee, will foreclose and legally enter upon his savings in the shape of "drainage" which he really owned all along. But even if A in this case were rightly accused of over-consumption, this over-consumption must be considered as balanced by the under-consumption of B, so that as regards the community of which A and B are both members there is no over-consumption.

Now, precisely the same line of reasoning applies if for the individual A we take the country of the United States. If it tries to increase its factories, machinery, etc., in excess of its ability to pay, it can only do so by borrowing from other countries; and if it cannot pay the interest on such loans, the "savings," in the shape of fixed capital which it has endeavoured to secure for itself, remain the property of the other countries which have effected the real saving which they embody, assuming them to have a value. If the action of the United States be called over-consumption, it is balanced by an under-consumption of England, France, or other countries of the commercial community. Mr. Price sought to avoid this conclusion by saying nothing about the individual from whom the landowner or the country from which the United States borrowed in order to increase the fixed capital. But as the landowner and the United States, *ex hypothesi*, did not make their improvements out of their own savings, they made them out of somebody else's savings, and that conduct which is styled over-consumption in them is balanced by an equal quantity of under-consumption in some other party. If thus we look at the individual landowner or the single country of the United States, we might say, accepting Price's view of consumption, that he and it were guilty of over-consumption, and that this was the cause of the commercial crisis. But since this over-consumption is absolutely conditioned by a correspondent under-consumption of some other member of the industrial community, it is not possible to conclude with Professor Price that over-consumption can even for a time exist in the community as a whole, or that such a condition can be the explanation of a crisis commonly felt by all or most of the members of that community.

What actually happened in the case of United States railways was that a number of people, either in America or in Europe, under-consumed or over-saved: their excessive saving could find no better form to take than American railways, which, *ex hypothesi*, were not wanted for use. A number of persons who might have made and consumed three hundred million pounds' worth more of corn, clothing, coals, etc., than they actually did consume, refused to do so, and instead of doing so made a number of railway lines, locomotives, etc., which no one could consume and which were not wanted to assist production. What occurred was a waste of saving power through an attempt to make an excessive number of forms of capital.

Even if, some years later, many of these forms obtained a use and a value, none the less they represent an excess or waste of "saving" to an extent measured by the normal rate of interest over that period of time which elapsed before they fructified into use. In a word, what had happened was not over-consumption, but under-consumption.

M. Guyot appears to think that in the community as a whole too much saving can be put into the form of "fixed" capital and too little into circulating capital, and that such a condition of affairs will bring depression. "Fixed capital," he says, "cannot be utilised if there is no available circulating capital. Ships and railways are useless if there are no commodities for them to convey; a factory cannot be worked unless there are consumers ready to buy its products. If, then, circulating capital has been so far exhausted as to take a long time replacing, fixed capital must meanwhile remain unproductive, and the crisis is so much the longer and more severe."[173]

To this there are two sufficient answers. The prevalence of low prices for goods of various kinds as well as for plant in a time of depression, the general glut of goods which forms one phase of the depression proves that the crisis does not arise from storing too much saving in plant and too little in goods. Where there exists simultaneously a larger quantity of plant, raw material, finished goods, and labour than the industrial society can find use for, no assertion of maladjustment, either as between trade and trade, country and country, fixed and circulating capital, will afford any explanation. Secondly, M. Guyot gives away his entire position by admitting "a factory cannot be worked unless there are consumers ready to buy its products." A "consumer" here can logically only mean one who buys finished goods for personal use, and if this be generally applied it amounts to a clear admission that under-consumption is the reason why there appears to be a glut of capital, fixed or other.

FOOTNOTES:

[146]Contemporary Review, March 1888.

[147]Report on Industrial Depressions, Washington, 1886.

[148]Report, pars. 61-66.

[149]Report, par. 106.

[150]Contemporary Review, July 1887.

[151]Contemporary Review, March 1888.

[152]Report of the Commissioner of Labour, Washington, 1886, pp. 80 to 88.

[153]D.A. Wells, *Contemporary Review*, August 1887.

[154]Lord Playfair, in the *Contemporary Review*, March 1888, gives a number of interesting illustrations of recent economies in transport and manufacture.

[155]Statist, 1879, quoted Bowley, *England's Foreign Trade in the Nineteenth Century*, p. 80.

[156]Essays in Finance, vol. i. p. 137, etc.

[157]For the view that over-consumption is cause, see Appendix II.

[158]"What is annually saved is as regularly consumed as what is annually spent, and nearly in the same time too; but it is consumed by a different set of people." (*Wealth of Nations*, p. 149*b*, McCulloch.) "Everything which is produced is consumed; both what is saved and what is said to be spent, and the former quite as quickly as the latter." (*Principles of Political Economy*, Book I., chap. v., sec. 6.)

[159]An able analysis of the nature of "paper savings" is found in Mr. J.M. Robertson's *Fallacy of Saving*. (Sonnenschein.)

[160]Chap. v. § 5.

[161]Bk. III., chap. xiv. § 3.

[162]The stock of a small retailer will not, however, in all cases vary proportionately with the aggregate sales of all classes of goods. A small shopkeeper, to retain his custom and credit, is often required to keep a small stock of a large variety of goods not often in request. If he sells them rather more quickly, he does not necessarily increase his stock in hand at any particular time.

[163]It likewise determines the quantity of plant and stock at *a*, *b*, *c*, *d* down each of the perpendicular lines, for the demand at each of these points in the production of plant and machinery is derived from the requirements at the points A, B, C, D, E. The flow of goods therefore up these channels, though slower in its movement (since in the main channel only goods flow, while fixed capital is subject to the slower "wear and tear"), is equally determined by and derived from the consumption at F. The whole motive-power of the mechanism is engendered at F, and the flow of money paid over the retail counter as it passes in a reverse current from F towards A, supplies the necessary stimulus at each point, driving the goods another stage in their journey.

[164]Böhm-Bawerk, *Positive Theory of Capital*, p. 67. See Appendix I. for conflict of opinion among English economists.

[165]Principles of Political Economy, Bk. I., chap. v. § 3; see also Bk. III., chap. xiv. § 3.

[166]It should be noted that an increased amount of consumption in the future does not necessarily compensate for a disturbance of the current balance of saving and spending, for an *increased proportion of future income* will have to be spent in order to compensate.

[167]It must be borne in mind that many articles of utility and enjoyment must in their final processes be produced for immediate consumption. The "saving" of perishable goods is confined to a saving of the more enduring forms of machinery engaged in their production, or in some few cases to a storing up of the raw material. So likewise that large portion of productive work termed "personal services" cannot be antedated. These limits to the possibility of "saving" are important. No amount of present sacrifice in the interest of the next generation could enable them to live a life of luxurious idleness.

[168]Ruskin, *Unto this Last*, p. 145.

[169]This does not necessarily imply a stimulation of new saving. A fuller vitality given to existing forms of capital will raise the quantity of real capital as measured in money. Mills and

machinery which have no present or future use, though they embody saving, have no value and do not increase real capital.

[170]Scope and Method of Political Economy, p. 162.

[171]Production and Consumption, chap. iv. § 2.

[172]Contemporary Review, May 1879.

[173]Principles of Social Economy, p. 245. (Sonnenschein.)

PREFACE

THIS work endeavours to construct an intelligible, self-consistent theory of Distribution by means of an analysis of those processes of bargaining through which economic distribution is actually conducted, the results of industrial co-operation being apportioned to the owners of the factors of production in the several stages of production.

The chief difficulty lies in coördinating the different factors of production, so as to bring the payments made respectively for the use of land, labour, and capital under a common law of price, and in showing that the same economic forces which determine the market and normal prices of commodities are applicable to the sale of all these uses of the factors of production.

The extension to all these cases of the terminology and modes of measurement hitherto confined to land, or extended tentatively and by analogy to certain other factors, involves a complete restatement of some of the problems of wages and interest. But this unification of the different processes of economic payment has long been felt to be necessary to the construction of a satisfactory theory of distribution, and various approaches in this direction have been made. This work claims to go farther and to reach a common law of price applicable to every sort of sale.

Some of the reasoning is difficult because it involves a necessary abandonment of commonly accepted terminology and the establishment of a new system of economic notation. If, however, the reasoning is valid, it establishes certain important theoretic conclusions, some of which are fraught with large. implications in the direction of progressive politics.

In particular, it claims to prove that all processes of bargaining and competition, by which prices are attained and the distribution of wealth achieved, are affected by certain elements of force which assign "forced gains" and other elements of "economic rent" to the buyers or the sellers. There is thus established the existence of a large fund, partaking of the nature of those monopoly and differential rents, long ago recognised in the case of land, which furnish no stimulus to voluntary industrial energy, and which can be taken for public service by taxation without injury to industry.

Much of the material of this work was given in the form of lectures to students of the London School of Economics and Political Science in 1897, and parts of several chapters have appeared in the *Harvard Quarterly Journal of Economics*. Since receiving the first proofs of this book, a little volume has come into my hands, entitled "The Theory of Wages," by Mr. H. M. Thompson, which works out independently some of the main points of my criticism of current theories, in particular of the fundamentally erroneous doctrine that "Rent does not enter into the Expenses of Production."

JOHN A. HOBSON.

CONTENTS

THE ECONOMICS OF DISTRIBUTION

CHAPTER I.

THE DETERMINATION OF A MARKET-PRICE.

§ 1. "I am unaware of any rule of justice applicable to the problem of distributing the produce of industry," wrote Professor J. E. Cairnes, and it is common to find in modern economic treatises general expressions of dissatisfaction with existing methods of apportioning wealth among those who have contributed to its production. But there is little agreement as to the nature of the defects in present modes of distribution, nor does the analysis of economic processes commonly adopted by those who indulge in these expressions of dissatisfaction fully justify any such general condemnation. The economic power of landowners, the establishment of trade monopolies or combinations, the weakness of poorer classes of labourers in bargaining with employers, are commonly regarded as defects of the existing industrial order. But the recognition of these defects is quite consistent with a conviction that the general and normal tendency of competitive industry makes for a fair and satisfactory

1

distribution of the fruits of industry. For the specific defects named above are seen to be closely associated with restraints of competition, and may plausibly be regarded as exceptions which by no means justify a general condemnation of the justice or utility of a system' of distribution based upon freedom of competition.

§ 2. In order to test the character of distribution fairly, we must study it under normal not under exceptional circumstances, and in its constituent acts. Distribution is composed of, or achieved by, transactions which, for lack of any better term, we call bargains. Much investigation has taken place of certain classes of bargains, particularly in reference to sales of the use of the factors of production, and special laws of rent, wages, interest, have been founded upon these studies. The general effect of these studies among earlier economists was to break up the unity of industry: first, by suggesting that bargains for the use of land, of capital, and of labour-power were subject to radically different laws ; secondly, by failure to relate these laws of the value or the price of the factors of production to the laws which were found to determine the price of the commodities which they contributed to produce. More recent economic writers have made considerable advances toward the integration or unification of a theory of Distribution, by relating the theories of determining the price of the several factors through an extension of the law of differential rents, and by a scientific formulation of a theory of value which is applicable to the determination of all prices, alike of uses of factors and of commodities.

But the completion of this work of unifying the theory of Distribution has been delayed by a refusal of economists to investigate sufficiently the nature of the bargain *per se*, so as to find what is common to its different species. So far as England is concerned, this refusal is due to a visible reluctance among students to engage upon purely deductive or speculative problems, except within a certain narrow field of mathematical analysis. The dominance of the historical spirit on the one hand, and the rapid advance of specialisation in economic study on the other, have unduly drawn attention from the root-problems of deductive economics, which are too often assumed to have been solved, or not to be worth the trouble of solution. To these influences I chiefly attribute the small amount of intellectual energy devoted to the investigation of the process of bargaining which lies at the base of the theory of Distribution.

Such study requires the moderate use of a method which is peculiarly disfavoured by English economists of the present day, and is stigmatised as "Crusoe economics." This recent revolt against speculations, which were barren or illusive because they commonly proceeded from false premises, has

gone too far. Such speculative analysis, with all
its dangers, is indispensable to the social sciences.
The conditions of inductive reasoning from experi-
ments, which exist in many branches of physical
science, are here notoriously lacking, and to supply this defect a process of fictitious experiment
is substituted, supposititious cases being framed
where unessential circumstances are eliminated, so
as to enable us to see more clearly the working of
certain simple forces.

To study problems of price or value, by plunging into the full intricacy of actual business, is not
really a practical but a most unpractical method.
To go back to a thoroughly uneconomic condition
is usually unprofitable; but to take, first, cases
true to the essential facts of life, though contained
in a simpler setting of circumstances than that in
which they are actually found, and afterward to
introduce the excluded circumstances gradually,
in order to see what difference is wrought, — such
substitute for the experimental method of the
physical sciences is both defensible and highly
profitable as a mode of gradual approach toward
a real issue. This method I propose to adopt in
opening up the nature of a bargain.

§ 3. Bargains are found commonly in clusters at
a market-price, being acts of sale or exchange at
this common rate. It is therefore first essential
to understand how this common price-point is
determined.

If A wishes to sell a horse and B is the only buyer, it is evident that, if the highest price B is willing to give does not reach the lowest point A is willing to take, there can be no price and no sale.

A asks £20 and fixes reserve at £15.

B offers £8 and fixes reserve at £12.

A's offers, <u>20 19 18 17 16 15</u>

B's offers, <u>12 11 10 9 8</u>

Next suppose A willing to take £15, while B is willing to give £18. If a sale takes place, the price will obviously lie in the common ground between £18 and £15. But at what point and how is the point reached? Professor Hadley assumes that a point will be reached and thinks it is determined by "relative skill in bargaining." [1]

A, <u>20 19 18 17 16 15</u>

B, <u>18 17 16 15 14 13 12 11 10 9 8</u>

But this attainment of a price by "skill of bargaining" implies ignorance of each other's mind in the case of A and B, or either. If A knows or thinks that B will go to £18 and B does not know that A will sell at £15, A will stand firm at £18 and get that price; if, *per contra*, B knows that A will sell at £15 and A does not know that

[1] Hadley's *Economics*, p. 73.

B will go to £18, B gets his horse at £15. If neither knows but each suspects the other will go further, "bluff" is the determinant; the bidding proceeds until either A or B believes that any further demand will outstep the limit set by the other in his mind and will lose him the bargain. The determinant here is superior cunning, or, as Hadley says, "skill in bargaining." Or it may be that while A is willing to sell at £15, he may know or suspect that it is more important for B to obtain the horse than for him to sell, in which case he is in the position to extort £18.

So far we have no element of competition : the process by which a price is reached, if it is reached, is one of bargaining from beginning to end.

Now introduce the competitive element upon one side of the transaction. A, the happy owner of the horse, which he will sell for £15 or as much more as he can get, is faced by B and C, who both want the horse and are furnished with effective demand in the shape of cash. Now B and C either set the same limit-price upon A's horse, or they set a different limit-price. If it is equally important to both to get the horse, and they are possessed of equal pecuniary resources, they may conceivably be both willing to bid up to £18 for the horse. In such a case it is a matter of absolute indifference to A whether, after making B and C bid against each other up to £18, he sells to B or to C. Indeed, the casuist would rightly argue that, since he could not sell to both, and there was no more reason why he should sell to one rather than to the other, he could not sell at all; but would stand like the Ass of the Fable, who starved to death as he stood at an equal distance from two equally attractive bundles of hay. But elbowing aside our casuist and allowing A to effect a sale at £18 to either B or C, guided by some personal preference or the prospects of future business with the respective parties, it is plain that the competition between B and C has simply placed A in the same position of bargaining superiority as he would occupy in dealing with B alone, on the assumption that he knew the limit-price B had set himself, while B did not know his limit-price. The actual price reached would assign to A the whole gain of the bargain, less the minimum required to compensate B or C for the trouble of bargaining.

But the chance of B and C fixing the same price-limit and adhering to it with equal persistency is infinitely small. In the actual business world we may take it that the two competitors fix a different price-limit, —

A, 20 19 18 17 16 15
B,   19 18 17 16 15 14
C,   18 17 16 15 14

B's limit is £19, and C will not go beyond £18. Here it will be evident that competition does not fix the price-point, but only a lower limit of price. The price actually reached cannot be less than £18, because B and C will bid against each other up to that point. It may be anywhere between £18 and £19 ; and the actual point will be determined, not by competition, but by those same forces of skill and force in bargaining which operated in the earlier case.

§ 4. Now arises the question : Is the method of determining a price essentially different when we place upon both sides of the transaction a number of genuine competitors, in other words, when we institute a free market ?

What is the determination of a market-price? It is curious to observe how the text-books of English economists have, almost without exception, shirked or slighted this practical question, hurrying the reader to the more abstract consideration of a normal price, and contented, as was Mill, to explain any particular divergence of market-price from normal price by vague reference to temporary fluctuations in supply and demand, which kept market-prices oscillating round a normal price, giving the advantage now to sellers, now to buyers.[1]

It has generally been considered a satisfactory account to say that the competition between owners of supply on the one hand and exercisers

[1] J. S. Mill, *Principles of Political Economy*, Bk. III, Ch. II, § 4.

of demand on the other hand will equalise supply and demand at some point of price. This is Mill's contribution toward the theory of a market-price,[1] and it may be said to be generally received in English economic text-books as a sufficient description of a market-price. Professor Marshall, in discussing the price of the corn market, finds it to be such as would "exactly equate supply and demand."[2] Professor Hadley, in his recent book, is content to say that "the market-price of an article under the modern commercial system is the price at which the demand is equal to the supply."

Now such a statement is doubly unsatisfactory. It neither defines a market-price nor explains how a market-price is actually reached. It furnishes no real answer to the question of the celebrated Oxford Professor who was reported to stop his friends in the street in order to ask them why a silk hat cost 20*s.* The text-book answer to this question consists in showing that the price of a silk hat cannot be 21*s.*, because in that case supply would be in excess of demand, there would be too many hats and too few people to buy them, and the competition of sellers would reduce prices; conversely, the price could not be 19*s.*, therefore 20*s.* is presented as a point of convergence between two opposing prices which reach at that

---

[1] Cf. *Dissertations and Discussions*, Vol. IV ("Thornton").
[2] *Principles* (2d ed., p. 392).

point a temporary equilibrium. The supply of hats was equal to the demand at 20*s*.

This statement that a market-price is one that equalises supply and demand explains nothing. What we want to know is why this equilibrium occurs at 20*s*. English economists have commonly shirked the direct significance of this question, which requires an investigation of the actual process of equilibration in a market, and have either betaken themselves to an examination of the costs or utilities which lie behind demand and supply, or to the logomachy regarding the meaning of these terms themselves. It is indeed too true that some economists have so used the terms "demand" and "supply" as to beg the question of an equilibration. "We desire," says Cairnes, "to know the circumstances which determine price; and we are told that the selling price is always such that the quantity of a commodity purchased in a given market is equal to the quantity sold in that market."[1]

[1] *Leading Principles,* p. 113. Cairnes, however, is wrong in imputing this fault of reasoning to J. S. Mill, though the latter, in the passages in which he expressly defines demand, is ill-advised in his language. In the formal definition (Bk. III, Ch. II, par. 3) he identifies demand with "quantity demanded." Unfortunately the expression might mean "quantity bought," or it might mean "quantity which buyers would be willing and able to buy at a given price." In a second passage (Bk. III, Ch. XVIII, par. 2) demand is held to mean "the quantity of it (commodities) which can find a purchaser," an expression involved in the same ambiguity, for it might be held that only

Where demand is equivalent to quantity demanded in the sense of quantity bought, and supply to quantity supplied or sold, it is evident that the boasted Law of Supply and Demand becomes nothing else than an identical proposition.

But while Cairnes was right in insisting upon the need of an exact explanation of the process by which supply and demand are equilibrated in a price, he was himself unable to throw any further light upon the process than to suggest that the final result depended upon "higgling of the market."

§ 5. The closest formal inquiry into the operation of two-sided competition in a market is that of Böhm-Bawerk. I propose here to take his illustration of the market and to present his reasoning in what I think is a simpler form than that found in his book.

A, B, C, D, E, F, G, H, are sellers of horses. All the horses are supposed to be of the same worth, and all the sellers to have an equal knowledge of the market. They have, however, minimum or reserve prices, which vary from £10 in the case of A, to £26 in the case of H.

the quantity actually sold "can find a purchaser," or it might include whatever quantity could be sold at a price, assuming it to be offered at that price. Mill's context and general treatment of a market-price, however, makes it pretty clear that he did not mean by "quantity demanded" quantity actually sold, but quantity which buyers were willing to buy if they can find sellers willing and able to sell at a price.

I, J, K, L, M, N, O, P, Q, R, are buyers in the market, with maximum prices which vary from £15 in the case of I to £30 in the case of R.

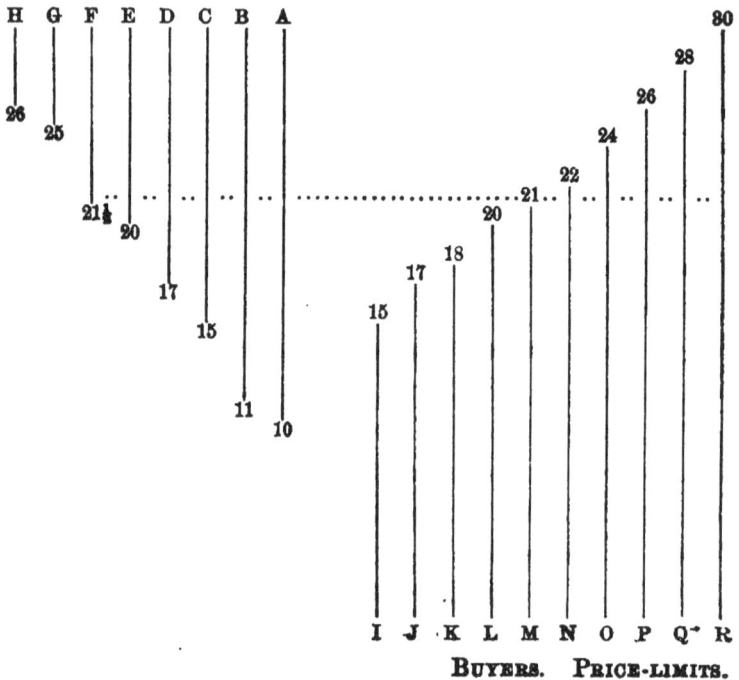

SELLERS.   PRICE-LIMITS.

BUYERS.   PRICE-LIMITS.

Let bidding open at £10. At this point only 1 will sell; 10 would buy, and since none will let the other have a bargain, they will overbid. At £11 there are 2 sellers, but the competition of 10 buyers will not allow a sale at that point, and bids still rise ; at £15 there are 3 sellers, but the other 7 will not allow 3 of their number to buy horses at £15, that sum being less than they would consent to give. At £15 10s. one of the buyers has dropped out, his limit-price having been exceeded, but there are still 9 buyers against 3 sellers; these 3 sellers could not fix a bargain with 3 of the buyers because, as they were settling it, the other 6 buyers, finding that they would be left in the cold, would offer better terms and upset the proposed bargains. At £17 10*s.* another seller enters in, and another buyer has dropped out, but there are still 8 buyers against 4 sellers, and no bargain can be struck. After £20 is passed, another seller will have entered, and another buyer have fallen out, leaving 5 sellers faced by 6 buyers. This state continues up to £21. A sale cannot take place, because the would-be excluded buyer, the odd man, will fasten on to any of the 5 possible sales and force up the price. If £21 is passed, however, this inconvenient odd man drops out, leaving 5 sellers and 5 buyers. Each man can make his bargain at £21 1*s.*, for 5 are willing to sell, 5 to buy, at that price. But though 5 would sell at £21 1*s.*, they would rather get more if they can; they can get more, for all 5 buyers would sooner pay up to £22 than fail to buy a horse. But if the sellers put up the price above £21 10*s.*, a 6th seller would enter the field, and there would be 6 willing sellers against 5 willing buyers — a state of things which would force the price down below £21 10*s.*

So whereas at any point just over £21 10*s.* there would be 6 sellers and 5 buyers, at any point just under £21 there would be 6 buyers and 5 sellers. In neither of these conditions is a price possible. On the other hand, at any point between £21 10*s*. and £21 there are 5 sellers and 5 buyers, and 5 sales can be made satisfactory to each party. In other words, supply and demand are equalised between £21 10*s*. and £21.

Competition of buyers on the one hand and sellers on the other hand has thus fixed rigid limits for a market-price.

But to fix limits for a price is not to fix a price, and curiously enough Böhm-Bawerk leaves his analysis at this interesting point. The bargain is made possible at any point between the valuation of the most capable of the excluded buyers, M, as lower margin, and the most capable of the excluded sellers, F, as upper margin ; but there is nothing in this analysis to show where it will lie between these margins. Indeed, we may say that if this were the whole process, no price could be fixed at all and no sale would be possible, at any rate by economic settlement. The unerring logic of competing self-interest which has found the price-limits will not find the price-point between those limits. The competition which was so effective when 6 sellers faced 5 buyers, or 5 buyers 6 sellers, seems to collapse when 5 buyers face 5 sellers, and there is no odd man to throw his weight on to an impending bargain. As far as Böhm-Bawerk's analysis is carried, there is no more reason for the market-price being fixed at one point between the limits rather than at any other point. Indeed, we appear to be landed in the same serious logical difficulty which encountered us before. The 5 sellers would like to get a price as near as possible to £21 10s., the 5 buyers a price as near as possible to £21: here we have a real discrepancy of interest between the parties and no machinery of competition to settle it.

We must plainly recognise that if the sellers and the buyers in this case were really acquainted, not merely with the outward condition of the market but with the subjective valuations which each of them puts upon the act of sale, no sale could be possible by economic means. If the sellers can fix the price near the upper margin, the advantage of one of the buyers is reduced to a minimum, and the whole body of sellers get the best of the bargain ; if the buyers can force the price to near the lower margin, one seller has his advantage reduced to a minimum, and the buyers get the best of the bargain. Why should either party give way? There is no economic method of reaching a price-point here ; it would be necessary either to agree to split the difference or to " toss-up," neither of which can be reckoned an economic settlement. This, we may take it, is not what would really happen, for the subjective valuations of the various buyers and sellers will not be known to one another. Although, in his elaborate analysis of two-sided competition, Böhm-Bawerk does not even indicate how the price-point is reached, he has hinted in an earlier treatment of "one-sided competition" which exhibits the same difficulty that the price-point will depend upon "skilful bargaining."[1] In other words, the work of competition is not to find a price, and there is no such thing as a "competition price": competition stakes off a ring, within which bargainers fight it out by force and craft. Taking our present instance, it seems essential to the fixing of a price that one of the bargainers should deceive the other as to the real facts of the case (*i.e.* as to his subjective valuation), leading the other to suppose that he will not give way any further. For instance, one of the sellers will conceal the fact that he would be willing to sell at £21, and will hold out for £21 9s.; one of the buyers believing him, and fearing to be left out in the cold, will show his willingness to accept; thus the bargaining at any price below £21 9s. will once more partake of competition, since only 4 sellers face 5 buyers, and the equation of buyers and sellers is thus falsely placed at £21 9s. By such fraud or force of superior bargaining the price-limits are drawn together so closely as to approximate toward a money-point, and the "standing out" of one of the 5 sellers may fix the price for all 5 sales at £21 9s. Some such

---

[1] *Positive Theory of Capital*, p. 200.

practice of fraud or force seems necessary to achieve a price-point.

Now, turning to those who have taken part in the process of determining a market-price, we can assign a different part to several groups.

(*a*) First come the ineffectual buyers and sellers whose limits have been too high and too low for them to take part in an actual sale. In this group fall G and H among sellers, I, J, K, and L among buyers. The desires and actions of these persons have had no influence whatever on the market or the price; their absence would not have caused any difference.

(*b*) Next come the effectual buyers and sellers, whose subjective limits lie above and below the limits within which a price-point is fixed, and who, though they take part in the bidding of the market, have no direct influence upon the price. These are A, B, C, D, among sellers, O, P, Q, R, among buyers.

(*c*) Thirdly come those members of the market whose subjective valuation fixes the possible limits within which 5 sellers would be willing to sell and 5 buyers to buy. Böhm-Bawerk holds that this group should comprise E and F among sellers, M and N among buyers, for he holds that the action of these two pairs fixes the upper and lower limits. "The upper limit is constituted by the valuation of the last buyer who actually exchanges (the last buyer) and that of the most capable seller excluded (the first excluded seller), and the lower limit by the valuation of the least capable seller who actually effects a sale (the last seller) and that of the most capable buyer excluded (the first excluded buyer)." So we get, he says, the very simple formula, "The market-price is limited and determined by the subjective valuation of the two marginal pairs." [1]

According to this, the upper limit is fixed by the valuation of F, the first excluded seller, and N, the last actual buyer : the lower limit by the valuations of M, the first excluded buyer, and E, the last actual seller. But N's exact valuation, £22, neither fixes nor helps to fix the upper limit, for if his valuation, instead of £22, had been £21 11*s*., it would have made no difference. Similarly, E's valuation at £20 does not help to fix the lower limit, for if, instead of being £20, it had been £20 19*s*., it would have made no difference.

It seems therefore that the valuation of N and E had no direct influence upon the limits which are determined directly and exclusively by the valuations of M and F.

(*d*) Lastly, within the price-limits we have the action of one of the effective competitors in assuming the attitude which draws the price to a point. There is, of course, nothing to inform us which one adopts this attitude. We will assume that it is

[1] *L.c.*, p. 209.

E, the last actual seller, whose limit-price is £20, and who perhaps may be considered the stiffest bargainer and the most likely to hold out for a price just below £21 10*s.*, which after all will give him a less subjective gain than will fall to any of the other sellers whose limit valuation is lower. Or else we may suppose that N, whose subjective gain is smallest among the buyers, makes the successful stand, and, cajoling the sellers into thinking he will not buy at a price much over £21, fixes the price just above that point.

§ 6. Our analysis, if correct, yields information upon two important matters : first, as to the method of determining a price or exchange-rate in a market ; second, as to the distribution of gain arising from a series of bargains at a market-price.

As to the method of determining a price, it proves (*a*) that competition does not fix a price, but only the approaches to a price ; (*b*) that within the limits a price-point is fixed by the superior bargaining power of a single buyer or seller.

As to the distribution of advantage arising from the series of sales at a market-price, that is seen to depend, first, on the superior force or cunning (bargaining power) of one of the buyers or sellers ; second, on the differential valuation of the several buyers and sellers as measured from this price-point.

According to the conditions of this market, a far larger aggregate gain is obtained by the sellers, because the market-price, whether fixed near £21 or near £21 10*s.*, widely exceeds the supposed limits of several sellers. At £21 price, the aggregate gain of the buyers stands at £25, whereas the gain of sellers stands at £32. If £21 10*s.* is the price, the buyers' gain falls to £22 10*s.*, and the sellers' rises to £34 10*s.*

No provision evidently exists, in the process of determining a price, for an equal or "fair" division of the advantage of exchange. In no case where a sale takes place at the market-price will the advantage to the two parties effecting the sale be equal. In every sale there must be some advantage to both parties, but it will not be equal. If the price stands at just under £21 10*s.*, N, the last effective buyer, will gain just over 10*s.*; while E, the last effective seller, will gain a little less than £1 10*s.* Whatever be the actual arrangement which couples the respective buyers and sellers making the 5 sales, no one of these 5 sales will give an equal gain to the two parties, though to both parties in each case there must be some gain.

§ 7. The net result of the investigation is to show that the gain which accrues to buyers and sellers in a market consists of two elements. First there is the difference between the higher and the lower limit of price, representing, in the case taken above, nearly £1 in each transaction. This is distributed according to the force or skill of the strongest among the buyers or sellers. It is not easy to decide how this gain may be most conveniently described. Regarded from the standpoint of origin it ranks as a "forced gain"; in so far as it denotes an advantage common to the whole body of buyers or sellers in the market, as distinct from the particular gains which accrue from differences of individual valuation, it may be spoken of as a "specific gain." It will be necessary to use both these terms in describing it.

The sellers and buyers, whose valuations lie beyond the limits within which the price is fixed, take in addition to the portion of this specific gain which may or may not fall to them, a differential gain which represents the difference between their individual valuation and the upper or the lower limit, according as they are buyer and seller.

For instance, on the assumption that the market-price was fixed at £21 9s., A would obtain a gain of 9s., representing the "forced" or "specific" element as measured from the lower limit of £21, and a gain of £11, representing the difference between £10, the least sum at which he would have sold, and £21, the lowest price which ordinary competition rendered possible.

Economic literature has, of course, made us very familiar with the idea of differential gains, classed commonly as producers' and consumers' rents, but the existence and nature of the other element, viz. forced gain, which clearly emerges from the analysis of market-price, has not received the attention it deserves.

It may be said to represent the failure of competition, alike in theory and in practice, to fix a price. If the competition between buyers and sellers were able to determine a price-point, the weakest buyer and seller would alike gain a minimum advantage from the sale, and there might be said to be a tendency toward an equal distribution of the differential gains of the bargain for the other parties. But the fair field of competition is seen to be incapable of reaching a market-price, and gives way in the last resort to that same arbiter of fraud or force that is seen to fix a price when a single buyer is bargaining with a single seller.

§ 8. In other words, if the example taken above is a sound one, force is the ultimate determinant of a market-price.

But is the example sound ?

Proceeding along our sliding-scale of instances from a primitive bargain, have we yet reached the true conditions of a modern market, and is the market-price really determined in the manner above described ?

It is evident that the example does not correspond to any actual or possible horse-market. It assumes that 8 horse-dealers are each offering for sale a horse which they all believe, and which all of the prospective buyers believe, to be of exactly equal quality, and that, this being so, the dealers yet differ so widely in their limit-price that while one is only willing to sell at £26, another will sell a horse he knows to be of equal worth at so low a sum as £10. An actual horse-market will offer a supply of horses, no two of which are estimated at the same worth by buyers or by sellers, and there will not be any close agreement as to that worth by any two of those taking part in the market ; neither will the actual conditions of bargaining be such that each knows what offers the others are making, unless the sale is of the nature of an auction, which really removes the case from a two-sided competition and places it among the one-sided competitions.

An actual horse-market, in which the several buyers and sellers bargained with one another, would not in fact result in the attainment of an exact market-price for a given quality of horse ; the prices actually paid not merely would fail to distribute equally the subjective gains of the bargains, but there would not be the objective equality afforded by our theoretic instance of equal money prices for equal "value." The individual craft of bargaining, the acts of concealment and of bluff, would, in fact, play a larger part than in our case. Taking the aggregate gains of a series of bargains in such a market, the differential element would be much smaller than in the theoretic case, and the "forced gain " much larger.

Böhm-Bawerk makes his differential gains dependent upon subjective valuations. In the case of horse-markets this is specious, at any rate, so far as buyers are concerned. But in ordinary trade markets, where the buyers buy to sell again, an objective basis of differential gains must exist. A can only value the same goods at 20% more than B, because he enjoys some trading or manufacturing advantage (objective) which enables him to put what he has bought to a larger *productive* use.

But these practical considerations do not appear to me to invalidate the general correctness or to destroy the serviceable results of the analysis. Our example has legitimately excluded minor conflicting circumstances ; all the material facts have been set in a clearer atmosphere, which enables us rightly to detect the real nature of the bargaining process.

§ 9. But there is one circumstance in the selected example which it is important to discuss. A horse-dealer must sell a whole horse at a time, and the buyer cannot buy less than a whole horse. In other words, the separate units of supply are dumped down into the market within distinct and fairly wide intervals of valuation between the several units. The last horse that is sold differs from the first horse that is not sold by a definite considerable sum, no less than 30s. Now if, instead of 8 horses valued at different intervals between £10 and £26, we had an infinite number of horses, it will be admitted that the competition (which I fear, however, would take an eternal time to compass) would bring the upper and the lower limit to a meeting-point (*i.e.* the interval between them would be infinitely small).[1] In that case the marginal pair would make their bargain upon equal terms without any element of " forced gain " entering the market-price.

Now this supposition that in a finite market there may be, not 8 or 80, but practically an infinite number of units of supply, valued at extremely minute intervals of difference, is not a pure work of the imagination, but is approximated to in certain markets. There is no possible interval between 1 horse and 2 horses in a supply of horses, but there is an indefinite number of possible intervals between 1 pound and 2 pounds of gold in a supply of gold. In the case of goods which are infinitely divisible, we might regard the supply in a market at any given time as consisting of an infinite number of

---

[1] Jevons, in his *Theory of Political Economy* (Ch. IV), plainly enforces the truth that the theory of competition, as determinant of price-point, rests upon the supposition of infinite divisibility of supply (cf. p. 108). In fact, the whole mathematical treatment rests upon the same supposition, and the fact that supply is not, in any case, infinitely divisible, impairs the practical service of the whole mathematical treatment.

units whose valuation in the minds of the sellers grades down by imperceptible intervals from the highest to the lowest limit-price. Such goods are gold or corn or cotton.

The importance of this is that, by taking our example of a market from such classes of goods, we seem to reach a market-price by pure competition of buyers and sellers. Look, for instance, at the local corn-market which Marshall uses to illustrate the determination of a market-price. Here we have a number of farmers, each (say) with 100 quarters of wheat to sell, and a number of corn-factors, who are buyers in this market. At a price of 36s. all the farmers would be willing to sell all their stock, but few, if any, buyers could be found at such a price: if 35s. was a possible price, most farmers would sell all they had; but a few would hold back part of their wheat, thinking to sell at a future market for 36s. Each lower price would, of course, reduce the effective supply and increase the effective demand; the price actually reached, say 27s., secures the so-called equilibrium of supply and demand, i.e. sellers are willing to sell (say) two-thirds of their wheat at 27s., and buyers will buy that same amount at 27s.

Now such a market differs in two respects from our horse-market. First, as to the units of supply and demand. In a horse-market less than 1 horse cannot be bought or sold; 1 horse is thus a minimum unit of supply; a dealer with 10 horses cannot offer to supply more than 10 alternative quantities. But a farmer with 100 quarters of wheat is owner of a much more elastic and divisible supply; though for purposes of rough reckoning he may divide his stock by tens of quarters and reckon it worth his while to sell 100 at 36*s*., 90 at 34*s*., and so on, there is nothing to prevent him calculating more minutely; in theory, at any rate, he would be willing to sell 79 quarters at a slightly lower rate than he would take for 80, in a rising market. At any rate, it is easy to see that there is a far greater elasticity in supply and in demand in a corn-market than in a horse-market, a far greater variety of possible prices with a far narrower interval between them. This signifies a far closer and more effective competition between buyers on the one hand and sellers on the other, the result being that the limits between which ordinary competition breaks down are much narrower.

The second point of difference is even more important. It consists in the fact that a local corn-market is in far closer touch with a wide world-market than is the local horse-market. Where commodities are in wide and general demand, valuable in proportion to their bulk and weight, so durable that they can be carried far without risk or waste, they are the subjects of a world-market. This means that wherever they are sold the price attained at any day in any local market is not determined wholly 'or chiefly by the present local supply and demand, but by the general supply and demand the world over. Not merely the 1000 quarters owned by the sellers, or the £1500 or so of purchasing power owned by the buyers, compete and find an equilibrium : both sellers and buyers are also influenced, in the quantity they offer or buy at the several prices, by the quotations from the wider market upon which the total, not merely of existing but of prospective, supply and demand of wheat is operating.

So in a local corn-market the possible limits of competition are circumscribed by conditions imposed from the national market, or those great centres where national economic forces are most fully operative ; while the national market is in its turn kept within tolerably small limits of fluctuation by the international market which takes close account both of the present and the probable future stock of wheat and the demands for the same.

§ 10. Every local market, even for highly perishable and cheap bulky commodities, is of course to some extent affected by wider market-areas, and to some extent by the general supply and demand of similar commodities. But, in respect of many commodities, this outside contact is so slight and slow that prices are chiefly the resultant of local forces of supply and demand. Common bricks or plums, for instance, will have a large number

of little market-areas, the prices of which may
vary widely. In the small local markets sellers
of bricks or plums have little power of withhold-
ing their supply or disposing of their goods elsewhere, while buyers are similarly restricted in
their demand : hence the pressure of local or
temporary circumstances, favouring either buyers
or sellers, will play a larger part in determining
a market-price, genuine competition will tend to
break down at any earlier point, and force or
superiority in bargaining-power will be a more
important factor. On the other hand, in the
market for gold, or even for cotton, wool, or
wheat, under normal conditions, buyers and sellers in a local market are less under pressure to sell
here and now, to buy here and now : the whole
world-supply, present and prospective, is taking
part in the competition as it affects each local
market, and the local market-price reflects the
greater delicacy and complexity of the world-
market. What this signifies is that in commodities belonging to a world-market, free competition
may be said to determine the price, because the
number of actually or potentially competing units
is so numerous that little scope remains for that
force or craft of special bargaining which plays
a considerable part in the small local market.

In fact, where the local market is in such close
and constant organic relation to the world-market,
the price attained in any part tends to be not

merely a market-price, but a normal price, that is to say, a price which will average the economic conditions of supply and demand over the whole present market, and, by discounting probable changes in future supply and demand, will similarly average the series of temporal prices.

For instance, in the market for gold or for leading securities of any kind, if the competition of buyers and sellers worked freely and were not constantly checked and falsified by the manipulation of rings of speculators, market-prices would tend to become average or short normal prices. The same is true of all goods for which there is a world-market. The competition here is between a vast number of competing buyers and sellers, whose units of supply and demand represent an indefinitely large variety of different equilibriums: under such circumstances competition would do its work so well that any local group of buyers and sellers would find there remained very little for the higgling of the market to achieve.

§ 11. When we have one of these wide highly organised markets, maintaining a genuine competition between very large numbers of buyers and sellers dealing with large quantities of divisible goods, the competition of buyers and sellers brings the price-limits so near together as to appear to establish a price-point. In theory, the case of the horse-market still applies, and a bargain under conditions of duress fixes the price-point here as elsewhere; but the influence is so slight that it may be practically ignored.

Moreover, in the cotton or the wheat market not only is this element virtually eliminated, but the differential gains of various buyers and sellers are reduced to much smaller dimensions than in the local horse-market. The markets which are in this highly organised state are generally those in which buyers and sellers are among themselves fairly on a level : sellers are producing under such equality of conditions that the supply sold at a given price yields a fairly equal profit to the different sellers; while buyers, as in the cotton or corn market, are buying not for use, but to sell again in some form or other under conditions which tend to equalise the subjective gains made on their bargains. The different buyers and sellers of raw cotton at Liverpool, at a given price, may be held to have made a subjective gain which will not differ widely in different cases, unless where the seller acts under some special pressure of financial circumstances.

§ 12. Whenever a market contains a considerable number of buyers and sellers, fairly equal in economic resources and in knowledge of commodities; where sellers obtain their supply under fairly equal conditions of trade or manufacture, where buyers are buying to sell again, not to consume; where the articles bought and sold belong to a wide market, are minutely divisible in quan-

tity and durable in nature, — these conditions
may be held practically to eliminate force from
a market-price and to make it the result of competition alone.

But these conditions are notoriously absent in
the great majority of cases. Take a rapid sur-
vey of the whole range of bargaining, examining
the various classes of goods as they exchange
hands in the different processes of production ; in
how many cases are the above-named conditions
present?

Take, first, the great extractive industries; consider the bargains made by farmers, miners, fish-
ermen, etc., with the merchants who buy their
produce or the railways that carry it; the constant attempts of shippers, importers, and produce-
exchange speculators to corner supply and to
operate in prices ; the advantages which superior sources of supply, patents or secret methods
of production, combinations to restrict output or
regulate prices have in most organised manufactures ; the oscillation of local corners and cut-
throat competition in most branches of retail
trade, — these and similar causes render the conditions of free and fluid competition inoperative
over the vast majority of the processes in the sale
of goods. Again, if we turn to the bargains for
the sale or hire of land, the conditions are notoriously absent. When we investigate the conditions under which bargains for the use of capital

take place, we shall perceive how narrow are the limits of the free field of investment where borrowers and lenders meet on equal terms. As to that huge class of bargains which take place at every spot in the industrial field for the sale of labour-power, in hardly any cases can we find the conditions of equal bargaining present, even where professional skill or other highly placed labourpower is the object of sale. Outside the ordinary range of industry, in cases where bargaining is between author and publisher, between mistress and domestic servant, between teacher and parent, hotel-keeper and guest, the competition is so slight and indirect, the knowledge of the two parties so imperfect, that an equal bargain is never struck except by chance.

It appears then that but a very small proportion of bargains can be referred to an open-faced, two-sided competition in a market where outside prices are so directly operative as to equalise the gain for the individuals who take part as buyers or sellers in the market.

§ 13. This brief investigation of the economic conditions of a market-price warrants the following conclusions : —

(1) Every economic buyer and seller in a market (*i.e.* every one guided by self-interest who knows what he is doing) makes some gain from his bargain. The notion supported by thinkers of such diverse character as Bacon and Ruskin, that

in a trading bargain "what one man gains another loses," receives no warrant from our analysis. It must, however, be admitted that in every series of bargains at a market-price, one of the buyers or sellers will make his bargain on such terms as will secure to him a bare minimum gain.

(2) There is nothing in the economic nature of a Market to secure equality of gain for any two bargainers.

(3) The amount of gain which comes to each will depend on three conditions : (i) the superior strength or skill of one final bargainer ; (ii) the ability of competition between buyers and sellers to fix the limits within which this strength or skill may operate ; (iii) the difference between the reserve-price of each buyer and seller and the actual price attained.

(4) Where the market-area is of wide space and time, differential estimates and power of bargaining will be of relatively small importance; where the market-area is narrow, they will be of relatively large importance.

APPENDIX TO CHAPTER I.

The Relative Strength of Buyer and Seller.

The analysis of the process of bargaining shows that sometimes the buyers, sometimes the sellers, are in the stronger position and are able to "get the better"

of the bargain. No law of direct and general application assigning this superiority of bargaining power is
discernible, but certain conditions are found to attach
to specific markets, which evidently make in favour
of one or other of the two parties. Setting aside for
separate and fuller treatment the markets for the sale
of the use of land, capital, and labour, and confining
ourselves here to markets of commodities, we find the
relative strength of buyers or sellers often associated
directly with (*a*) the greater or less urgency of the
need to buy or sell, (*b*) the greater or less strength or
skill in the art of bargaining.

Where the buyer does not buy for personal consumption, he is generally held to have an advantage in the
process of bargain or exchange, partly because he is
the holder of money — the least specialised commodity — pitted against the holder of some specialised
commodity, partly because the urgency of a trade-
use is less than the urgency of a personal need. But
where the buyer is a direct consumer, this advantage
is often more than offset by the present pressure of
personal needs which obliges him to buy now from some
one who is not obliged to sell now. So, for example,
the venders of refreshments or books in a railway
station enjoy a distinct advantage in bargaining.
The general rule, however, assigns superiority to the
ownership of money, which for many commercial
purposes is more desirable than a nominally equivalent value in specialised wares. It seems strange
that the advantage of the extra stability of value and
exchangeability attached to money should not be
fully discounted in actual prices; but it is found in

practice that any owner of goods for sale who names their "value" "would rather have the money." If, however, the consumer who cannot delay consumption is liable to the disadvantage attending a forced purchase, the producer under modern commercial conditions is often subject to the inconvenience of a "forced sale," either because his expenses of production are incurred on credit (*i.e.* he needs money to pay for raw material bought with bills, to pay interest on borrowed capital or mortgage, or to pay wages or other current business expenses), or else because the goods he has to sell spoil or lose value by being kept. A striking example of a class of producers subject to the conjoined force of these disadvantages is the agriculturist, but all sellers of quickly perishable goods are liable to this handicap.

If the owners of money be held to have an advantage as compared with owners of goods for sale, the sellers of raw materials which are needed for many different industrial uses, and of other less specialised commodities, will seem to have an advantage in selling to various groups of buyers who, because they belong to different trades, will not act closely together. The seller of timber, wool, or iron (other things equal) seems to hold a stronger position than the buyer. It is, however, possibly incorrect to attribute the greater desirability of holding money over holding goods to the general command over commodities attaching to the latter. For if there were a ready and perfectly reliable demand for goods, their possessors, though one step further removed from the ownership of any other class of commodities than the possessors of money, would have a compensation for this remoteness by owning something of more direct service in consumption. If the owner of corn or wool or leather could rely upon the speedy sale of his goods at a calculable price, his command over commodities in general would not really be weaker than that of the owner of money, but only a little slower in its operation. In that case the buyer who offered money could not be deemed to be to any appreciable extent the stronger bargainer. It is therefore the uncertainty of finding a purchaser at a calculable price which must be accounted the weakness of the seller as compared with the buyer. This weakness is plainly enhanced by certain tendencies of machine-production and machine-transport, which seem to keep many markets in a constant or a frequently recurring condition of congestion: the eagerness of sellers to find purchasers is attested both by the extraordinary energy in pushing and advertising goods and by the cutting of the marginal profits upon each sale to a minimum. The wide prevalence of these conditions is irrefutable proof of an admitted weakness in bargaining on the part of owners of goods as compared with owners of money.[1] This superiority, perhaps normal over a

[1] It is curious that Mr. and Mrs. Webb, who, in the chapter on "The Higgling of the Market" of their *Industrial Democracy*, emphasise and illustrate so powerfully the superior position of the buyer "at each link in the chain of bargaining," fail to perceive that no other "economic" explanation of this fact is possible than that a general excess of producing power exists beyond what is required to supply the current demands of consumers. If it is a fact that "at each link in the chain of bargainings the superiority in 'freedom' is so overwhelmingly on

large field of industry, may be modified by the nature
of the money-offer of buyers. Where credit is freely
given, the buyer loses part of his advantage as owner
of money — a fact which may be otherwise expressed
by saying that a buyer will bid higher when he need
not pay ready money.

The mode of bargaining or the conditions under
which bargains are made have much to do with the
success of buying and selling. It may be broadly
stated that makers are at a disadvantage in bargaining with traders, in so far as the art of bargaining
forms a larger part of the trader's activity, so that he
must be deemed more highly specialised in dealing.
Where the productive processes are conducted under
conditions which remove the producers from wide commercial training, and especially where, as in farming,
they are not themselves large buyers of raw material, ·
etc., the merchants or dealers who buy their produce
have a clear advantage. Purchasers of retail goods are
in this respect at a disadvantage in comparison with the
sellers. They are less effective bargainers in so much
as they must be regarded as amateurs bargaining
with specialists for any particular class of goods they
require for consumption. Again, the conditions under
which the retail market is commonly conducted tend

the side of the buyer that the seller feels only constraint;" if
"it is highly significant that it is always the seller who bribes,
never the buyer" (Vol. II, p. 676), this can only signify a constant tendency for the effective supply of markets to exceed the
effective demand, only another way of stating the fact of an
excess of producing power. It is significant that Mr. and Mrs.
Webb have no economic explanation to offer of the curious
phenomenon they note.

to secure this advantage to the retailer. As Cairnes points out: "In the wholesale market the sellers and purchasers meet together in the same place, affording thus to each other reciprocally the opportunity of comparing directly and at once the terms on which they are severally disposed to trade. In retail dealing it is otherwise. In each place of sale there is but one seller; and though it is possible to compare his terms with the prices demanded elsewhere by others, this cannot always be done on the moment, and may involve much inconvenience and delay." ("Leading Principles," p. 112.)

One of the peculiar advantages of the large over the small business in manufacture is that the scale upon which the large business is conducted enables it to employ skilled specialists in buying and in selling.

These are differences in the economic strength or the skill of bargaining. One further point bearing upon the process of bargaining deserves mention, viz. the relative disadvantage of the party who names a price. In retail shops the habit of ticketing goods, of using price-lists, or even of naming a price upon request, gives to the buyer a certain advantage, the nature of which is apparent from our analysis of the horse-market. The bargainer who at the outset names a price gives some indication of his subjective valuation; the buyer might be willing, if necessary, to pay a higher price than that named, if both parties were equally ignorant of the estimate they set respectively upon the bargain. In open bargaining it is a clearly recognised point of skill to get the other party to name a price, even though that price has little or no chance of being satisfactory to both parties.

Finally, it must be remembered that, where the conditions of a perfect market exist, in the sense that all buyers have the same valuation and all sellers likewise, while the knowledge of the arts of bargaining and other special advantages are equally divided, the issue is determined by numbers. In such a case one side (that with the shorter number of competitors) will get the full gain of the bargain, the price being determined at or close to the higher or the lower limit. A reference to the case of the horse-market set forth in the text will make this evident. Change the conditions of this market so as to present 10 willing sellers at a minimum price of £20 a horse and 9 willing buyers who would consent, if necessary, to pay £21, the price will be at or just above £20, because the tenth seller, afraid of failing to effect a sale, will, by competition, beat down the price to that point. This consideration means that under existing industrial conditions, where there are generally more willing sellers at a price than willing buyers, the latter enjoy a normal advantage.

CHAPTER II.

§ 1. Before proceeding further with the analysis of market-price and the element of forced gain
contained in it, it is desirable to clear some misapprehension which attaches to the differential
gains which play so prominent a part in the analysis. Differential rents have received much attention from economists in their investigation of the
relations of producers and consumers. Now these
producer's and consumer's rents, as they are called,
have been a source of grave misapprehension, by
reason of the mode of measuring them, which has
been generally adopted. The nature of this error
will be best understood by examining concrete
examples.

Take the instance of the passengers who purchase tickets for 32s. 8d. to go from London to
Edinburgh by a particular train. Here we have
a number of buyers who pay the same price for
their tickets, but who, presumably, will differ
widely in the importance which they assign to the
purchase of a ticket. A is reluctantly leaving
business at an awkward time in order to visit his

41

relatives, and we may assume that if the price of
a ticket were any higher than 32*s*. 8*d*., he would
refuse to go.   He ranks as the marginal buyer,
whose differential gain or rent is *nil*.   Turning to
the other extreme we find B, who will make a
business profit of £1000 if he can put in an appearance at Edinburgh within a certain number of
hours.   B would pay for a ticket any sum short of
the whole difference between 32*s*. 8*d*. and £1000,
if he had no option.   His differential gain, therefore, appears to stand at (say) £998.   This is the
common mode of measuring producer's and consumer's rents.   Yet it is plainly fallacious.   For
B's supposed gain of £998 upon his transaction
with the railway is derived truly, not from that
transaction, but from a certain business advantage
he obtains in a business bargain in Edinburgh.
This sum will evidently appear as a differential
or a specific gain in the market to which the latter transaction belongs, and if the purchase of a
ticket to Edinburgh stands as a separate action, the
same gain will be counted twice.   This is clearly
inadmissible.   The fallacy consists in a false independence assigned to the purchase of the ticket.
This purchase is in reality one of a number of
acts complementary, or, in this case, subsidiary, to
the business transaction from which the gain
of £998 emerges.   In order to reach Edinburgh
in time, he may be obliged to send a telegraph, to
take a cab, and to make sundry other small out-

lays; each of these may be a necessary means to his end, in which case, according to the accepted mode of estimating differential gains, the £998 will be counted over again many times. Evidently this method of detaching each transaction is illicit. A number of related actions must be taken to form an organic group, and the true differential gain will be the net differential gain upon the group. The business custom which would reckon the price of the ticket and other incidental outlays as expenses, to be deducted from the gain of the transaction toward which they were contributory means, is clearly the logical mode of procedure. Where expenses may be incurred, partly on their own account, because they contribute some direct satisfaction to the spender, and partly as a means to secure some ulterior gain, it may be difficult or even impossible to make a true assignment of differential gains. A business man's expenditure during a given time may not easily break up into separate groups centring round some distinct business "deal"; even where a large number of transactions are clearly recognised as incidental, the main deals, from which the "gains" directly proceed, may be closely connected or mutually dependent.

But, however difficult it may be in practice to find the true group-unity in a number of dealings, theory requires that we reckon differential gains upon the group, and not upon a falsely isolated item.

.The fallaciousness of the separatist treatment is still more glaring when we take the common instance of the differential gain attributed to the purchaser of some necessary of life. Each time a man buys his necessary supply of food or clothing, he can appear to make a differential gain measured by the difference between the price he pays and the price he would be willing and able to pay if he were compelled to do so. "All that a man hath will he give for his life," so that the difference between the price actually paid and the total possessions of the purchaser will rank as differential gain *on each occasion* when a necessary is bought.

§ 2. These reflections seem to require important modifications to be made in the treatment of producer's and consumer's rents. The common presentation of consumer's rents assigns to the consumer a rent upon that portion of his income spent as necessaries, which is infinitely great when measured in utility, and which, when measured in money, is equal to the whole of the remainder of his income which he would have consented to add to the price actually paid for necessaries, had he been compelled to do so. So, if we suppose a case of a man spending an income of £400 a year, the first £100 going for necessaries, the second for conveniences, the third for comforts, the fourth for luxuries (taking the convenient distinction usually made), the consumer's rent obtained on the outlay of the first £100 would be £300, upon the second £200, and upon the third £100, while the last can yield no consumer's rent, for he had no reserve out of which he could have paid a higher price for the luxuries he bought. Such analysis yields a consumer's rent of £600 out of a total expenditure of £400. Taking a nicer discrimination in the relative subjective valuations of different portions of each group of goods, we should, of course, obtain a more complex measurement (all luxuries, for instance, except the least valued, yielding some rent); but the rough estimate will serve to illustrate our point, which is this : If the man be supposed, at any given time when he is making a purchase, to have at his command his whole income of £400, on each separate occasion when he buys a weekly store of necessaries he will appear to make a consumer's rent, measured by the difference between what he pays and £400, and the net rent during the year will depend upon the number of times he buys necessaries. The same will hold of his other non-necessary purchases. Or again, if this man has £100 saved in the bank, this £100 will rank as rent every time he makes a purchase of necessaries, for he would and could pay it in addition to the price he actually pays, rather than go without a necessary. This also will hold of his other purchases, of conveniences, etc., for he would consent to pay a portion at least of his saved £100 rather than fail to get them.

It is evident from this that the assignment of a consumer's rent upon a particular purchase is illicit. A consumer's rent can be rightly reckoned only by considering the totality of purchases over a given period and the totality of the current income during such period. When, therefore, Professor Marshall says,[1] "The excess of the price which he would be willing to pay rather than go without it, over that which he actually does pay, is the economic measure of this surplus pleasure, and may be called consumer's rent," his definition is doubly fallacious. In the first place, the mere *willingness* to pay cannot be a source of consumer's rent, nor indeed does Professor Marshall intend that it shall be so understood. The willingness to pay must be backed by the power to pay. But this power to pay, as we have shown, cannot be rightly reckoned upon the single purchase. In order to measure it, we need to take a related group of purchases, and if we are dealing with rent derived from the expenditure of an income supposed to cover a period of time, the group must consist of the whole number of purchases within that time.[2]

---

[1] *Principles*, Bk. III, Ch. VI, § 1.

[2] Professor Nicholson (*Principles of Political Economy*, Vol. I, p. 58) effectively discloses the illusory nature of the attempt to measure total utility by price.

§ 3. It may, indeed, be questioned whether this mode of reckoning, thus logically forced upon us, does not invalidate the utility of consumer's rent altogether. For if we suppose that (*a*) either the whole of the year's purchases are made at a single time with the whole of the year's income, or that (*b*) each piece of income as soon as it is received is laid out in a purchase, it will appear that no consumer's rent emerges, either upon the totality of purchases in the one case (*a*), or upon any individual purchase in the other case (*b*); for in neither case is there any residue of money in the hands of the purchaser which he could and would have paid rather than fail to get what he buys. If I spend my income literally as fast as I receive it, no consumer's rent emerges. It is only the spare cash in my purse after I have made a purchase, all or part of which constitutes consumer's rent: if my income were doled out to me for each specific purchase, though my income over a period of time were just as large, no consumer's rent could appear.

One qualification to this conclusion seems to be required. If I do not spend, but save, a portion of my income, that saving rightly appears as consumer's rent, even when the totality of purchases is set against the total income; for I would have sacrificed the whole of this saving rather than have dispensed with a necessary, and some of it rather than go without a convenience.

I suggest, therefore, that savings may be the only legitimate consumer's rent, when we take an organically related group of purchases measured over a period of time and compare them with the income received during that time.

It may, indeed, be arguable that the term "consumer's rent" should continue to be applied to the £300 which our man would have consented to spend upon necessaries, had he been obliged to do so; but there seems little advantage in this application of the term. Our first rude reckoning of consumer's rent upon the supposition that the first £100 of an income of £400 was spent on necessaries, the second £100 on conveniences, the third on comforts, and the fourth on luxuries would, we found, yield a total rent of £600,— £300 on the first, £200 on the second, and £100 on the third division. But this reckoning must also be discarded, for it is evidently just as illogical to make an artificial severance of expenditure into four groups, and to treat the whole income as if available for each group, as it would be to take the whole £400 into account whenever a single purchase of a necessary or a convenience was taking place.

If it is still held convenient to retain the category of consumer's rent, it must be understood that, in the instance we have taken, the total consumer's rent on purchases during the year will only amount to the £300 spent on other things than necessaries. Thus conceived, consumer's rent will be measured, not on the individual transaction, but upon total expenditure over a period of time, and will be equivalent to that portion of the income which is either spent on other things than necessaries, or is saved.[1]

§ 4. Now let us turn to producer's rent. The excess of price actually obtained over the price which the seller would have consented to take forms producer's rent. Differential advantages for production may be said to be the origin of these rents in competitive trade. Let us suppose that among cycles competing for sale at £18, the most expensively produced cost £15 to make, while some others — made by makers enjoying superior economies of production — may be produced at £12; in this case £3 ranks as producer's

[1] This conclusion may be illustrated by a more detailed examination of the illustration of consumer's rent Marshall takes (Bk. III, Ch. VI). He takes the case of a man who buys 7 tons of coal at £1 per ton. This man would have paid £10 rather than fail to get one ton, £7 rather than fail to get a second ton, £5 for a third ton, £3 for a fourth, £2 for a fifth, 30s. for a sixth. Since he only pays £1 for each ton, his consumer's rent on the 7 tons amounts to £22½. Now, though none of this cost can rank as a "necessary" (for in that case he would have been willing to pay the whole £7 + £22½ for the first ton), it ranks as a prime convenience of life. When, therefore, we say that this man would have willingly paid £22½ more in order to get the coal, we mean that he would have sacrificed the other comforts or luxuries upon which he has already spent £22½ (or the £22½ savings, if he has saved it). But if, instead of coal, we took bread or any necessary, it is

rent. At first sight this rent seems to be calculable upon a single act of sale, but it is not really so. For this maker can produce at £12 not the , particular cycle which is sold for £18, but this cycle in conjunction with a large number of others. It is only produceable at £12 as one unit in a large output. Thus the consumer's rent of £3 is based upon an assumption involving a large number of other sales. Expenses of production cannot be taken as any definite amount in reference to a single sale, just as utility of consumption reckoned in money cannot be taken as a definite amount in reference to the purchase of a single consumable.

The true basis of calculation for producer's rent will be the total output of a particular business over a period of time, as in the case of the

easy to see that this same £22½, plus all the part of his income spent on conveniences, comforts, and luxuries, will figure as consumer's rent upon the purchase of bread. Let him have an income of £1000 a year, £40 of which is spent on necessary food, the rest of the £960 will appear as consumer's rent upon purchases of food, for he would have paid it all rather than fail to get the food. This same sum, or part of it, cannot rightly be reckoned over again as more consumer's rent upon coal and other commodities which the consumer appears to value at a higher price than he gives.

The total consumer's rent cannot exceed £960, and would, in fact, appear to correspond to that portion of his income spent upon non-necessaries, including any savings he might make.

Marshall's mode of reckoning would enable the same money income to count over and over again, as often as a purchase was made.

consumer's expenditure of income. So the net profit on a given business over a month or a year may be legitimately taken as the basis of measurement for a producer's rent.

The term "net profit" is proverbially ambiguous. The producer's rent, however, may be taken to be any excess of profit that may accrue in a business during a given period over and above the minimum profit required to induce the continued application of industrial power. This excessive profit doubtless emerges in each act of sale; but it cannot be rightly calculated on the separate sales, since the expenses of production of one article are organically related to those of other articles. The true producer's rent thus represents the money value of a differential economy of production, as compared with the economy of the least effective producer competing in the market, and is estimated upon the total business over a period of time. The true consumer's rent represents a differential economy of consumption, expressed in the money value of that portion of consumption and saving which takes place during a given period, over and above the necessary margin of subsistence. Thus we place the two rents in line with one another: the producer's rent measured from a marginal expense of production (*i.e.* the smallest sum necessary to recoup the costs of production of the portion of supply produced under the least favourable circumstances); the consumer's rent measured from a marginal expense of consumption (the smallest sum necessary to maintain the consumer's life under the least favourable circumstances).

§ 5. Consumer's rent is sometimes stated in direct relation to reductions of price of a commodity. For instance, a fall in the marginal expenses of producing cotton goods represented in a fall of prices is described as yielding a consumer's rent. This treatment, however, involves an assumption of the stability of money income of consumers which is not legitimate. It may be that a fall in price of commodities is also an economic cause of a fall of income to a class of consumers ; in that case the fall of price does not yield to members of this class a true consumer's rent, for the margin for purchases outside of necessaries is not increased. Though it may be true that a fall of money prices does commonly increase the purchasing power of consumers and so raise their consumer's rent, the fixity of money income is not rightly assumed in a community where incomes are ultimately paid out of the prices received for sale of commodities.

§ 6. This consideration of producer's and consumer's rents shows a tendency on the part of differential rents of buyers and sellers in a market to assume an exaggerated size by reason of an assumption of independence and isolation of a small local or temporal group of transactions.

The criticism of consumer's rent may at first sight appear inapplicable to the differential gains of buyers who buy not for "consumption" or direct personal enjoyment, but in order to sell again or to use as a means of production. But when buyers are manufacturers who buy raw materials of manufacture, or are retailers, their differential gains may either be accounted analogous to consumer's rents, — consumers' utility being imputed to the various production-goods which are required in the different stages of production, in accordance with the analysis of Wieser and the Austrian School, — or they may be taken as a source of future producer's rents in the manufactory or the retail business to which the buyer devotes the goods he buys. The latter is perhaps the more convenient mode of reckoning. Where the buyers are manufacturers purchasing their materials of manufacture, any differential gain they make will be represented by a differential gain which the lower expense of production in their business will enable them to obtain from the sale of the manufactured goods into which these materials shall pass.

Since the residual element of forced or specific gain in a market-price is dependent on and measured from the differential valuations of the limiting buyer and seller, the character of quantitative exactitude imputed to it in the illustration of a market, borrowed from Böhm-Bawerk, will be subject to a similar process of qualification.

In fine, the group of transactions taken to constitute a market at a given place and time has had ascribed to it an independence which is unreal, with the result that a false definiteness appears in the gains which the different parties are assumed to make from their transaction.

But the recognition of this truth does not impair the fundamental validity of the analysis of a market. The two elements of differential and specific gain which this analysis discovered in the market are really there, though the actual conditions of a market prevent them from being subject to the precise measurement ascribed to them in our falsely isolated instance.

CHAPTER III.

PART I.

§ 1. It has appeared that the process by which
a market-price is reached makes no provision for
the equal distribution of the advantage of a bargain in the case of any of the pairs which effect a
sale in the market. It is equally clear that the
amount of gain which accrues to each party respectively in a number of bargains at a market-
price will be determined by certain forces which
lie outside and beyond the machinery of competition and bargaining in the market, and which
assign to the body of buyers and the body of sellers the economic power which is represented in
the actual gain each gets from the transaction.

If, putting the matter in general terms, we say
that the relation of supply to demand determines
the market-price, we are driven for further explanation to examine the forces which give power
to supply and to demand.

First, a word further as to normal price. It is
sometimes suggested that though a market-price

may, by virtue of passing or local circumstances, lean in favour either of buyers or sellers, there exists something called a normal price, round which market-prices oscillate, which averages the fluctuations of market-prices over a period of time, and which in the long run divides equally the advantage among buyers and sellers. Now this term "normal price" has its uses. But it must be kept in mind that a normal price is nothing. but an average of market-prices, itself varying according to the number of different market-prices it averages. The notion, therefore, that in a normal price the inequality of competing or bargaining power between buyers and sellers will be eliminated, and that the normal price represents absolutely free competition, is utterly chimerical. The identification of the normal or average price with what theoretic economists sometimes still call a natural price, whereby exchanges take place with absolute reference to cost of production or some other standard of value, has no validity. For we have no reason to assume that a normal price, which represents market-prices of wheat or horses over a period of a year or two years, is a price which, if it were constant through that period, would divide equally among buyers and sellers the total gain of the transactions. If the advantage which one party may possess in a market were simply due to chance (to some sudden or unaccountable facts), and there were an

equal probability of this chance favouring one
side or the other, on that supposition an average
or normal price would be one which eliminated
the advantage in a market. But how, if the superiority of competition belongs to one side or the
other, not merely in a single market-price, but
over the whole series; if one side has an advantage on the average? Evidently the normal
price will not eliminate, but will reflect that advantage, and a normal price will in no sense be a
natural, or a " free competition," price. If one of
the two sets of bargainers enjoys a constant advantage in the power to manipulate a profit by
passing circumstances, or a power resting on some
superior source of supply, it follows that a normal price which merely averages actual market-
prices will include an element of inequality.
Average the dealings of small money lenders with
their clients over a term of years; you obtain a
normal price of such loans, but that price reflects
a normal advantage possessed by such money lenders. For certain purposes, theorists are doubtless at liberty to ignore these normal advantages
and to consider industry under a condition of absolutely free competition of capital and labour.
But much intellectual harm has resulted from
economists leaving the consideration of an actual
market-price, and hastening to the consideration
of a normal price, which in one breath they regard as an average, in another as a " natural,"

price expressing the relation of commodities under purely ideal conditions.

§ 2. The laws of distribution which underlie the bargain are best studied as they govern the forces operating in the market. Some of those very factors, which it is believed a normal price eliminates, are essential to the study.

Let us, then, return to our market-price. We have seen how it is actually determined in the market, given certain buyers and sellers with their valuations ; but we want further to know what outside economic forces determine such and such buyers and sellers to enter the market and bargain at such valuations.

Now these deeper economic forces, which govern market-prices, are best examined as they are operative in a change of price.

What is the cause of a price-change? The question sounds a simple one, and economists generally agree in the terms of their answer. A price-change is directly motived by a shift in the quantitative relation between supply and demand at the previous price. But what is here suggested by supply and demand? The supply which thus operates in price-change evidently does not mean the total stock of goods in existence, but the quantity which sellers are willing and able to sell at the former price. Similarly with demand. If we are to place it in true relation with this supply, demand must mean either the quantity of goods

which buyers are willing and able to buy at the
former price, or the quantity of money buyers are
able and willing to pay for goods at the former
price. If, however, taking these meanings of the
terms, we turn to the mechanism of the market,
we find them defective in that they furnish
a merely statical setting to a dynamic problem.
Supply and demand thus conceived are stationary
amounts. Now, price-change is a process, and in
order to understand this process, what we have to
estimate is the rate at which the stock of goods is
increased and depleted — a flow and not a fund.
But, if we conceive supply and demand as quantities of goods (or money) regarded àt a particular time, we conceive them as funds. In order
to study price-change properly, we must express
supply and demand as flows, *i.e.* measure them
as processes taking place in time. Consistently
with this purpose, supply may mean the total stock
offered for sale at a price during any given time,
and demand may mean quantity of purchases at
a price within a given time, or quantity of money
expended at a price within a given time. But it
will be more convenient to define the terms more
narrowly, confining supply to the rate of increase
of stock; demand to the rate of withdrawal from
stock (or the rate of payment of money in with-
drawing from stock). Thus alone do we rightly
come to regard supply and demand as processes
or "flows," and the supply and demand with

which we concern ourselves will be equivalent to the rate of production and of consumption.[1] Where goods flow out of a stock at the same pace as they flow in, the price remains firm, and demand and supply will be said to be equilibrated; where the inflow is faster than the outflow, prices fall, and supply will be said to exceed demand; where the outflow is faster, prices rise and demand exceeds supply. This setting regards demand primarily as a rate of outflow of goods. But if we regard demand as a power exercised by the purchaser, it signifies and is measured by an inflow of money. The quantitative relation of supply and demand may be expressed in either measure of demand. But in dealing with the mechanism of exchange, it is best to regard demand as an action proceeding from the buyer and to measure it in the terms of purchasing power.

Any increase or decrease of money, expended upon goods at a given price within a given time, implies a corresponding increase or decrease in quantity of goods bought, so that no error will arise from substituting the money-measure for the goods-measure of demand, and regarding it as an

---

[1] The term "consumption" is here used in the loose business sense, in which, for instance, it is said, cotton-yarn or iron is consumed when it is utilised in manufacturing processes. In strict statements of economic theory, it is desirable to confine consumption to the use of retail goods by so-called consumers.

inflow of money from the purchaser instead of an outflow of goods from the seller.

Keeping clearly in mind this conception of supply and demand as a rate of flow, it is hardly possible to misstate the law of price-change.

So long as a body of sellers in a market, maintaining the same stock of goods, can sell those goods at the same pace at which they have sold them hitherto, they will not lower and cannot raise the price. If they lower the price, this act means either a fall off in the pace at which buyers ask for goods, or it means that they have increased their stock, and in order to make sales correspond with this increased rate of supply, they must stimulate demand by lowering prices ; if they raise their price, it means either a reduction of supply in face of a constant or an increasing demand, or it means a growth of the rate at which purchases are made from a constant or decreasing supply.

Thus there are two immediate causes of a rise of price, — viz. a relative decrease of supply or a relative increase of demand; two causes of a fall of a price, — a relative increase of supply or a relative decrease of demand.

§ 3. This somewhat pedantic formulation of the law of price-change is rendered necessary by the fact that in working out special problems, economic thinkers not infrequently ignore the law and adduce distant forces as causes of a change of price, without showing how they operate in altering the quantitative relation between the flow of supply and of demand. I might illustrate from every page of the elaborate controversies upon money. Generations of economists have argued the influence of quantity of gold or of money upon prices, without recognising that they are ⎦ under any obligation to show how an increase or a decrease of money will affect the rate of supply or the rate of demand for commodities : this final link required to connect quantity of money with price-change is almost always either jumped or ignored, the real issue being begged in some more or less ingenious manner. Persons who so confidently affirm that an increased quantity of gold or other money would of necessity raise price, are required to show that this increase of money necessarily means an increased rate of purchase of commodities, or a decrease in the supply of commodities; this they seldom or never attempt to do.

Of course there are numerous forces (and monetary ones among them) which can be rightly spoken of as causing changes of price, but they all act through, and can be tested by, their influence upon rate of demand or supply.

§ 4. Turning then to our issue, price-change, we see sellers and buyers as repositories of supply and demand.

Whatever force proceeding from either side disturbs the existing balance of supply and demand affects price. It also affects value. Nearly the whole of the trouble about value has arisen from separating unduly the consideration of value from that of price. Once keep clearly in mind the fundamental truth that price is value expressed in terms of money, it will then appear that the most profitable way of studying the nature of value is to study the forces which cause price-change. The notion that value is some inherent and abiding property of wealth, which escapes at any rate the minor fluctuations of market-changes, has no validity whatever.[1]

Once expel from the mind the idea that value

[1] Still more fallacious is the signification which so hard-headed a thinker as Professor Hadley adopts, identifying value with "a proper and legitimate price as distinct from an unfair and illegitimate one."

"The price of an article or service," he says, "in the ordinary commercial sense, is the amount of money which is paid, asked, or offered for it. The value of an article or service is the amount of money which may properly be paid, asked, or offered for it."—Hadley's *Economics*, p, 92.

Now this involves a double-barrelled error. First, whatever value is, it is not "an amount of money," though it may be measured by an amount of money. Secondly, the idea that it is a "proper" or "legitimate" price involves, as indeed Hadley admits, a reference to some ethical standard which he does not attempt to establish. There is no justification whatever for assigning to value (exchange-value) any more permanency than attaches to price. The value of any stock of goods (the quantity of other goods they will exchange for) will vary with everything that affects the market-price.

is an inherent quality or enjoys any more permanency than does market-price, and it becomes
evident that the study of price-change is the
surest approach to the true understanding of
value.[1]

§ 5. The one-sided theorists who have made
value dependent either solely upon "cost" of
production or upon "utility," commit a similar
error. Though they formally describe value as
a relation between commodities, they realise it as
a property attaching to commodities. Those who
attribute to cost of production the cause or determination of value, realise goods as possessing value
in the shape of the productive power of labour and
capital which has been used in making them, and
are thus driven to deny the direct influence on
value of causes which do not operate through
cost of production. The Utility School similarly
comes to regard and speak of value as a property
or force stored in goods, by reason either of the
direct satisfaction they can afford, or because of
their contribution toward the production of goods
which give a certain quantity of satisfaction, only
admitting causes from the cost side in so far as
they are seen to operate upon utility.

Considered in a broad, historical light, the two
opposed theories of value are of great interest.

---

[1] Böhm-Bawerk, who insists on distinguishing value and
price as conceptions, admits that "the laws of these two
coincide." (*Positive Theory of Capital*, p. 132.)

Economics, after it left the liberal hands of Adam Smith, was moulded into the structure of a science of commerce by the classical economists with Ricardo at their head. The characteristic note of this school was to regard the production of commercial wealth as the end or final cause of industry: to this intent they twisted the whole terminology of political economy. Consumption itself was justified as a means to an end — the furtherance of production.[1] Not merely was the theory of Consumption or Human Satisfaction left wholly undeveloped by this school, but it was equally germane to their conception of the science to ignore utility and to consider cost of production as the cause of value. This is essentially the commercial point of view. The commercial man has no direct concern with the utility of his goods — that is the purchaser's lookout (*caveat emptor!*) ; his chief business is to look after the cost of production and the sale. The treatment of labour as a mere commodity — one " cost " of production — belongs to the same attitude. On the other hand, Jevons and his fellow-thinkers in England, Austria, and America assign utility as cause or determinant of value, because they have abandoned the commercial standard and substituted a " human " standard. Economic activities are regarded as

[1] The froo trado theory did, indeed, formally recognise the supremacy of the interests of the consumer, but it never affected the main structure or the terminology of political economy.

contributing, not to "business," but to satisfaction : the end is no longer production, but consumption. So, just as it was natural for the commercial economist to look upon "costs" as a force generated in various processes of production, accumulating and vested in goods as making them "valuable," so it was natural for those who look down the line of industrial processes from the other end, from consumption, to take the consumer's test of the valuable — utility — to refer it back as a property potentially existing in different classes of commercial goods which are on their way to blossom into really useful goods when they reach the consumer.

Stand at one end of the stream of industry, you see goods gathering cost as they pass from process to process in production, and then cost appears to be the value which is growing : stand at the other end, value seems only to emerge from the contributions which productive processes make toward the supply of consumables, and to consist of nothing else than this utility of consumables reflected back upon the earlier processes — a potentiality of satisfaction.

Now both these views of value are due to an almost materialistic conception of value as a property or force stored in material forms of wealth and transmitted from one end or other of the chain of industry. By an unwise departure from the actual operations of the market, they

have developed an abstraction as unreal as the
"oddity and quiddity" of the mediæval school-
men. Like the latter, too, they have developed a
dogmatism in the assumption of their theory,
which would be ridiculous if it were not so injurious. Of course all holders of a "cost" theory
of value admit that valuable things must be useful, but this utility is only a condition, while cost
is the efficient cause: "utility" men allow that
cost affects the value of all freely produced goods,
but they maintain cost is the condition, utility the
efficient cause.[1]

§ 6. Now if, leaving abstractions, we turn to
shifts of actual prices and recognise that with

---

[1] Admitting, as Böhm-Bawerk does, that "for the emergence
of value there must be scarcity as well as utility, — not absolute
scarcity, but scarcity relative to the demand for the particular
class of goods," — it is hard to understand why he should refuse
to scarcity (and through scarcity to cost) an independent influence as a direct determinant of value. He does not really
dispose of this independent influence by making economic
scarcity "relative to the demand"; for while change of demand
may undoubtedly affect the "relative" scarcity, changes produced by natural causes or human arts, stimulated by no change
of demand, may also affect this relative scarcity. It is difficult
to comprehend why a change in the value of a stock of wheat,
due to a favourable season or a new railway, should be attributed to demand, which has either not changed, or the change
of which has been clearly consequent upon an enlargement of
supply. Yet if "scarcity" thus affected may be legitimately
regarded as a true determinant of *change* of value, why may
not "scarcity" and the cost factor behind it rank as a true
determinant of value? (*Positive Theory*, Bk. III, Ch. II,
p. 135.)

each price-change the value of a stock of goods
is changing, we perceive that value is affected,
and directly affected, by forces proceeding from
either side, and that this distinction between
causes and conditions of value has no ultimate
validity.

Only by turning to the actual play of economic
forces in a market can we perceive the organic relation between cost and utility operating
through supply and demand, which is required
to establish the truth that value is determined by
the interaction of the two. It is the most serviceable achievement of Professor Marshall to
have clearly established the equality and the in-
terdependence of cost and utility as the determinants of value. This he did by working out
through supply curves and demand curves the
laws of the regulation of prices. With the theory
of value as distinct from that of prices he has
dealt very briefly, but his brief treatment contains a refutation of the Jevonian theory of "final
utility" as crushing as even Mr. Hyndman could
desire. With characteristic academic modesty
Professor Marshall has placed this criticism of
Jevons in a small print note, the very title of
which is but a slight indication of its matter. It
is called a "Note on Ricardo's Theory of Value";
but though it contains an exposure of the insuffi-
ciency of the cost theory, its chief importance
consists in its brief and absolutely conclusive ref-

utation of the syllogism into which Jevons somewhat rashly cast his doctrine of value. The fact
that many students of economics still speak of
themselves as Jevonians in their interpretation
of value, I can only explain by supposing that
Professor Marshall's note has escaped their attention. As Professor Marshall points out, Jevons,
with the ingenuousness of the professional logi-
cian, provides his own refutation. His theory
that the value of a supply of goods is determined
by the final utility, *i.e.* the utility which attaches
to the least serviceable portion of the supply which
is already consumed, he sums up in the following
syllogism : —

> "Cost of production determines supply,
> Supply determines final degree of utility,
> Final degree of utility determines value."[1]

Now, setting on one side the careless and inac-
curate statement that cost of production determines supply, whereas final cost is the immediate
determinant, this syllogism, as Marshall points out,
really gives away the most distinctive feature in
Jevons's treatment. Jevons wishes to insist that
final utility, not final cost, is the real controlling
force. But his syllogism, though alleging that
value is directly dependent on final utility, shows
that final utility is controlled by final cost, so that
the latter is made, after all, the master.

[1] *Principles* (2 ed.), Bk. IV, Ch. XV.

The whole statement, as Marshall shows, can be utterly upset by inverting Jevons's syllogism and substituting the following, which is "rather less untrue " : —

"Utility determines the amount that has to be supplied,
The amount that has to be supplied determines cost of production,
Cost of production determines value."

The fallacy of attributing the determination of value (or price) to final cost or to final utility is one and the same. Final utility cannot be the ultimate determinant of value, because final utility will depend upon how much is bought, and how much is bought will depend upon the quantity that is offered at different prices, and this in its turn depends upon final cost. So, conversely, final cost cannot determine value, because the cost of producing the last portion of supply will depend largely upon how much is produced, and that will depend on the effective demand at different prices, or, ultimately, on the final utility attending different quantities of consumption.

Professor Marshall has summed up the matter with perfect accuracy by comparing the two in their action to the blades of a pair of scissors. "When one blade is held still, and the cutting is effected by moving the other, we may say with careless brevity that the cutting is done by the second ; but the statement is not one to be made formally and defended deliberately."

The fact is, that both sides commonly imported a particular concept into value which begged the question. The commercial economist saw that goods fetched a high price because they were difficult to get hold of (scarce) or "costly" to make; the humane-minded economist found the common meaning of value more akin to utility. The same transaction is often regarded in common life by two parties with the same difference of view. Take the case of the cab-runner, who demands a shilling for carrying your box into the house. He values his action at a shilling, looking at it from the cost side; he has run two miles against a horse, with the risk of being refused the job after doing all this work; a shilling is not an outrageous charge for his effort and his risk. On the other hand, you would almost as soon as not take the exercise of carrying your own box up the steps, so the actual good you get from the cab-runner is very small indeed. Or, again, take the case of Mr. Beecham, who sells us pills which he perhaps correctly observes are "worth a guinea a box" to us, and yet, with a rare spirit of self-denial, consents to take 1s. 10d., regulating the price rather by consideration of the cost to him than the utility conferred on us.

The confusion which has thus attached to value arises almost inevitably when a popular abstraction is taken into scientific terminology.

§ 7. Another curious instance of the inveterate

one-sidedness of the adherents of final utility in
recent times is furnished by the use which Böhm-
Bawerk and others of his school have made of the
term "subjective value" in seeking to identify it
with the old use value.   " It is important," writes
Böhm-Bawerk,[1] "that we give right names to
those things which tradition has handed down to
us under the inadequate designation of use value
and exchange value.   The two groups of phenomena, to both of which popular usage has
given the ambiguous name 'value,' we shall distinguish as value in the subjective and value
in the objective sense.   Value in the subjective
sense is the importance which a good, or a complex
of goods, possesses with regard to the well-being
of a subject."   And this "well-being" he proceeds
to identify with the "satisfaction of a want."   Now
by thus identifying subjective with use value he
has begged a most important issue.   I may put
the matter in the form of a question and ask, Why
should not the term "subjective value" be applied
to the whole subjective or human facts which lie
behind objective or exchange value—facts which
relate not only to the utility of the good possessing the exchange value, but to its cost as well?
The forces which directly operate in determining
objective value proceed both from costs and from
utility.   Why, then, should the term "subjective
value" reflect only the subjective aspects of those

[1] *Positive Theory of Capital,* Bk. III, Ch. I.

which proceed from utility? The "well-being of a subject" is just as much concerned with minimising costs as in maximising utility. Subjective value, if it is to have any proper or intelligible correspondence to objective value, should express the relation of subjective cost to subjective utility. It is perhaps not curious that Böhm-Bawerk should proceed to mate this error by giving also the same one-sided interpretation to objective value by which he says is meant "the power or capacity of a good to procure some one objective result. In this sense there are as many kinds of value as there are external results with which man may be connected. There is a nutritive value of food, a heating value of wood and coal, a fertilising value of manures, a blasting value of explosives, and so on." [1] Now there is, perhaps, no sufficient reason why Böhm-Bawerk should not apply the term "objective value" to these objective utilities. But when he seeks to identify it, as he does in the paragraph just quoted, with exchange value, I can only say that he is departing from the meaning consistently and universally accorded to that term by past economists.

The fact is that in his preliminary process of defining objective and subjective value he has identified them with objective and subjective utility, denying the validity of all "cost" considerations. This, occurring as it does in the opening

[1] p. 131.

pages of a treatment of value, is sheer "*petitio principii.*"

§ 8. But, though in the specific problem of direct determination of value final or marginal utility exercises no power, the like of which is not exercised by final or marginal cost, there is a sense in which a superior control may be claimed for utility as " *causa causans.*" Were "economics " expanded into a broader science, which should take cognizance of all forms of vital wealth, the economic antimony of production and consumption would be merged in the deeper unity to which biology and ethics testify, when they insist that work, or production, can be as genuine and vital a source of satisfaction as consumption itself. From such a standpoint Böhm-Bawerk's insistence, that the causal connection "runs in an unbroken chain from value and price of products to value and price of costs," appears defective, for we perceive "utility" or other vital satisfaction emerging directly from processes of production in the finer arts and handicrafts.

A really philosophical analysis from the physiological or the psychological standpoint would seem to bring together into such close organic relation the processes of productive and consumptive work and enjoyment, that neither in the purely biological nor in the conscious realms could they be severed or priority of importance accorded to one of them.

But taking economics within the limits generally assigned to it, the Utility Schools are entitled to ignore these considerations, and to insist that the theory of value is not concerned with the ultimate rationale of function and fruition, effort and satisfaction, but only with such pains of production and pleasures of consumption as actually figure in present human estimates of value. So, any labour, which is itself a joy, and is recognised as such, involves no economic "cost," and such "goods" as it produced would, unless the labour were hampered by scarcity of material, possess no "value," but would be "free" goods. The utility theorist rightly urges that, since economic costs are ex-hypothesi "painful," they cannot be regarded as undergone for their own sake, but only as means to the end of attaining some utility. Thus the conscious motive force which directs the volume of productive force emanates from the demand of consumers, and utility of consumptive goods becomes the ultimate cause why value attaches to any stock of productive goods.

We may even affirm that from utility, through demand, proceed the very forces which direct and evoke costs, drawing industrial energy into the right channels and stimulating those very improvements in organisation and the industrial arts which subsequently appear as chief causes of changes of value from the cost side.

But though utility thus figures as the final cause

of value, it is not rightly taken as the sole efficient cause or as the sole determinant of quantity of value attaching to a stock of goods. The distinction here made is not a barren one. The economic problem of value is one in which we are rightly concerned, not with final, but with efficient, causes, and the mistake of the Utility School is that they substitute the former treatment for the latter. As a direct, independent, efficient cause of the value of a given stock of goods, cost ranks on a level with utility. The attribution of final causality to utility has no serviceable bearing on the problem of determination of values and prices. Böhm-Bawerk sometimes seems to feel this, and is driven to claim for utility a superior power, not only as final, but as efficient, cause, insisting, for instance, that value "runs from iron goods to iron, and not conversely." Now the iron goods appear to impose value upon iron and to determine the "how much" of the value, only so long as we ignore the influence of costs (through scarcity of supply) upon the iron goods. When, however, that influence is taken into consideration, the value of the supposed sole determinant is seen to be itself determined partly from the cost side. In other words, the flow of accumulating costs drawn from the iron and coal is perceived to be just as much an efficient cause of the value of the iron goods as the utility of the latter is of the value of the iron. So that even were we to admit that the value of iron was imputed from the value of the iron goods, cost is not banished as an efficient cause of the value of iron. The somewhat intricate and complex reasoning by which Böhm-Bawerk has sought to get rid of costs as direct and separate influences on value of productive goods, receives more detailed consideration in an appendix to this chapter. The breakdown of the attempt to repudiate the separate efficient causal influences of "costs" in determining the value of consumptive goods and productive goods is there made manifest.

§ 9. A brief summary of the actual relations which subsist between costs and utility and between the value of productive and consumptive goods will take the following shape : —

Taking industry as "a going concern," and bearing in mind the present condition of the industrial arts in the several processes, we shall find that a definite quantitative relation exists between the amount of value of the productive goods and instruments at the several stages, and the amount of value of the consumptive goods which issue from them. If we consider, as we reasonably may, consumptive goods as the conscious goal of industry, it will appear that productive goods receive their value as means to an end, and that the amount of this value is dependent upon the amount of value of the consumptive goods. If, then, the value of these consumptive goods could

be rightly considered to be determined by their
final utility, this latter would be placed in the position of the true determinant of all values. But
even Böhm-Bawerk, when confronted with the
question, admits that the final utility of consumptive goods is itself determined by the relations between "wants and provision." Now behind "provision" or "supply" stands the force of costs.
So that where the value of consumptive goods seems
to determine the value of productive goods, it is
not more because the final utility of consumptive
goods determines that of productive goods than
because the final costs of productive goods have
already determined the costs of the consumptive
goods, and so helped to determine the very value
which appears to be reflected back. If we choose
to disregard the "suction" exercised by demand
for consumptive goods and to follow the mere
"flow" of the industrial stream from the early
processes onward toward consumptive goods, it
seems equally plausible to represent the value of
productive goods as determining that of consumptive goods.

In fact, the flow of the accumulative force of
utilities and costs is in opposite directions. So
far, then, as the actual determination of the value
of a stock of productive goods is concerned, we
must insist that there are two sets of efficient
causes, — those operating through final utility,
derived from and dependent on the final utility

of consumptive goods, and those operating through final costs (except where natural scarcity takes the place of costs).

§ 10. While, therefore, in a scientific physiology of industry, final utility is of supreme significance as indicative of the true source of industrial life, the motor power which flows from the effective demand of consumers of commodities, and which by the pressure of its "final" or "marginal" activity directs and attracts the requisite productive powers in every channel of industry, it cannot rightly take the place which is claimed for it in the specific problem of the determination of the value of any stock of useful goods at any point of the industrial stream. Our setting of the problem of price-change and of value, concerned as it is with "efficient" causes must, therefore, hold the balance equal between final utility and final cost.

To achieve such a task careful terminology is essential, and, in order to clear our mind as much as possible from controversial misconceptions, I propose, first, to substitute for the term "value" a generally admitted equivalent, which the discussions of the Austrian School have brought to the front.

The value of a supply or of an article of supply means the "economic importance" attaching to it. There are two advantages in substituting the term "importance" for value.[1] In the first

---

[1] Menger is, I think, the first to identify value with "importance," in a distinct definition of the term.

place, it is *prima facie* impartial, so far as a theory of value is concerned, whereas the term "value," from common association, leans toward utility. Secondly, it gets rid of the notion of "value" as a quality or property of goods, and gives emphasis to the true notion of it as an aspect or relation. This impartiality, indeed, is not quite absolute, for we find Austrian economists, in their adoption of the term, already imputing into it a bias toward utility as the source of "importance."[1]

If, however, taking the following table of terminology, we approach the central conception of economic importance in relation to the concrete problem of determination of price, the equilibration of prices from the cost and the utility sides will be established beyond all controversy.

"Die Bedeutung, welche concrete Güter oder Güterquantitäten für uns dadurch erlangen, dass wir in der Befriedigung unserer Bedürfnisse von der Verfügung über dieselben anhängig zu sein uns bewusst sind." (*Grundzüge*, p. 78.)

This is paraphrased by Professor Smart as follows, "Value is the importance which a good acquires as the recognised condition of something that makes for the well-being of a subject, and would not be obtainable without the good." (Introduction to the *Theory of Value*, p. 14.)

[1] Böhm-Bawerk, for example, proposes to define value "unambiguously and exactly," as: "That importance which goods or complexes of goods acquire, as the recognised condition of a utility which makes for the well-being of a subject, and would not be obtained without them." (*Positive Theory*, Bk. III, Ch. II.)

TABLE OF TERMINOLOGY FOR THEORY OF VALUE.

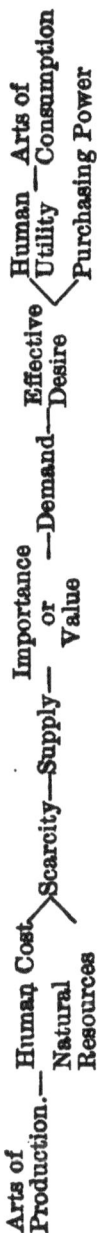

```
                                  ⎧ Human ⎧ Arts of Consumption
                     ⎧ Effective ⎨ Utility ⎨
Importance ⎧ —Demand⎨   Desire   ⎩         ⎩ Purchasing Power
   or      ⎨
 Value     ⎩ Scarcity—Supply—
                     ⎧ Human Cost ⎧ Natural
Arts of    ⎨         ⎨
Production ⎩         ⎩ Resources
```

The importance or value attaching to a stock of goods changes directly with any change in the relative rate of supply and demand. But supply and demand, in order to be economic forces, in order to affect importance, must be governed by certain forces behind them. A supply infinite or indefinitely large has no economic significance. Comparative scarcity is the governor of supply. Similarly, demand receives its economic significance and power from effective desire (a willingness and ability to give something in order to get). Just as there is no economic supply of free goods because there exists no scarcity, so there is no economic demand for them, because there is no willingness to give something to get them. Effective desire is in effect a "scarcity" on the demand side.

Scarcity of supply itself is conditioned: sometimes by a restriction, which may be natural, as in the case of certain kinds of land; or the product of circumstances, as the scarcity of food in a siege, or the scarcity due to an organised corner or syndicate. The scarcity of "old masters" etc., may also be regarded as "natural."

In most goods, however, scarcity is due to the fact that human costs must be incurred to produce a supply. How far the fact that human effort is required to produce goods will make them scarce, depends very largely upon the relation of human effort to natural sources of supply. Where there is some natural limit of good or easily accessible material, more human effort must be expended in each increase of supply.

Here scarcity is apt to assert itself and forces rising importance to press from the cost side. Where there is abundant access to natural sources of supply, less human effort may be expended in each increase of supply. Here the pressure of scarcity is abated, and the forces operating on supply make for a reduced value or importance in each article. Here we have the familiar Laws of Increasing and Diminishing Returns.

Turning to the demand side, we see a similar mechanism of economic forces. Effective desire regulates demand in the same way in which scarcity regulates supply. Effective desire means desire backed by purchasing power; it is the product of two factors, *a*, human utility, or, more strictly speaking, the craving for satisfaction arising from utility, and *β*, purchasing power.

Human utility has to demand the same relation that human cost has to supply. The economic forces which operate on cost are the arts of production. The practice of the arts of production, otherwise efficiency of production, will depend in part upon scientific considerations, the amount of knowledge of the industrial arts, partly upon the character or quality of the men who exercise these arts, their individual and their collective power to avail themselves of the knowledge of the arts. Given the same absolute knowledge of natural forces in relation to matter and of the modes of working, differences of physique, race, climate, social and political institutions, and a variety of other influences will affect the actual cost of producing a given quantity of wealth. Again, the effectiveness of the practice of industrial arts, as we have seen, is always qualified by the limits imposed by nature upon the supply of matter and natural energy.

Closely analogous in working are the forces which play upon demand. As the arts of production stand behind cost, so the arts of consumption stand behind utility or satisfaction. Any given stock of valuable goods will of course depend, for the real satisfaction they afford, upon the degree of development of the tastes of the consumer and the habits of consumption he has formed. There is a skill of consumption which rests upon physical laws relating partly to the constituents of consumable goods, partly to the nature of the consumer, and which consists in a right and delicate harmony or adjustment of power in securing different kinds and quantities of consumption, just as the skill of production consists in the delicate manipulation by human and natural energy of variously adjusted quantities of raw material. As human cost or effort is null and void in its contribution to supply, except so far as it has access to natural sources, similarly human utility or satisfaction is void unless it can find its means of expression in purchasing power. This latter condition makes desire an economically effective force, just as limitation of natural supply makes productive effort effective.

Remove the limits of matter and of natural forces, and the cost of producing any stock of goods may shrink to an indefinitely small amount. Similarly assume an infinite amount of available income or purchasing power, and the smallest amount of desire will express itself in an indefinitely large demand.[1]

§ 11. The use I claim for this table is not merely that it suggests a settlement of disputed terminology, but primarily and chiefly because it forces a recognition of the organic relation between cost

---

[1] This assignment of a subjective basis of value does not conflict with or impair the objective signification which identifies value with the quantity of other goods for which a good will exchange. If we prefer, we may accept the distinction made by Wieser of objective exchange-value and subjective exchange-value, understanding by the former the quantity of other goods for which it exchanges, by the latter the importance assigned to it by considerations of scarcity and utility. The relation between the two is, that the subjective importance is

and utility, and the strictly equal or analogous part each bears in determining value.

It convinces us that there are forces constantly passing from both sides to affect the value or importance of a stock of goods.

It rejects the compromise sometimes suggested, whereby the value of some kinds of goods is said to be determined by cost, the value of others by utility.

There are doubtless certain goods which may be classified in such a way as to show an absolute scarcity or limit of supply, with regard to which all changes of value will appear to be the product of forces from the side of demand. Pictures of old masters, food in a siege, are familiar examples. Here human costs appear to exercise no direct influence in determining value, which is fixed by the relations between absolute scarcity and effective desire, and, since the latter is the only changing factor, it may be said to be the sole direct regulator of the value of such goods at any given time. It might perhaps be urged that even in these cases cost, though reduced to a minimum, is not absolutely excluded as an influence

measured by the objective exchange-value, which is expressed either in terms of other goods, or more conveniently in terms of money as price. It is, however, more accurate to say that the quantity of goods for which a good will exchange, constitutes not its value, but the measure of its value, though that measure is itself commonly referred to an accepted standard of money.

on value. Supply-markets are not absolutely
separate one from another, for the demands which
cause them to be classified are not kept in water-
tight compartments. It might, then, be urged that
there is neither a supply nor a demand for old
masters which is entirely separate from the supply
and demand of other pictures, or of art goods in a
wide sense. To take a concrete example, "copies"
of old masters or "spurious" old masters must cer-·
tainly be held to cater to the same tastes as the
limited supply of genuine pictures, and may therefore rank as an increase of "supply," which will
moderate the absoluteness of the "scarcity." Since
"costs" will operate upon this portion of supply,
as in other "freely produced" commodities, the
influence of these "costs" will presumably have
some effect upon the value of "old masters."
Similarly, the effective supply of food in a be-
sieged city is not an entirely inelastic quantity;
the amount of it which figures as supply on any
given day will depend upon the economy with
which individuals have used the stocks in their
possession, and the high human "cost" of keeping
food for a later period of the siege will have some
influence as a determinant of its value. It is
scarcely possible to eliminate altogether the influence of "cost" upon value save by recourse to
some impossible hypothesis.

In both these instances, it may be rightly
claimed by those who emphasise utility as the

final cause of value, that human desires, operating through demand, are the real forces which evoke the "costs" that are necessary to break down the absoluteness of monopoly by enlarging the effective supply. But this admission of an ultimate causality assignable to human desires ought not, as we have shown, to affect the economic setting of the cases. The influence of human costs and natural scarcity cannot be eliminated as direct efficient causes of price and value, even by reference to extreme and almost extra-economic instances.

But even if it be admitted that human costs in such cases have no influence on supply, and so on value, the power of supply as a determinant of value is still represented by "scarcity." Whether we are dealing with a natural or an artificial scarcity, it is never absolute and constant; the material of every supply is continually perishing or receiving accessions, so that, though the pressure of demand appears to be the sole source of changes of value and of price, there is always some slight vital influence proceeding from the supply side. Though one of the blades appears to do all the cutting, to adopt Marshall's illustration, and the other to stand still, if we look closely enough, we shall see that the latter nevertheless moves. Scarcity is never a mere statical "condition" of value, but always exerts an active force.

Neither can we take the other side and conclude with Mill that the value of freely produced goods is derived from and determined by cost. For purposes of commercial convenience it may be better to compare the values of most free goods by reference to relative costs or expenses; for whatever forces operate from the demand side will be reflected in normal costs, just as the forces from the cost side will be reflected in utility. But the selection of costs for the more convenient measure of values and price-changes must not be understood to imply that either theoretically or practically the forces operating through cost are more important than those operating through utility.[1]

Professor Marshall, indeed, suggests that "we may say that, as a general rule, the shorter the

---

[1] The folly of recognising two Laws of Value — one where Supply is limited, another where it is capable of increase — is well exhibited in the controversy which Böhm-Bawerk has carried on with Professor Dietzel, in the pages of Conrad's *Jahrbücher für National-Oekonomie*, during 1890–1892. Though Dietzel had several times plainly formulated the true theory which assigns the determination of value neither to cost nor to utility, but to the relations between scarcity and utility (cost being one source of scarcity), he weakly abandoned to the Marginal Utility School the class of limited goods, admitting their value to be determined by marginal utility alone, whereas he ought to have stoutly maintained that though no "cost" entered here as cause, "scarcity," otherwise determined, played the same part as a determining factor as in the case of freely produced goods. The fact that, in the one case, the "scarcity" is rigid, in the other, flexible (by the application of new costs), has no effect upon the universality of the Law of Value, though for practical purposes of measuring change of value and of price, it throws the stress upon the utility side of the equation.

period which we are considering, the greater must
be the share of our attention which is given to the
influence of demand on value; and the longer the
period, the more important will be the influence
of cost of production on value."[1]

But even this distinction, sound as it is for practical purposes, must be rejected if it implies that
ultimately cost is the more important regulator or
determinant of value. The operation of a change
of taste, the growth of a new habit into a standard
of comfort, will exercise as strong and as abiding
an effect on the value of a class of goods as any
change which takes place in the method of producing these goods.

It may be the case that a larger number and
variety of more enduring forces operate upon
value from changes in the arts and conditions of
production than from the side of consumption,
but it is not easy to establish the fact. There
are of course certain classes of goods the value of
which is more frequently and more largely affected
by forces which come from one side or the other.
We may say that the value of wheat is more influenced from the supply side, but the value of
fashionable dress-goods is influenced chiefly from
the demand side; and in the practical considerations of market-price and bargaining these facts
must receive due weight; the study of the relative
importance of these different forces as they operate

---

[1] *Econ. of Ind.*, p. 223.

on market-price is the most delicate, the most difficult, and the most practically important work of the modern profit-seeker.

Taking the wider theoretic view, however, an absolute equality in the relation of cost and utility toward value must be posited.

§ 12. The most curious feature in the recent history of economic theory is that Jevons, who perversely insisted in trying to upset the cost theory of Value by plunging into an opposite falsehood of extremes, is also the English writer who more than any other has laid the true subjective foundation of a correct analysis of value. In his chapter on "Theory of Labour" he works out a theory of the relation between cost and utility for the individual which is irrefutable. He shows exactly how a worker, engaged in supplying himself with commodities by his own efforts, will accurately balance the pain or disutility of production against the pleasure or utility of consumption; that the number of hours he works, the intensity he imparts to his effort, the distribution of working energy over different kinds of work, will be carefully balanced against the different amounts of satisfaction derived from consuming different quantities of goods produced by the day's labour.

It is, indeed, conclusively shown that the economic value of the day's product is similarly and equally affected by the disutility or cost of production and the utility or satisfaction of consump-

tion; to such a man it will be a matter of equal
consideration whether he increases his day's effort
by one unit or reduces his day's satisfaction by
one unit.

His analysis of disutility or cost is similar to
his analysis of utility or consumption. He offers
a complete setting of the individual economy; in
reality he lays down the true theory of Value,
which he misrepresents elsewhere. The objection may perhaps be raised that the theory of
Value cannot be given in terms of the individual
economy, because no act of exchange takes place.
But the individual problem contains all the essential factors; if we like, we may treat the case as
one of exchange worked out between the two sides
or selves, — the idle self, which shirks effort, the
greedy self, which seeks satisfaction. The mode
of balance will be similar, though more accurate,
than that established in an exchange of commodities between two bargainers. The strange thing
is that Jevons does not apply this theory of Exchange in the individual to society. His formal
theory of the Individual Economy establishes two
most important truths: (1) the equal importance
and the continuous organic interaction between
final cost and final utility; (2) the essentially
subjective nature of the problem of exchange.[1]

---

[1] His analysis, p 189, of his *Theory of Political Economy*, lays
the foundation of the subjective treatment of cost and utility,
which Austrian and American economists have built upon.

Yet Jevons, in his "Theory of Exchange," ignores the influences which emanate from cost, or counts them as indirect agents operating through final utility. His treatment of "disutility" in this part of his work refers, not to cost, but to damage or pain incidental to certain classes of consumption.

In his final chapter, one imperfect glimpse of the true problem emerges, where Jevons affirms, "The problem of economics may, as it seems to me, be stated thus: Given, a certain population with various needs and powers of production, in possession of certain lands and other sources of material; required, the mode of employing this labour, which will maximise the utility of the produce." If Jevons had added the words, "and minimise the 'disutility' of producing them," his statement would have been complete. But in fact his work, as the work of all those who attach themselves to utility as the special measure and determinant of value, is one-sided and defective.

The perception that cost and utility, resolved into their subjective elements of effort and satisfaction, are essentially, organically, related in the individual economy, must be followed by the plain admission of a similar relation in the social economy which expresses itself in social value and in price. And a scientific statement of value must assign a similar relation to the forces affecting value from both sides.

PART II.

§ 13. This wide excursion into the theory of
Value may seem to some to have a too remote
bearing upon the more definite problem of price-
point and price-change. But this is not really
the case. Until the precise equality of final cost
and final utility as determinants of value is established, we cannot fully appreciate the process of
competition and bargaining which results in a
price.

I began by pointing out the fact that behind
the supply, which figured in any market, there
were a number of forces relating to scarcity and
cost of production in the wider market, which
determined the quantity available at the different
prices. The same forces bring it about that some
portions of the market supply are produced more
cheaply than other parts. The owners of the more
cheaply produced goods would consent, if necessary, to sell them at a lower price than the owners
of the more expensive portion of supply would
consent to take. In other words, the difference
of price-limit, which we saw the different sellers
put upon their goods, arises from differences in the
cost or expense of producing them. If the supply
is thus graded according to the cost of its different
parts, the price which is eventually reached will,
it is maintained, be such as only just to cover the

expenses of the most expensive portion. Those who lay stress upon this side say that the price is determined by the expense of producing this last part, or the marginal expenses of production. Similarly, the different valuation which was imputed to the buyers is attributed to the superior "effective desire" which some exhibit as compared with others. The attainment of the horse or the quarter of wheat will either satisfy a stronger desire in some than in others, or an equally strong desire backed by a fuller purse. Those who lean upon this side say that utility (effective desire) of the last portion that is bought determines the value of the whole supply.

§ 14. Now let us turn to our diagram of market-price and ascertain how marginal cost and marginal utility actually express themselves. We shall find that they can be identified with the final pair before whose valuation competition of buyers and sellers gives way, leaving the price-point to be determined by the bargaining of the two.

The competition and "higgling" was seen [1] to result in five acts of sale, in which A, B, C, D, E, were the sellers and N, O, P, Q, R, the buyers, at a price which was finally determined by the higgling of a single pair within limits imposed by competition. The final pair, whose action determined the price-limits, and eventually the

[1] Ch. I, pp. 11–19.

price, were seen to be F, with a limit-price of sale amounting to £21 10*s.*, and M, with a limit-price of purchase amounting to £21. F is the one among actual sellers whose limit-price is highest. He cannot afford to sell at less than £21 10*s.* Why? Because he reckons that price will only just cover

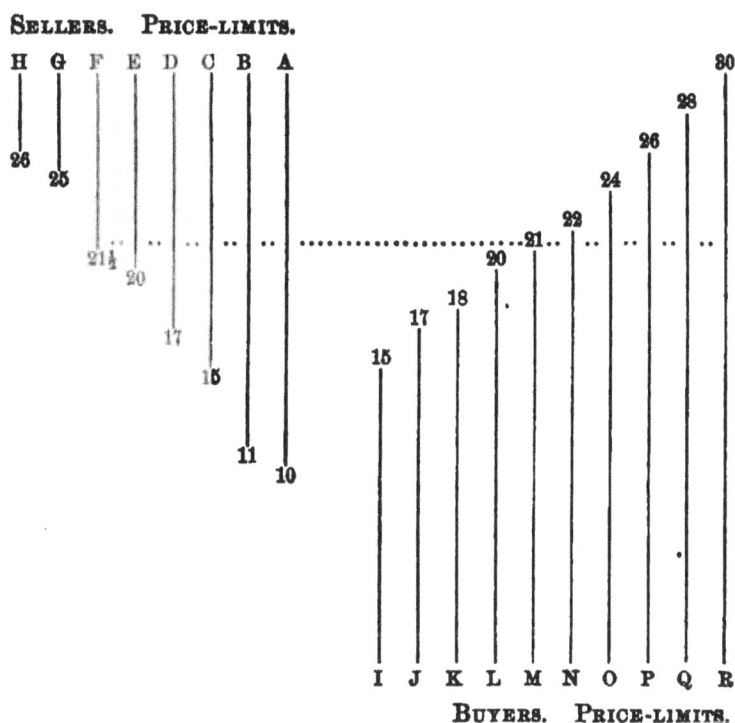

his cost of production, or, more strictly speaking, will only give him the minimum gain required from a single sale. In other words, F represents the most expensive portion of possible supply, final or marginal cost. R is the actual buyer whose limit-price is highest; he will pay more than any other buyer, because he wants a unit of supply most, or because he has more money at his disposal, so as to make his "effective desire" the greatest. In other words, R is the person who imputes the highest utility, and M is the representative of final or marginal utility. The differential advantages obtained by A, B, C, D, E among the sellers, and N, O, P, Q, R among the buyers, will thus be found to correspond to real differences of cost (expenses) of production on the one hand and utility on the other hand. If, without making any other change, we transfer our illustration from a horse-market to a market of some manufactured wares, it will easily appear that the larger gain which D, C, B, and A make as compared with E upon each sale effected signifies and rests upon the special advantages possessed by each in economy of manufacture. Similarly, it will be recognised that the special gains made by O, P, Q, R, in their capacity of purchasers, as compared with M, is based upon special amounts of utility attributed by them to the same goods for trade or for consumption.

On each side, among the buyers or the sellers, the differential gain or "rent" is to be measured from the position of a member of the final pair representing marginal cost or marginal utility. In our diagram the dotted line which connects F with M enables us to see at a glance the relative size of these differential gains, which include those portions of A, B, C, D, on the sellers' side, which fall below the price line; and those portions of N, O, P, Q, on the buyers' side, which rise above that line.

A certain awkwardness in the setting forth of this analysis arises from the fact that F and M, the final or determinant pair representing marginal cost and utility respectively, do not figure in the actual sales effected, but are excluded margins. This is due to the fact that our example has placed for convenience certain definite intervals between two valuations of buyers and sellers respectively. Under conditions of perfect competition the intervals will be infinitely small, and E and N, the extremes of actual supply and demand, would be legitimately taken to represent marginal cost and marginal utility. But for present purposes these margins must be understood to lie just outside the actual supply and demand.

We may summarise the bearing of this analysis upon the theory of Value and Price in the following words: Granting the assumption of the mathematical economist that the supply and demand of a market are infinitely divisible, the marginal or final pair, whose transaction directly determines price, earn, both of them, an infinitely small gain. In such a case either marginal cost or marginal utility may be taken with equal correctness to measure or determine price and value.

If the various contributors to supply and demand
are likewise supposed to enjoy precisely similar
advantages of production and to be subject to precisely equal pressure of needs, no differential gains
would emerge, and the market-price would distribute the gain, which would be, however, infinitely small on each transaction, with exact
equality among all who took part. The actual
circumstances of a real market are found to be
very different from this. Whether we take a
short or a long period, a "market" or a "normal"
price, we find that neither marginal cost nor
marginal utility exactly determines price or
value as an independent cause, though in any
given market one or the other will furnish a true
measure of price or value. In the transaction
of the marginal pair which determines price and
value an element of "forced gain" always emerges,
smaller where the market is large and free, larger
where it is small and restricted. The variation
of the economic resources of the different buyers
and sellers increases the inequality of distribution
effected by sales at a common price, by adding to
this forced gain a differential gain.[1]

[1] The notion that cost is a more serviceable *measure* of
value, even if it ranks equally with utility as a *cause* of value,
based upon the belief that different costs can more easily be
reduced to and expressed in some common term, such as
"labour-power" or "labour-time," has no warrant. Labour-
time, ignoring kinds and intensities and other conditions of the
giving out of labour-power, is no more a measure of "cost" than

FIRST APPENDIX TO CHAPTER III.

The Subjective Basis of Value.

In order to mark the essentially subjective nature of the theory of Value, it is desirable to distinguish more definitely subjective cost and utility from objective cost and utility.

Subjective cost must be taken to consist of the actual effort of workers measured in terms of disagreeable feeling and regarded as a quantity, *i.e.* disutility in work, as estimated by the individual consciousness of the worker. Objective cost must be taken to mean the productive energy which attaches to this effort, referred for measurement to some objective standard, *i.e.* hours, foot-tons, etc.

Subjective utility will represent the pleasurable feeling got out of consumption by the consumer, regarded as a quantity, *i.e.* the quantity of pleasure got from eating a loaf, or burning coals for warmth. Objective utility will measure the services of consumable goods by some objective standard, *i.e.* the power of

abstract "satisfaction" is a measure of utility; and the fact that the former is more usually, and, for certain purposes, conveniently, measured by the clock than the latter, gives it no practical advantage as a sound and accurate measure of value. It is curious to find so keen a writer as Dietzel resorting to this crudest fallacy of the Marxian analysis, in his criticisms of the marginal utility theory (*Jahrbücher für National-Oekonomie,* B. xx, SS. 587-8), and concluding that, "Whether I reckon by cost-value or use-value, the result is the same. But I reckon more simply and more accurately by cost-value than by use-value."

sustaining life, or furnishing physical power contained in a bushel of wheat, the actual heating-power in a hundred-weight of coal.

The distinction is of supreme importance in the art of economics. For while the subjective cost and utility which attach to the production and consumption of wealth are evidently the true measure of economic prosperity and adversity, as interpreted by the present conscious estimates alike of individuals, classes, or societies, it is equally evident that the operations of the actual industrial world, as expressed by many valuations, have direct reference only to objective cost and objective utility.

Now it will easily appear that a given quantity of objective cost may be related to indefinitely divergent quantities of subjective cost, according as it is distributed. A given quantity of labour-power will imply a quantity of painful effort which varies (1) With the nature and conditions of the work, *e.g.* according as it is monotonous, taxing continuously the same muscles or nerves, or varied, according as it implies danger of disease or accident from the conditions under which it is carried on. (2) With the mode of its apportionment among the workers, *e.g.* according as it falls upon strong men or upon weaker women and children, according as it is given out in a long or short day's work, etc.

A corresponding analysis of utility will show that a given quantity of objective utility will vary indefinitely when reduced to terms of subjective utility according to (1) the nature and conditions of consumption to which the objective utilities lend themselves, *i.e.*

the capacities and methods of enjoyment possessed by the actual consumers ; (2) according to their distribution among the consuming public, *i.e.* food will vary in subjective utility from infinity to zero, according as it passes into the possession of a starving person or a fully-fed one.

In this analysis, be it observed, no departure is made from the commonly accepted economic standard. The appeal is not to any such ethical or vital standard of values, as Ruskin seeks to substitute for market valuations. The present estimate is based strictly upon what "is," not upon what "ought" to be; the existing conscious valuations of desirable and undesirable, on the part of workers and consumers, are taken as the standard.

Referred to our theory of Value or Importance the terms will take the following setting : —

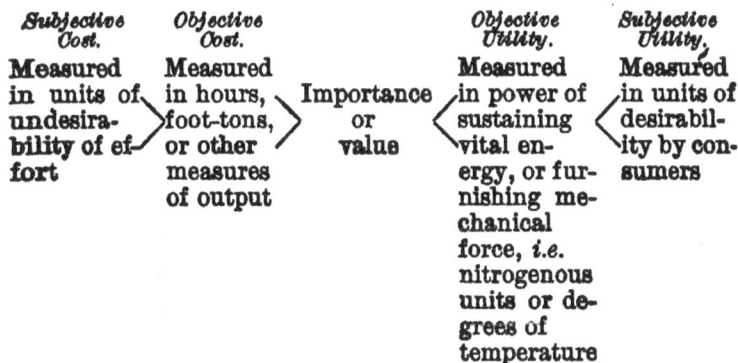

Subjective Cost.	*Objective Cost.*		*Objective Utility.*	*Subjective Utility,*
Measured in units of undesirability of effort	Measured in hours, foot-tons, or other measures of output	Importance or value	Measured in power of sustaining vital energy, or furnishing mechanical force, *i.e.* nitrogenous units or degrees of temperature	Measured in units of desirability by consumers

Professor Smart[1] suggests a serviceable illustration from the production and consumption of a given quantity of coal.

[1] *Value*, p. 6.

Subjective Cost.	*Objective Cost.*		*Objective Utility.*		*Subjective Utility.*
Painful effort of miners	Hours' work in raising coal	Supply of coal	Heating-power		Satisfaction gained from the heat

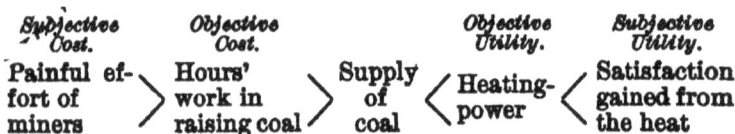

The efficacy and fruitfulness of this distinction of subjective and objective value may be illustrated by showing how it clearly explains one difficulty which besets the ordinary commercial view of value. Take a Supply of commodities: the first portion that is sold goes to satisfy the strongest desires of consumers, the next portion a somewhat weaker desire, and so on until the last portion that is sold satisfies the weakest desire, or, using the ordinary language, has the smallest utility attached to it. Yet all portions have the same price and the same value. Those who insist on taking utility as the essence of value find it difficult to explain how, with a diminishing utility attached to the successive portions sold, the value and price of the part which serves the fullest use are as great as that which supplies a necessary of life.

But our tabulation, which makes value = importance, shows that the importance attaching to all portions of supply that are sold is equal. For as the subjective utility furnished by consumption of the later units of supply diminishes, the subjective cost of producing these has increased. The first unit of consumption which satisfies the strongest-felt need is rightly considered as taking off that portion of supply which would be produced if no other were produced, because it can be produced most easily. Each later portion taken from supply satisfies a weaker need, but is produced at a greater cost, and since cost plays the same direct part in assigning importance or value to an article as does utility, there is no diminution of value by a reduction of utility accompanied by a corresponding rise of cost. The last portion of supply with the least subjective utility has the highest subjective cost.

This has been illustrated by pointing out that the last bottle of wine at the millionnaire's feast, which furnishes the smallest satisfaction to the drinkers, is the bottle, the products of which represents the last hour's labour of the hardest-worked producer, *i.e.* has the highest subjective cost attached to it.

Thus it can be simply shown how it is that each separate unit of supply, though it has a different cost and a different utility from any other unit, has the same value or importance.

Professor Scott, of the University of Wisconsin, in a letter which discusses the relative importance of the influence of "human costs" and "human utilities" on value, makes the following interesting and pertinent remarks concerning "the density and elasticity of the medium through which 'human costs' produce their effect on value."— "Under modern conditions of production there is a long road between human sacrifices and changes in the supply of goods. The people who furnish these sacrifices are, for the most part, labourers, and not infrequently a change of supply, which may mean greater sacrifice for them, may not mean greater costs for the man whose acts are directly responsible for changes in supply. Human costs may, therefore, change without producing any change in supply or value." This failure of human costs to register their

changes accurately in expenses of production, and so
to operate through supply on value, is of practical importance, and when in a later chapter I discuss the
special conditions of the labour-market, the reasons
for this failure will be evident.

SECOND APPENDIX TO CHAPTER III.

Böhm-Bawerk's General Theory of Value.

The elaborate attempt made by Böhm-Bawerk in
his important work, "The Positive Theory of Capital," to derive all "value" from the utility of final or
consumptive goods, and to refute the "cost" theory of
Value by showing the ultimate dependence of costs
upon utility, deserves separate consideration. The
keen, and sometimes brilliant, analysis by which he
has traced the flow of utility from consumptive goods
through the veins of industry in all the productive
processes, and has thus impressed upon his readers the
organic unity of the entire industrial system, has induced many to accept his interpretation of causality
in value as a sound and conclusive result of close
reasoning.

Let us, however, test Böhm-Bawerk's steps, starting
from his identification of "value" with economic
"importance," adopting, as far as possible, his own
statement of his case.

In the mere identification of value with "importance" there is nothing to indicate whether or how
far the "importance" of a good is derived from, and
depends upon, the costs of making it or the satisfaction

of consuming it. But no sooner has Böhm-Bawerk adopted "importance" as a synonym of value than he proceeds to "bias" it toward utility. When we read (p. 138) that, "If the value of a good is its importance to human well-being, and if this 'importance' means that some portion of our well-being is dependent on *our having* the good, it is clear that the amount of the goods value must be determined by the amount of well-being which depends on it." These words make it evident that "importance" is already conceived as a quality of goods which comes to the possessor, and that "well-being" is regarded purely as an effluence of consumption. So when the question is once more fairly put on the following page (139), "What is the gain to our well-being that in any given circumstances depends upon a good," the answer already imported into the question is "Utility." This, indeed, he openly avows, declaring that "the measure of *the utility* which depends on a good is, actually and everywhere, the measure of value for that good." We have then at once and plainly identified "utility" with "importance."

He next proceeds (p. 140) to identify this "well-being" or "utility" with "the satisfaction of a want," and to insist that the amount of this "well-being" derived from a "good" is found in the answer to two questions, — "First, *which*, among two or more wants, depends on it? and, second, what is the *urgency* of the dependent want or of its satisfaction?" (p. 140). It might be thought that his own use of the word "urgency" (which, though called in to explain, only repeats the notion originally conveyed by "impor-

tance") might have bade Böhm-Bawerk pause and
reflect whether the "urgency" of obtaining a particular good might not depend upon the cost of obtaining
an alternative good as much as upon the intensity of
the desire of the consumer. But by this time the
"importance" of a good has exclusive reference in
Böhm-Bawerk's eyes to the satisfaction in consumption; and he proceeds to a careful and highly serviceable analysis of the kinds of wants, on the one hand,
and the degrees of wants on the other. Then upon
this basis he develops and illustrates the theory of
Marginal Utility in relation to different kinds and
quantities of consumables.

Then, strangely enough, after utility has already
been identified with value and "importance," and marginal utility has already been taken as criterion, the
whole issue is once more thrown into the melting-pot
by starting the question, "What determines marginal
utility?" It now appears (for a little while) that
the "importance" (or value) of goods is not, as was
just affirmed, identical with their utility in consumption. On the contrary, Chapter VI opens with a sane
statement of the Law of Value which, though loosely
worded, is essentially correct.

"Usefulness and scarcity are the ultimate determinants of the value of goods." Now, not only is
scarcity thus fetched up from the supply side of the
equation as a determinant of value separate from
utility, but it is made the determinant of "marginal
utility" itself, for "it is the scarcity that decides to
what point the marginal utility actually does rise in
the concrete case" (p. 160).

Now, since "concrete cases" are precisely those to which the theory of value must apply, Böhm-Bawerk is surely affected by a suicidal mania in placing "marginal utility" at the mercy of "scarcity." For "scarcity" depends, so far, at any rate, as most goods are concerned, upon marginal costs of production, and it therefore appears that marginal costs will in these cases determine final utility. Here we perceive that Böhm-Bawerk has made an abandonment of his position very similar to that which Jevons, by the showing of Marshall, had made before him. Nor is this a momentary *lapsus calami,* for the writer proceeds to develop a theory which, though it no longer maintains "scarcity" in the dominant position just accorded it, equally repudiates the dominance of marginal utility for the time being. We are now told that "the height of marginal utility is determined by the relations of wants and provisions" (p. 160).[1]

But though Böhm-Bawerk goes so far in a footnote as to make a perfectly straight declaration of a sound theory of Value in affirming that "the relation of wants and provisions is the ultimate universal deter-

[1] "Classical economists," as Dietzel remarks, "have some ground for dissatisfaction at having served up to them, at the end of a long process of investigation, a Law of 'Marginal Utility' which turns out after all to be the familiar 'Law of Supply and Demand.'" "The value of a good depends upon the amount of its 'marginal utility': the latter upon the relation of needs and provision," says Böhm; "the others, with their formula that price depends upon the relation of demand (want) and supply (provision), come to the same result." (*Jahrbücher für National-Ökonomie,* Neue Folge, Bd. XX, S. 570.)

minant of the value of goods" (p. 160), he gives no
analysis of the ideas of "scarcity" and "provision"
to which he has given such a commanding place, and
traces no connection between them and "costs." On
the contrary, in the following chapters, VII, VIII,
and IX, he returns to his application of the theory of
Determination of Value by Marginal Utility, just as if
he had never interrupted or abandoned it. It is not
until Chapter X that he confronts the real issue of
"costs." It soon becomes evident that he is destined
to adopt the same "question-begging" method as that
by which "importance" was originally identified with
utility. The "value" of productive goods is what
we have really to investigate, for the "costs" which,
according to cost-theorists, dominate value, are expressed and contained in productive goods. Now,
instead of proving that the "value" of productive
goods, like that of consumptive goods, is derived from
utility, Böhm-Bawerk simply asserts it as "self-evident." "On the lines of our conception of value it
must be self-evident that a productive good, like any
other good, can only obtain value for us through our
recognition that on its possession or non-possession
depends our gain or loss of some one utility, of some
one satisfaction of want. And it is equally self-
evident that its value will be high when the dependent
satisfaction is important, and low when it is unimportant. The only difference is, that, in the case of goods
for immediate consumption, the good and the satisfaction stand beside each other in a direct causal relation,
while, in the case of productive goods, there is inter-
posed between them and the satisfaction finally

dependent on them a more or less lengthy series of intermediate members, their successive products" (p. 181).

We have, then, elaborate illustrations of the way in which the utility of consumptive goods is reflected back upon the productive goods and constitutes their value. "The value of each group has its immediate measure in the value of its product, the succeeding group" (p. 182). So "from stage to stage the name of the determining element changes, but under the different names it is always the same thing that acts — the marginal utility of the final product" (p. 183). We have now a perfectly smooth and intelligible theory in which all claims of "costs" to determine value disappears (though later on it will be revived for "a particular case" of value). In Böhm-Bawerk's own words we may piece together and thus condense the argument. "Costs are nothing else than the complex of those productive goods which have value — the labour, concrete capital, uses of wealth, and so on, which must be expended in the making of a product" (p. 183). "The amount of this, their (referring to 'means of production,' and so to costs) common value, is regulated for all, in the last resort, by the amount of the marginal utility of their finished product." (p. 182). "To put it generally: the value of the productive unit adjusts itself to the marginal utility and value of that product which possesses the least marginal utility among all the products for whose production the unit might, economically, have been employed" (p. 186).

Here is a perfectly consistent statement of the doctrine of marginal utility as the final determinant of value of all productive goods. But what has become of "scarcity" and the dominant place once assigned to it, and where has the interrelation of "wants and provisions" disappeared?

To get rid of "costs" by merging them in "productive goods,"[1] and then to declare that it is "self-evident" that the value of productive goods depends upon the marginal utility of the consumptive goods they are designed to make, is one of the most curiously bold *petitiones principii* which I have met in the annals of illogic. The judiciously minded reader will, at any rate, insist upon recalling Böhm-Bawerk to the "scarcity" and the "provision" which he has admitted to be determinants of that marginal utility of consumptive goods which he now seeks to make the be-all and end-all of economic activities.

If his argument in the chapter entitled "What Determines Marginal Utility" is intended to stand, we must insist on taking up the assertion there made that "it is the scarcity that decides to what point the marginal utility actually does rise in the concrete case," and the allied, though inconsistent, admission that "the height of marginal utility is determined by the relations of wants and provisions," and we must press for an examination of the bearing of "costs" upon scarcity and provision. If scarcity is a direct

---

[1] Dietzel pertinently remarks that "had the marginal-value theorists given their consideration to the 'power of production,' instead of to that of the possession of 'a supply,' they could not have so falsified the necessary relation between the value of the product and the value of productive or 'cost' goods." (*Jahrbücher für National-Oekonomie*, N. F. Bd. XX, S. 580.)

determinant of marginal utility, and so of value in consumptive goods, it must likewise be a determinant of the value of productive goods, not merely the scarcity of the consumptive goods reflected back, but the particular scarcity of each supply of productive goods. For it can hardly be suggested that scarcity of fire-irons affects the value of iron ore, but that scarcity of iron ore itself does not affect its value. If the relation of wants and provisions, or in current economic language, demand and supply, govern marginal utility and value in consumptive goods, as Böhm-Bawerk declares them to do, surely it is unreasonable to say that the relation of these same forces does not govern the value of productive goods. It would be an idle inconsistency to affirm that the value of consumptive goods is determined, not by marginal utility, but by the relations of " wants and provisions," but that the value of all intermediate goods is determined by the marginal utility of consumptive goods. This position Böhm-Bawerk does not, indeed, directly assume, but by words from his own pen he can be driven into it.

The entire trouble arises from his refusal to analyse " scarcity " when he has declared that it determines "marginal utility" in "the concrete case." Had he done so, he could hardly have failed to admit that " costs " are the direct determinants of " scarcity " in most classes of goods. In the first pages of Chapter X a partial restoration of " costs " as a " regulator " of value takes place. But even here, where the law of costs is admitted, " costs are not the final, but only the intermediate, cause of value. In the last resort they do not *give* it to their products, but receive it

from them" (p. 189). The example adduced to make
this perfectly clear is perhaps the most convincing
evidence of the *petitio principii*, with which I charge
Böhm-Bawerk in his initial dogmatic identification
of "importance" with "utility." "That Tokay is
not valuable because there are Tokay vineyards, but
that the Tokay vineyards are valuable because Tokay
has a high value, no one will be inclined to deny,
any more than that the value of a quicksilver mine
depends on the value of quicksilver, the wheat field
on the value of wheat, the brick kiln on that of bricks,
and not the reverse" (p. 189). On the contrary, this
is precisely what the major number of thoughtful
economists have always denied; while admitting that
the utility of Tokay vineyards depends upon the
utility of Tokay, they refuse to make the assumption
that value is identical with utility, and are inclined to
insist that the "high value" of Tokay is itself, in
part, determined by the limited quantity of Tokay
vineyards. This, Böhm-Bawerk has admitted when
(p. 160) he makes marginal utility depend on "scarcity." What natural scarcity does in the case of
Tokay vineyards, "costs" do in the case of freely
produced goods. Böhm-Bawerk is right in declaring
"costs are not the final, but only the intermediate,
cause of value." But the economic problems of value
are concerned with intermediate or efficient, and not
with final, causes. We may yield to Böhm-Bawerk
the final causality of utility all along the line, but insist that the relations between cost (or scarcity) and
utility are what economists should regard as "causes"
of value.

CHAPTER IV.

THE LAW OF RENT AS THE BASIS OF COÖRDINA-TION OF THE FACTORS OF PRODUCTION.

PART I.

§ 1. In discovering the method by which a price of goods is determined, we have practically learnt how a ratio of exchange is established between one class of goods and any other class. For the sale of goods for money is admittedly not more than half a transaction; when ₜthe money that is received has been expended in an act of purchase, the transaction is complete; goods have been exchanged for goods.

But in order to understand more fully the nature of this bargain, we must regard any two commodities which have been exchanged as complexes of the various quantities of factors of production that have entered into them in the various productive processes.

A bargain for the sale or the exchange of finished commodities will depend, so far as supply-forces are concerned, upon the conditions of a number of preceding, underlying bargains for the use of different kinds and quantities of land, capital, and labour power. How far does our analysis of market-price (and value) of commodities apply also to the transactions for purchase of the use of these factors?

The market-price of commodities contained, over and above the measure of marginal cost or marginal utility, a residuum of "forced gain," and also allowed a series of differential gains to accrue to the stronger buyers and sellers, measured from the position of the marginal buyer and seller.

§ 2. Do the same conditions hold for the purchase of the use of the factors of production? If we regard the hiring of factors of production as equivalent to the sale of their use, we are confronted with the investigation of the market for the sale of the use of various supplies of land, labour, and capital.

Now these markets differ in one radical respect from a market for commodities, in the mode of measuring the supply. In our setting of the horse-market, and any other market for goods, a supply was reckoned for purposes of bargain as consisting of a number of units of equal quantity and quality. · Where the wheat or wool in a market consists of different qualities or kinds, it will, in theory and usually in practice, rank as a number of separate supplies subject to separate bargaining. Our differential gains in such a market measured the different valuations set by buyers or sellers upon goods which were held to be identical in size and quality. Now in a market for the sale of the use of labour and land no formal reduction to equal sized units takes place. Though the real object of sale is a quantity of productive power vested in land or labourers, what is nominally bought and sold is the use of so many acres, or so many labourers, containing each of them an indefinitely larger or smaller quantity of productive power. But while the bargainers express themselves in terms of acres and labourers, the real object of their bargain is the use of land-power and labour-power, and they are continually engaged in reducing acres and labourers to units of productive power when they buy and sell. The maintenance of this awkward mode of measuring land and labour, and the necessity of finding some standard of reference in order to ascertain the quantity of productive power contained in an acre or a labourer, has given rise to a grading of these factors of production which has played a large part in economic theory. In particular, it has given rise to the habit of taking the least productive land and labour as a standard of reference, and reckoning the productivity of better land and labour by comparison with this. Thus the better land and labour in a supply is held to obtain a differential gain or rent which measures the excess of its productive power over the worst land or labour. If an acre of the worst land in use contains 4 units of land-use, then an acre of better land containing 8 units has a differential rent of 4 units imputed to it. Now it is important to observe that these differential rents are in no sense equivalent to the differential gains which arose in a market of goods. The latter represent the different valuations put by different buyers and sellers upon *similar* objective quantities, the former represent valuations of *different* objective quantities. In order to place the sale of factors of production upon the same level with markets for the sale of goods, it will be necessary to eliminate these objective differences which rest⃰ upon customary modes of measuring the repositories of productive power.

But since economic theory has felt obliged to adopt for many purposes the conventional modes of measuring productive power, and has derived thence certain laws which play an important part in the theory of distribution, it is necessary to accept provisionally the current custom of measuring land by its acreage per annum, labour by the labourer per hour or week, and capital by its money value, in £100, until we have discovered a method of common measurement of the factors which any satisfactory theory of distribution requires.

The general tendency of economic science, especially in England, has been to assimilate the theory of the sale of capital-use and labour-power to that of the sale of goods, but to mark off the sale of land-use as subject to quite other economic laws.

I propose to bring the sale of the factors of production under the general laws of value and of price as disclosed by the investigation of bargaining for commodities.

For this purpose it is necessary (1) to coördinate the three factors with respect to the conditions which regulate their price; (2) to show that their sales are in essence identical, as economic processes, with the sale of commodities.

It is most convenient to approach the first of these tasks by examining the validity of the claim to assign a separate law to the determination of the rent of land.

The separatist doctrine may be thus summarised. Ricardo's fundamental assumption, upon which it still rests, is that the use of land is the use of certain "inherent and indestructible properties of the soil," certain fixed supplies of land of given fertility and position; that the efforts of man cannot increase or diminish these supplies. So, whereas the price of the use of capital and of labour may be determined by processes of competition and higgling based upon the will of individual bargainers to increase or reduce the effective supply, the price of land-use will be determined directly by circumstances not relating to land but to the efficiency of capital and labour in those industries into which land-use enters. That is to say, rent is a surplus, land taking in payment for its use whatever residue is left after human efforts and sacrifices are remunerated at a competitive price.

§ 8. Now, since the determination of price is our objective, it will be most profitable to test the validity of this separate treatment of land by examining the arguments which are adduced to support the doctrine that rent of land forms no element in prices, "does not enter into price," and does not help to determine prices.

Two lines of argument have been used to support this conclusion: the first has reference to extensive cultivation with a margin represented by the worst pieces of land in use; the second to intensive cultivation with a margin represented by the worst productive power in use, contained in a particular piece of land.

These two arguments are often adduced as contributory to the same result and as consistent with one another. This, I propose to show, is not the case.

The first argument is that with which we are familiarised by Ricardo's presentation in Chapter II of his "Political Economy." We are to suppose different quantities of land taken successively into cultivation to contribute to a single supply: the "marginal" land in use at any time will pay no rent; the produce raised on this mar-

ginal land with the largest expenditure of labour
and capital per unit of produce will be the "regulator" of the price of the whole supply. Since no
portion of the value of the produce of this marginal
land is taken for rent, "rent is not a component
part of the price of commodities." Ricardo leaves
it to be inferred that since the worst quantities of
labour and capital engaged in production pay some
wage and interest to their owners, wage and interest must always be component parts of the price
of commodities.

Now this reasoning, so far as it relates to differential rents, measuring the superiority of particular lands over the margin, is, of course,
irrefutable. But its assumption that a margin of
cultivation is composed necessarily of no-rent
land, has been exposed by Adam Smith in anticipation and by numerous writers since Ricardo.
It is quite unnecessary to have recourse to the
historical arguments which Carey and others have
used to show that the extension of the margin of
cultivation is not necessarily, or in point of fact,
from better land to worse. These arguments are
faulty in that they ignore the part which position
for market takes in determining the goodness or
badness of land.

The assumption that the extensive margin is
necessarily a no-rent margin arises from a fallacious simplicity in the abstract setting given by
Ricardo to his problem. If all land is considered

as contributing to a single supply, *e.g.* wheat, and
if this supply contains more land than is required,
some of which is slightly inferior to the worst
land in use, the margin will be no-rent land.

But neither of these assumptions is absolutely
warrantable.

Suppose that an increase in the population and
the demand for wheat brings into cultivation all
the land available, the worst land in use may or
must pay an actual rent. This will not be a
differential rent, but a forced or scarcity rent
limited in its rise only by the pressure of the need
for land, and representing the power of the stronger
bargainer in the final pair that determines the
market-price.[1] Such forced rent would evidently
be reckoned as an expense incidental to all portions of the wheat supply, and would enter into
the prices.   But this may be held to lie outside
of practical economics for a country in open commercial relations with the world supply of land.

What really invalidates the Ricardian treatment
is the fact that most land in use has several alternative uses or can contribute toward several
different supplies.

Though the worst grazing land may pay no

---

[1] The adjective "monopoly" has been often applied to such
scarcity rent by economists; but, though bearing some analogy
to a monopoly or "one-man market" by reason of the dicta-
torial power held by the marginal owners, this marginal rent
is best described as a scarcity rent or forced gain.

rent, the worst wheat land might be better for
grazing than the worst grazing land, in which
case it can only be obtained for growing wheat by
paying a little more than its differential rent for
grazing purposes; this rent for the worst wheat
land will be a positive rent, and will enter into
wheat prices; again, the worst market-garden land
competing for a given market may be tolerably
good wheat land, and, if so, the rent which it could
get for wheat forms a marginal rent for market-
garden land. So as we ascend to the higher and
more special uses of land, we find that the differential rents must be measured, not from a no-rent
margin, but from a minimum specific rent of a
higher and higher order, until we get to city
ground, which is measured from a minimum which
must exceed the rent which that land could obtain
for the best agricultural use to which it could be
put.

The accompanying figure will serve for illustration. Suppose the city A to lie in the middle
of a fertile plain surrounded by belts of land devoted to different uses. The outermost belt, E,
is rough pasture, improving in quality and position as it approaches D, so that whereas the
pasturage at the outer belt of E pays no rent, a
gradually rising differential rent emerges as we
approach the circle D. Similarly, let us suppose
the belt of land between D and C to be engaged
in growing cereals, the worst cereal land being at

D, and the land as we approach C gradually improving for cereal use. If the worst cereal land at D would be of equal value for grazing to the grazing land midway between D and E, it will be rented for cereal use at a rent which is equivalent to or slightly higher than the differential grazing rent paid by the land midway between D and E. Thus the marginal land for cereals will be found paying a positive rent, and the differential rents

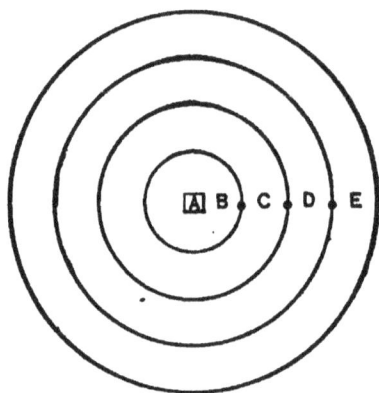

for cereals will be superimposed upon that marginal rent. Again, as we come nearer to the city, crossing the circle C, we come to a belt of land utilised for market gardens, improving in quality and position as we near the circumference B. If the worst of this market-garden land in C is capable of being cereal land of middling quality, the marginal market-garden land will pay a rent equivalent to the marginal cereal rent and the differential cereal rent for middling quality of

cereal land. In the same way it will appear that
the worst land of the next belt, B, devoted to
suburban uses, will pay a still higher marginal
rent, based upon the fact that the worst suburban
land at B may be capable of drawing a high differential rent for market-garden purposes. When
we finally reach A, the city itself, the worst ground
may draw a ground rent higher than that drawn
by the margin of suburban land.[1]

For the sake of simplicity I have assumed that
the marginal rent is directly and exactly determined by the alternative use of the worst land in
cultivation for each use. But this, of course, is
not necessarily the case. It is not necessary that
the worst land should have an alternative use; it
may be some better land, enjoying a differential
as well as a marginal rent, which occupies that

---

[1] This argument which makes "marginal rents" hinge upon
"alternative *uses*" of land may appear to lean unduly toward
the doctrine that "marginal utility" determines values. But
though the marginal utility theory can neatly illustrate the
variation of values connected with different uses, natural varia-
tions in their bearing upon scarcity of supply can afford a
similar "illustration" from the other side. The existence of
"alternative uses" with different values may be explained
either by the different chemical and other qualities of the soil
(the intensity of various wants being given) or by the growth
and intensity of different human wants (the differences in qualities of soil being assumed). The true explanation makes the
value of "alternative uses" directly dependent on the relation
between natural qualities of soil and human wants. Here, as
elsewhere, "marginal utility" may be regarded as the final
cause of value, but not as the sole efficient cause.

position. The worst wheat land might obtain a
marginal rent of 20*s.* per acre; superior qualities
of wheat land might take higher rents rising to
40*s.* Suppose that some of the land rented at
30*s.* had another use which would yield a rent of
29*s.*; it is evidently this land which fixes the marginal rent; it must receive 30*s.* in order to induce
it to contribute to the wheat supply, and the 20*s.*
taken by the worst land measures its inferiority
of wheat-growing power as compared with the 30*s.*
land. It is possible that the 20*s.* land might continue to grow wheat, however little rent was paid;
its rent is directly determined by the cost of keeping in the supply of wheat land the superior land
at 30*s.* In such a case it will be the 30*s.* land and
not the 20*s.* land which is the direct determinant
of price for the supply side in the market for sale
of wheat-growing power. The Ricardian analysis
has, in fact, laid undue stress upon the worst land
contributing to supply, the so-called margin of
cultivation. It is important to understand that
this margin has no particular significance except
as furnishing a convenient measure for the ready
reckoning of differential rents; it has no determinant importance. It is the land with an alternative use, which may or may not be the marginal
land, that not only determines price from the supply
side, but determines the whereabouts of the margin.
This can easily be shown by a closer examination
of the illustration just taken. It is admitted that

what is really sold in the bargaining between landowners and cultivators for the use of wheat land
is units of wheat-growing power. The fact that
the nominal subject of bargain is acres of different
kinds of wheat land must not blind us to this
under-truth. Suppose now that the price per unit
of wheat-growing power, as determined in a market
set forth after the manner of our horse-market,
turned out to be 5*s.* per unit. This price, we will
further suppose, is determined by the owner of the
30*s.* land, which yields 6 units per acre of this
wheat-producing power, and which, by the possession of an alternative use at a price just below 30*s.*,
has assumed the position of seller in the "final
pair." The price 5*s.* has been determined on the
supply side by the fact that it is required to induce
this particular land to contribute toward the supply of wheat land. Now what about the 20*s.* land,
the worst wheat land in occupation, the margin
of cultivation, which ex-hypothesi only yields 4
units of wheat-power per acre? It is quite legitimate to suppose that the owner of this land, having no available alternative use at any price
approaching 20*s.*, might have been willing to contribute to supply even if the price per unit had
been fixed at 4*s.*, and the rent per acre consequently
had been at 16*s.* instead of 20*s.* In such a case it
will be evident that it is the owner of the 30*s.* land
who, in fixing for the supply side the price per
unit at 5*s.*, determines the amount of rent per acre

of the land at the margin of cultivation. In dealing with the price of land-use, as of any other kind
of goods, it is to the strongest bargainer that we
must look for the direct and final determination
of a price, and the differential gain of the others
should rightly be measured from him. It is only
the conventional modes of selling and regarding
the sales of uses of factors of production that
obliges us to depart from this rule, and in the
case of land makes it convenient to measure differential rents from the worst land in cultivation
which contributes to the market.

But though the differential rents thus calculated, not from the subjective valuation of the
"final pair" of bargainers, but from the margin
of cultivation, are not equivalent in amount to
the "differential gains" reckoned according to our
market for sale of ordinary commodities, their
economic nature is not essentially different, for
they are determined in the same way. In so far
as the price of uses of factors of production is
reached by competition and bargaining (and this
is our hypothesis throughout), the mode of determining rent, interest, and wages will be essentially the same as that of determining the price
of horses or wheat, and in order to understand the
theory of Distribution we must, while accepting
for convenience the different grading which charac-
terises the former, penetrate to the essential units
beneath. In land, we must recognise that rent or

price of land-use is determined, just like the price
of commodities, by the relative economic strength
of buyers and sellers bargaining for a given quantity of land-use and not for a given sized piece of
land, though the language of these proceedings has
reference to the latter. The subjective valuations
of a single owner and a single tenant (the final
pair) fix the limits for the price of a unit of this
land-power, the stronger of the two fixing the
price-point. This done, the rent per acre is determined by the net yield of land-power in each grade
of land. If the higgling of the market fixes the
price of a unit at 20s., the best land available for
that supply may yield 2 units of power per acre,
in which case the rent per acre is 40s., the worst
land only ½ an unit with a rent of 10s. per acre.[1]

Thus it appears that the determining increment

---

[1] The treatment of rent as purchase money of so much land-
power or use of land will only be fully justified when the full
theory of coördination of the factors in production is grasped.
One surface objection, however, may be removed here. In
speaking of rent as the price of quantities of land-power, it
may appear as if I had committed myself to the view that all
land with some quantity of productive power could command a
price. To avert the appearance of this error I have used the
term "net yield of land-power" to indicate the power which
could command a price. Unless the value of the productivity
of a piece of land exceeds the expense of working it, there is
no "net yield of land-power," and, therefore, no price for such
power. The term "net yield of land-power" represents in the
use of land what emerges in the case of a machine or other piece
of concrete capital after expense of working is defrayed.

of supply is not necessarily identical with the worst land contributing to that supply, commonly known as the margin of cultivation. If the slackness of demand for wheat land causes a fall of rent, it is not necessarily the 20*s.* land which passes out of cultivation; it may be the 30*s.*, if the latter has an alternative remunerative use and the former has not.

The actual determination of rent by this method is, of course, complicated by the fact that as a rule not merely one part of the land supply, but many parts, have alternative uses to which they would succumb, were the price for one use to fall below a certain figure. But it is reasonable for us to assume that the price per unit of land-use is always determined by the common position of one part of supply, which at that price is just induced to contribute toward that supply in preference to some others; the fact that at a different price per unit some other land would occupy this position need not concern us.

Now since it is convenient to retain the term "margin of occupation or employment" to describe the worst or least efficient part of supply, some other term is needed to mark that part which occupies the determinant place in any given market. I propose to speak of this portion as "the determining portion of supply," and of its owner as "the determining owner." The worst land in cultivation for a particular supply will be described, in accordance with usage, as "marginal land," and its rent as "marginal rent." "Differential rents" will be the rents obtained by lands of superior productivity contributing to this supply, and will be measured from the margin.

It will, however, be useful sometimes to substitute the terms "specific" and "individual" for "marginal" and "differential," or to conjoin these adjectives in order to emphasise certain aspects of our application of the Law of Rent.

One further distinction requires to be made. Whether the determinant portion of supply of land be the worst land or not makes no difference; the price of land-power, and so the rent of different qualities of land, appears to be directly determined by the fact that some of the land has an alternative use, and that it may refuse to contribute to the supply unless a certain price is paid. But though the alternative price that can be got for some other use determines a lower limit of marginal rent, there is nothing to prevent the marginal rent rising higher than this. If the 30s. land has an alternative use, it is possible that use might yield only 25s.; now, though the owner of that land would consent to take 26s. rent, he may be able to get 30s., because there is, for the time, an absolute scarcity of land available for this supply. In a word, he may be able, as the final seller, to take a forced gain of 5s., which corresponds precisely to the "forced gain" in the price of the horse in our analysis of a market for commodities.

In such a case it might be best to distinguish this 5*s.* from the other 25*s.*, and to class it as a third form of rent. Thus, if we took the highest rented land at 40*s.*, we should describe 25*s.* as marginal rent, 5*s.* as forced or scarcity rent, and 15*s.* as a differential rent measuring the superior productivity of this land over the land at the margin of employment for this use. This would signify that 25*s.* was the price necessary to make this land abandon some alternative use and enter this particular supply; that its economic force as a bargainer, within the market of this use, enabled it to exact 5*s.* more, and that 15*s.* measured its superiority over the absolutely worst land contributing to this supply.

Though the actual distribution of land-uses in a country will never be so regular as that represented in our illustration, the latter approaches far nearer to the actual facts than does the Ricardian hypothesis, and compels us to perceive that for many, if not most, purposes land at the margin of cultivation will pay a positive rent.

The argument from extensive cultivation, though quite valid for showing that differential rents do not enter price, lets into price any rents which are paid for the use of marginal land contributing to any supply. Land may be graded according to its economic uses; the differential rents will be excluded; the positive marginal rents will be included in the market (and even in normal) prices.

§ 4. Yet, though Adam Smith, in dealing with wine lands and other cases of limited supplies of land, J. S. Mill, in the formulation of the Laws of Value, Jevons, and other modern economists have explicitly affirmed that scarcity prices of land all enter into prices, Professor Marshall and not a few thinkers reject this view.

It is of the utmost importance to understand the grounds upon which this rejection is based. Jevons admits that a marginal rent enters into expenses of production, "If land which has been yielding £2 per acre rent, as pasture, be ploughed up and used for raising wheat, must not the £2 per acre be debited against the expenses of production of wheat?"[1] Marshall, in commenting upon this passage, urges that "there is no connection between the particular sum of £2 and the expenses of production of that wheat which only just pays its way."[2] That is to say, though the

---

[1] Preface, 2d ed., *Theory of Political Economy.*

[2] Book V, Ch. VIII, par. 6 (note). There is, however, a curious passage in the sections immediately preceding this, in which Marshall himself seems to admit that a marginal rent does affect price. One of the chief conditions affecting the normal value of oats will be "the amount of land which is capable of growing oats, but for which there is so great a demand for other purposes that it affords a higher rent, when used for them, than when used for growing oats. *For the expenses of production of those oats which only just pay their way are greater than they would be*, were it not that much of the land which would

worst land contributing to the wheat supply pays a rent of £2 per acre, no portion of that rent enters into price. This rejection of marginal rent from price is achieved by turning from the extensive to the intensive margin of cultivation.

Upon this mode of reasoning those economists rely who assert that in no case does rent enter into price, and who extend the principle from agricultural rent to all other rents. The argument, first plainly formulated by James Mill, briefly and occasionally used by Ricardo, runs as follows:—

return the largest crops of oats to the smallest outlay is diverted to growing other crops that will enable it to pay a higher rent than oats would afford; and therefore the rent that land on which oats could be grown can be made to pay for other purposes, *though it does not enter into the expenses of production and the normal value of oats, yet does indirectly affect them.* (Bk. V, Ch. VIII, par. 5.)

Marshall does not explain how it "indirectly affects them." The passage seems to admit that the positive marginal rent of oat land, arising from alternative uses, will raise the price of oats, somehow, without entering into the marginal expenses of production, although this is inconsistent with the opening words of the same paragraph, where it is said that "the expenses of production of those oats which only just pay their way are greater than they would be" if marginal oat lands could be got at no-rent. The fact is that Marshall is quite wrong from his standpoint in admitting that "the expenses of production of those oats, which only just pay their way, are greater than they would be," etc. The application of the "dose" principle to an intensive margin of cultivation, upon which he relies through his main argument, will oblige him to ignore altogether the positive rent which must be paid for the extensive margin of oat land.

Take a given piece of land, apply to it "doses" of capital and labour remunerated at the ordinary rates of interest and wages. The produce raised by the earlier applications of capital and labour will leave a residue, after the fixed payments of interest and wages, which will figure as rent. The economic tillers of the soil will increase the number of these "doses" of capital and labour until the last dose yields just enough to pay interest and wages, leaving nothing for rent. Since no part of the produce obtained by the application of the last "dose" can be reckoned as rent, while the expense of raising this last part of the produce measures the price of the whole supply, it follows that rent does not enter into the price.

Economists have often evinced some hesitation in applying the doctrine that rent does not enter into prices to manufactured goods; but Professor Marshall has clearly shown that a fair expansion of the older argument requires us to hold that "ground rent does not enter into the expenses of manufacture."[1]

Now the most curious feature of this illustration is that it can be similarly applied to show that interest and wages do not enter into price.

Instead of taking a given quantity of land and applying additional doses of capital and labour, let us take a given quantity of capital and apply additional doses of labour, neglecting for the

---

[1] *Principles of Economics*, 2d ed., p. 462.

present the consideration of land. Let our piece of
capital be the premises, stock, good-will, etc., of
a shop. Apply to this capital additional doses
of labour in the shape of shop assistants. The
assistants first engaged will earn not merely their
wages but a considerable surplus, which will go
as interest and profit to the owner of the business.
Assuming there is plenty of labour available, the
shopkeeper will go on increasing the number of
his shop assistants as long as the last-engaged
produces more value than is represented in his
wages. At last he will come to a "marginal"
assistant, who only just produces the value of
his wages. Now the shop goods into which this
"marginal" assistant puts his work pay no interest
or profit; but they are sold for the same price as
the other shop goods, and being produced under
the least favourable circumstances, *i.e.* at the margin of labour, must be considered to measure the
price. Since no portion of the value added to
these goods in the retail process can figure as interest, so interest on shop capital is no component
part of the price. Or, again, take the machinery,
stock, good-will, etc., which constitute the capital
of a given factory. Here, too, after a certain point
in the application of labour is reached, the same
law of diminishing return is found to apply; each
"hand" beyond a certain number yields a less and
less surplus of value over and above his wages,
until a "hand" is reached whom it is just worth

while to engage because the value of his work just covers his wages. The "goods" made by this last hand evidently pay no interest or profit, and as they are precisely analogous to the grain produced by the application of the last dose of capital and labour to a given piece of land, they govern price, and therefore interest does not enter into the price of manufactured goods.[1]

Marshall, indeed, in one passage, applies the "dose" illustration to show that one of the shepherds employed upon a large sheep farm is to be regarded as a "marginal shepherd," whose productivity only just earns his wages.[2] But curiously enough he fails to recognise that he has proved the expenses of raising sheep to be determined by this man's wages, and that interest or profit of farm capital does not enter into the price of sheep.

Finally, we can take a fixed quantity of labour-power and apply to it successive doses of capital or land. First take the energy and skill of a single business man who borrows doses of capital for a commercial enterprise. The last dose he borrows only yields to him a minimum or nominal

---

[1] I may here state that I use interest for the return made for use of concrete forms of capital and not merely for capital valued in money. When necessary, I distinguish the two as "real" and "money" interest. Thus alone can one evade the Protean term "profit."

[2] *Principles*, 2d ed., Vol. I, p. 567.

return after paying its necessary interest, *i.e.* he cannot *profitably* utilise any more. It therefore appears that the last increment of the goods he handles in his business yields no earnings of management. Therefore earnings of management form no element in expenses of production or of price.

Or take the case of an agriculturist in a country where there is plenty of available land of a given quality at a fixed or customary rent. The produce raised by such a man upon the few acres he first rents may yield him, after paying the stipulated rent, a large surplus which he will take as wages. Let this labourer increase the acreage he rents; beyond a certain point he will find that the proportion of the produce obtained by each successive application of more land, which is left for wages, becomes less and less, until he reaches an application which, after paying rent, does not increase the net surplus which he takes as wages. In other words, the produce obtained by this marginal application of land to labour "pays" no wage. Since this marginal produce measures and indicates the price of the whole supply, wages do not enter into that price. Now in respect to the supply-price of agricultural produce in any given market, it is held that rent does not enter into price because a portion of that supply is obtained under conditions which preclude any part of it from counting as rent. So it must be held that wages do not enter into the price because another portion of that supply may, as we have seen, have been obtained under conditions which forbid any of it from contributing to wages, while interest does not enter into price because a third portion is raised under conditions which require that it all go for rent and wages and none of it for interest. We have only to suppose three producers — the first of whom has a fixed quantity of land, and keeps adding fresh doses of capital and labour; the second with a fixed quantity of capital, which he spreads over increasing quantities of land and labour; and the third with a fixed quantity of labour, to which he applies ever increasing quantities of land and capital — to arrive at the conclusion that neither rent, interest, nor wages is a component part of "price."

To this *reductio ad absurdum* we are inevitably brought by following out the line of argument usually adduced to show that rent does not enter into price.

§ 5. This line of reasoning, however, though it compels the admission of a fundamental error in the "dose" illustration as applied to intensive cultivation, does not explain the nature of that error. The truth is that a certain harmony of combination of factors of production exists for various productive purposes. In a given case, a certain proportion of the three factors of production is most productive. If, however, there is a short supply of one of them at the former quality and price, a more than proportionate increase of one or both of the others may be substituted, involving, of course, an increased cost per unit of the increment of supply.

So when the final dose of capital and labour on a given piece of wheat land achieves a product which yields no rent, it means that with the same quantity of land-use as sufficed for a smaller product, a larger quantity of capital and labour-use has been combined; that as no more land-use was employed, none was paid for.

˗ Or, if it seems more reasonable, we may consider a piece of land as containing various land-powers, some high, some low — some powers so low that they require so large a proportion of capital and labour to utilise them that they only just pay to work. These low natural powers yield no net economic powers of production.

Now take the case where a portion of the final increment of a supply of wheat is raised on the extensive margin at a positive rent of 2 units, and a portion upon the intensive margin where it is held to pay no rent. It is evident that the cost of production is the same in each case, though rent forms 2 units of cost (out of say 10) in one case and none in the other. Where the intensive margin is taken, 2 more units of cost of use of capital and labour are found. The man who chooses between paying for worse land-use or for more capital- and labour-use exercises a choice between the factors of production which implies their interchangeability. Either land-power or capital- and labour-power may do the extra work required to raise the last increment; if the former is preferred, rent is paid; if the latter, rent is not paid, but more profit and wage. This interchangeability is a fact of prime importance in understanding the theory of distribution.

If, because land-use can be replaced by capital-use, we choose to say that rent does not enter money-cost of production, we are, strictly speaking, justified in doing so. But by a similar argument it is possible to show that interest and wages need not enter money-cost of production.

The last increment of cotton cloth in the supply may be the produce of the worst loom in the worst-equipped mill (*i.e.* raised on the extensive margin of capital), or it may be the produce of a good loom in a good mill working overtime: in the former case it is partly produced by capital-use, which may be paid by interest; in the latter case there is no extra call on capital. (Or taking the analogy of lower un-paid powers of land, we may say that lower power of capital entered in unpaid.) In the former case, the final increment of cotton cloth yields an interest; in the latter case, it only just pays overtime wages; by taking the latter case, we prove that interest forms no element in the price of cotton cloth. But it must be observed that the money-cost and the price of the final increment of the cotton cloth will be the same, whether it is said to include profit or not.

§ 6. We have shown how rent need not enter money-cost of production and price of wheat where the final increment is produced on the intensive margin. By a similar application of the Law of Substitution it can be shown that wage may or may not enter into the price of this same final increment of wheat. Suppose it is raised by a tenant-farmer as part of the result of an extra last hoeing and ploughing on his land, it pays extra wages but no rent; if, however, instead of this extra hoeing and ploughing the farmer decided to hire one more acre of the same quality of land and spread the same amount of labour-power over the larger area, the product of this last acre pays its rent but no wage.

Or, again, take the case of a 4-loom weaver [1] who decides it is just worth his while to undertake a 5th loom; the product of the 5th loom, after paying a profit and a compensation for extra wear and tear to the weaver, yields him no true increase of wage. The real wage, or net advantage, which he obtains by working 5 looms only exceeds by a nominal amount the net advantage of working 4 looms.

---

[1] The assumption here is that the weaver is on time wages. The rarity of such an occurrence need not be taken to invalidate the illustration.

The labour of working the 5th loom or the last acre of land is certainly remunerated by wages, and at the same rate as the other looms or other acres. Why, then, does it appear from the "dosing" illustration that the product of the last loom or last acre pays no wage?

Only two replies are possible. First, it is possible to suppose that the weaver's capacity was underrated, and that he had been put to 4 looms when his normal energy was equal to 5 looms. Now it is evident that if a 5-loom weaver is set to work 4 looms, there is an absolute waste of labour-power; if the mistake is discovered, and the waste stopped by adding a 5th loom, the weaver, assuming he were on time wages, might receive no additional wage. Similarly, we may suppose that the farmer underestimates the number of acres upon which he may most profitably spread his labour-power; discovering his mistake, he may add the extra acre which seems just to pay its rent and leave nothing for his wage.

Now the sophistry of these examples is patent. If an employer hires a worker and misapplies his working power, he must pay as much as if he had properly applied it; if a farmer does not understand the economy of his labour-power, he may expend upon a smaller area the same quantity of power which he ought to have bestowed upon a larger area. If a tenant hires a piece of land and puts 5 doses of capital upon it when he ought to have put 6, he pays a rent based upon the supposition that he will make a full economic use of the land, *i.e.* that he will put 6 doses on it. If, discovering his error, he afterward adds the sixth dose, he only appears to pay no rent out of its produce, because he has all the time been paying a rent based upon the supposition that he was working his land with 6 doses.

The conclusion is a peculiarly simple one. If we make an uneconomical use of a factor of production, we must pay the same price for it as if we made an economical use of it.

Some of the "dosing" illustrations are thus vitiated by treating the owner of a factor of production as if he were not an "economic man," whereas the just application of a principle, like the Law of Diminishing Returns, does not permit such an assumption to be made.[1]

§ 7. But the "dosing" illustration is vitiated by a more fundamental flaw. By assuming the separate action of each dose, it ignores the organic relation of parts in industry. It is not necessary to suppose that the 5th loom was added to the

---

[1] If I rent a piece of land in Piccadilly, in which all houses are 3 or 4 stories, the rent I shall pay will take into consideration the capacity of the ground for building a 3- or 4-story house. If I choose to put a 1-story house upon the ground, the rent I pay will be the same as if I had more fully utilised the site. If afterward I add stories, it will seem that I pay no rent for this extra accommodation, but in reality I have been paying it all the time.

weaver because it was found out that he had been paid as a 5-loom weaver while he had been working at 4 looms. We may suppose that he is in full knowledge of the facts and has a full exercise of choice; as a consequence, he estimates that it just pays him to work 5 looms instead of 4. Now why will it appear that, whereas the weaver, when working 4 looms, made a net wage on each of them, he makes a merely nominal wage on the 5th loom? The 5th loom, after it is added, is found to be just as productive as any of the other 4 looms. The answer is plain. The 5th loom only just pays because its addition has injured his work with the other 4 looms; he must work 5 looms at slower speed than he worked 4, stoppages will be more frequent, more time must be spent on tuning, cleaning, etc. If he gives out the same working energy to 5 looms as formerly he gave to 4 (which supposition is involved in our hypothesis that to a fixed quantity of labour-power is added a fresh increment of capital), the effort of adding the last loom can only be estimated by taking account of its influence upon the productivity of the other 4 looms.

So, reverting to our illustration of a fixed quantity of shop-capital which for its most profitable working requires 10 shop-assistants. The tenth shopman, whichever he may be, appears only just to produce enough to pay his wages, because it is evident that it would not pay to put in an eleventh shopman. But the productivity of this last unit of labour cannot be rightly separated from the productivity of the other units, as is supposed when a particular additional increment of product is attributed to his presence. The service of this final unit of shop-labour largely consists in enabling the shop to be better ordered, and a better division of labour to be adopted; in other words, it helps to raise the general efficiency of all the labour employed.

The same is true, though within narrower limits, of the effect of the last dose of capital applied to a given piece of land; its effect is not a separate one, but partly consists in the greater efficiency imparted to earlier units. Suppose the last unit of capital to be represented by improved fencing or drainage; this has evidently an important influence in increasing the efficiency of the earlier units of capital.

There is a false separatism in the "dosing" illustration which ignores the organic unity in a business. No light is thrown either upon the theory or the practice of industry by treating one Factor of Production as a constant quantity and two as variables.

§ 8. Thus we perceive that the fallacy of the "dosing" illustration consists in assigning a particular amount of productivity, and therefore of "product," to a particular dose. Professor Marshall, in treating the marginal dose of labour in agriculture (*e.g.* the last hoeing applied to a field), admits that "the return to that last dose cannot be separated from the others," but he adds "we ascribe to it all that part of the produce which we believe would not have been produced if the farmer had decided against the extra hoeing." (Bk. IV, Ch. III, par. 2.)

Here we probe the heart of the "dosing" fallacy. It is claimed that the product of the last dose of labour is to be measured by the reduction in the aggregate product of the farm which would have attended the refusal to apply this last dose of labour. Now this is not justifiable. The withdrawal or refusal to apply this last dose of labour would have meant a diminished productivity, not only of the other units of labour, but of the units of capital and of land, and part of the result of this diminished productivity of other units is wrongly attributed to the last unit of labour.

For let us see how this mode of measuring the productivity of the last increment applies. Let us suppose that a farm business is composed of 4 doses of labour, 6 doses of land, 3 doses of capital, this being the combination of the factors which is economically advantageous. Now in order to measure the productivity of the last dose of labour, let us remove it. The diminution of the total product may be 8%. This 8%, according to Marshall's method, we ascribe to the last dose of labour. If now, restoring this dose of labour, we withdrew the last dose of capital, the reduction of product might be 10%. This 10% is regarded as the product of the last dose of capital. Similarly, the withdrawal of the last dose of land might seem to reduce the product by 10%. What would be the effect of a simultaneous withdrawal of the last dose of each factor? According to Marshall's method, clearly 28%. But is this correct? Is it not likely that this simultaneous withdrawal might reduce the product not by 28%, but by (say) 18%? According to Marshall, the whole of the 8% which disappears on the withdrawal of the last dose of labour is to be regarded as the product of that dose. But part of that 8% will consist in the reduced productivity, not only of the other labour-doses, but of the doses of capital and land. The withdrawal of the last dose of labour may well be supposed to reduce in particular the utility of the last dose both of capital and of land, which factors are now in excess. Similarly, the withdrawal of the last dose of capital will affect the productivity of the last dose of labour and of land. The withdrawal of a dose of land will act in the same way upon the last doses of labour and capital. We should thus find that the simultaneous withdrawal of the last dose of the three factors would be considerably less than the 28% which Marshall's mode of measurement requires. For the withdrawal of the last labour-dose involves a nullification of a part of the productivity of the last unit of capital and of land, and a part of the result thus attributed to labour is due to the diminished productivity of the other factors. Put the same experiment upon its broadest footing, and the overlapping fallacy becomes obvious. Take the labour, capital, and land as consisting of a single dose of each; now withdraw the dose of labour, and the whole service of capital and land disappears. Is the destruction of the whole product a right measure of the separate productivity of the labour-dose alone? Obviously not; for if the dose of capital had been withdrawn instead, or the dose of land, the same effect would have ensued.

§ 9. Causation may indeed be proved by what is called in logical text-books the Method of Difference, but the composition of causes prevents quantitative effect from being proved in this manner. The "dose" illustration is nothing else than a slightly more intricate example of the fallacy which confuses mechanical composition with organic coöperation. Where it is essential to productivity that land, capital, and labour shall all coöperate, it is impossible to assign to any one of them a product based on the supposition of a separate productivity. Similarly, where there exists a necessary organic quantitative relation between the factors, no separate product can be put down to any single dose of each.

The root-fallacy of the "dose" illustration consists, then, in a false separation which ignores the

organic nature of production and the Law of Substitution. The real determinant of price of a
supply from the "cost" side will be found to
reside in the comparative advantage of employing
various combinations of the factors of production.
In considering how a new increment of wheat
supply, evoked by rising prices, will be produced,
nothing is learnt by supposing it to be raised by
applying a new unit of capital and labour to wheat
land already in use. The real problem for consideration will be, "What changed proportion of
the several factors will most easily turn out the
increased supply?" Should more labour be applied to the same land, or should more land be
worked by the same labour, or should more capital
be added, or what should be the conjunction of
additional factors?

The net result of this argument is that the
application of the Law of Rent to the intensive
cultivation of a single factor must be rejected as
fallacious.

The chief use of the "dose" illustration has
been to support the theory that rent of land
differs radically from all payments for uses of
other requisites, in that it is a surplus which,
being measured from a no-rent margin, does not
form an element of price. Whereas it appeared
that land at the extensive margin of cultivation
for all higher uses paid a positive rent, it was
sought to exclude this rent from price by arguing

that a portion of the supply might be raised upon an intensive margin, where no rent was paid even for supplies toward which no-rent land did not contribute.

§ 10. The complete breakdown of this intensive margin throws us back once more upon the extensive margin for the sole legitimate application of the Law of Rent.

We have already recognised what qualification of this law is necessary. While the generally accepted statement of the law holds good in the case of the lowest or least remunerative use of land where the margin of cultivation pays no rent, it must be qualified in the case of land put to higher uses by the recognition of a series of higher margins of cultivation where a positive rent is paid for the worst land in use. The differential rents for each particular piece of land will be measured from the no-rent margin only in the case of lands competing for the lowest use; the differential rents of lands for higher uses will be measured from a specific margin which pays a rent. While these differential rents will form no element in prices, the marginal rents will enter as an expense of production that is common to the whole supply. If the marginal hop land in use pays a rent of £2 an acre, a portion of that sum will be represented in the price of each pocket of hops.

PART II.

§ 1. While there has been a growing tendency among recent economists to extend the term "rent" and the application of the Law of Rent to capital and to labour, as a rule this has been done tentatively, rather by way of analogy than as a recognition of the application of a common law.

A true coördination of the factors of production which shall enable us to bring them all alike, in respect to the sale of their uses, under the general laws of price which are operative in the markets of commodities, requires that we first show how the law of rent in its extensive application is valid for each factor.

The difficulties which confront us in this work chiefly arise from the adoption in economic treatment of a terminology which expresses loose popular modes of regarding land, labour, and capital, and are mainly two.

§ 2. The first difficulty arises from a radical difference in the common mode of representing capital on the one hand, labour and land on the other. Whereas the two latter are regarded in their concrete forms, the land in its acres, the labour-power in its daily or weekly output of energy, we commonly regard capital not in the concrete shapes of plant, raw material, and goods, which are its serviceable forms for industry, but in its money value of so many £100's. Whereas the payment to land and· labour is payment for the use of the concrete forms, payment for capital is payment for the use of so much of this abstract force measured by £100's.

Now it is evident that no common law of price or value can be applied to the use of the three factors, unless we place them upon a common footing. Either we must measure land and labour by their abstract or money measurement, capitalising them and regarding rent and wages as payment for the use of so many £100's of this land-capital or labour-capital, or else when we speak of capital, we must speak of the concrete forms, of goods, plant, etc., which are used in industry. The actuality of a science of industry as distinguished from a science of finance requires us to take the latter course, and. to treat capital as consisting not in money but in concrete forms of wealth serviceable in production.

The payment for the use of this concrete capital is interest. Since this latter term is by usage closely confined to the price, not of concrete capital but of money capital, I should have preferred to adopt some other term. But none other is available excepting the still more slippery term "profit." I propose, therefore, to use the term "interest" for the payment of the use of concrete capital, distinguishing it where necessary from financial interest by appending the term "real" to the former, "money" to the latter.

It is, of course, evident that no coördination of capital with land by application of a law of rent is possible where capital takes the fluid form of money. For no "rents," either specific or individual, could emerge from such uses of capital. It is, of course, incorrect to say that £100 of capital in one employment earns 2½% interest and another £100, elsewhere employed, 5%. The extra 2½% in what seems the better investment will either not be interest at all, but compensation for special risks, or it will by its very existence raise the capital from £100 to £200. For under present circumstances £100 of capital simply means so much capital as will bring £2.10s. interest per annum to its owner. A proper business valuation of all capital is a valuation based upon the rate of interest. *Ex hypothesi*, therefore, there can be only one true rate of interest for all this fluid abstract capital. Business habits often persist in speaking of capital as £100, when the increased annual value of the concrete forms represented has raised it to £200, so that one £100 share may be spoken of as paying 5%, but the market or selling value of course would be £200 and the true interest still 2½%.

No relation is possible between this capital and our other factors of production. We must deal with the concrete forms which are thus valued. What is paid for their use is real interest.

§ 3. When we have placed the factors of production upon the common concrete basis and agreed upon a term to describe the payment of the use of concrete capital, we are confronted with another difficulty. In measuring the value of land, a margin of cultivation is found to be of essential importance, and our examination of the law of rent has clearly indicated the need of substituting a joint-margin, composed of all the factors, for a margin of land only. But can we legitimately extend the conception of a margin of employment to capital and labour? The initial difficulty takes this form. The worst land in cultivation for the lowest use (say grazing land) pays no rent; can we say that the worst placed capital will yield no profit and the worst labour in employment obtain no wage?

First, as to capital, whether it be true or not that the prospect of obtaining interest is a necessary motive to induce the creation of capital, it may distinctly be affirmed that interest is not necessary to secure the economic maintenance of forms of capital which have been brought into existence. What is needed for the continuous existence of forms of capital is a provision against wear and tear or depreciation; this charge upon gross profits is not interest, but is a deduction prior to payment of any interest. A business paying the minimum or merely nominal interest on its invested capital must, if it is properly conducted, have made provision for the maintenance of its plant and other forms of capital. Though some positive interest may be necessary to bring into use new forms of capital, it is not required to maintain old forms. This Walker has rightly recognised by insisting that the idea of no-rent land must be extended to no-profit businesses, and that the profits of better businesses may be measured from this margin, as the rents of land are measured from a no-rent margin.

Indeed, the more closely we look at the real supply of land and capital, the more artificial and the more unjustifiable appears the abrupt distinction made by earlier economic theories. Mere land does not figure in supply. Land in its natural state — "prairie land" — is not really a factor of production. Its so-called "inherent and indestructible properties " have no value until the land is cleared and broken in, until some expenditure of labour is made upon it. In this sense there is a cost of producing a supply of land roughly corresponding to the cost of producing capital.[1] Again, just as the continued existence of capital is secured by a constant provision

---

[1] Professor S. N. Patten has shown (*Premises of Political Economy*) how this cost of production of land impairs the exactitude of the measurement of rent, because "the laws which regulate the bringing of new lands into cultivation, and

against depreciation, so the powers of land for most purposes are not indestructible, but demand a constant outlay. The abstraction of an economic land for which economic rent is paid is on the whole a singularly futile and confusing one. The worst capital and the worst land in economic use alike require a provision against wear and tear which is neither interest nor rent, while the interest and rent paid for their use is a merely nominal amount.

§ 4. Now the case of labour seems different, but the difference arises merely from the adoption of inconsistent terminology. Whereas the fund for keeping forms of land and capital in existence is not termed rent or profit, the fund for keeping in economic existence repositories of labour-power is included under "wages." Thus it comes to pass that while the margin of land is no-rent land, the margin of capital no-interest capital, the margin of labour is (say) 15s. labour.

In order to clear the problem of price in distribution, it is essential to remove this anomaly. This 15s. wage does not in any sense correspond to interest or to rent. It is simply a wear-and-tear fund of labour, the expenditure necessary to replace the labour-power given out in a day's work,

those according to which land will be withdrawn from cultivation, are very different," affording "a large margin within which the price of produce may vary without a change in the quantity produced."

and to maintain the labouring population at their present numbers and at their present efficiency. The logical coördination of factors of production requires that this wear-and-tear or depreciation fund shall be distinguished from the additional payment which most labourers receive. It is wages above 15s. that correspond to positive rent or interest. If the term "wage" could be applied exclusively to the fund of maintenance, and some other term, such as "rent of labour," could be used to describe the higher payments, the coördination would be complete.

We should then be able to apply with a fairly close degree of accuracy to all three the general statements which have been often reserved for land.

§ 5. The fact that while land may be in existence unutilised below the limit of cultivation, no forms of capital continuously exist below the no-profit limit, and no labour-power can be assumed to exist below the bare subsistence limit, does not in the least impair the setting. For just as land below the margin has only a potential economic existence, and can only be brought into supply by prices which give a positive rent to marginal land (lowering the margin of cultivation), so there must be deemed to be a potential fund of capital which will become actual, provided marginal capital receives a positive interest, while any rise of payment to the marginal 15s. labour will increase the supply of labour-power, either by raising the population rate or by improving the efficiency of labour, or by both.

The causes which raise and lower the margin in all three cases will be similar in operation. The investigation of these causes, however, lies beyond our present inquiry. What payments for use of land, capital, labour, enter as elements into market-price of goods? was our leading question. The coördination of land, capital, and labour leads us to conclude that just as rent of land need not form an element of cost or price in agri-cultural produce, some of which is raised on no-rent land, so interest need not figure in the cost or price of manufactured goods, some of which are produced by no-interest businesses, while similarly no cost of labour above the 15s. depreciation fund need enter into the price of commodities partly produced by marginal labourers.

The same reasoning which shows that differential rents of land need not enter price shows also that differential payments for capital and labour need not enter price.

§ 6. Can a market-price then be composed of these depreciation or maintenance costs, without any element of positive rent or interest?

It might be the case. If a part of the supply of wheat in a market was raised upon no-rent land by farmers who obtained no interest for their capital and paid the minimum subsistence wage to their labourers, such wheat raised under the greatest economic difficulty might regulate the market-price.[1]

But normally the last and most expensive portion of supply which rules the supply-price will not be produced under conditions which exclude all rent and all profit. Where a number of farmers working under widely different conditions, some in old, some in new countries, are contributing to the same wheat supply, it is more likely that the last portion of supply will be produced, partly on no-rent land, but paying an interest on capital and perhaps a wage far above 15*s*., partly by tenant-farmers paying rent but earning no interest on invested capital, partly by peasants paying rent or mortgage interest, but living on a bare subsistence wage. That is to say, the Law of Substitution has always to be taken into account. The possibility of this choice or substitution of method shows the futility of arguments based on the single Ricardian application of the Law of Rent. If the history of the most expensive portion of a wheat supply could be closely traced, it might well be found that some quarters of it were raised on no-rent land, others on no-profit capital, others on subsistence wages; but that an average

---

[1] This assumes that the marginal buyer is stronger than the marginal seller in the wheat market, and that therefore the price is pressed down to the lower limit so as to include no element of "forced gain."

quarter of this most expensive portion contained some element of rent or interest or higher wage, or all three.

In other words, the Law of Substitution requires that in measurement of price we should substitute for the margin of cultivation of land a composite margin of employment of land, capital, and labour, at which is paid not necessarily the minimum rent, interest, and wage, but the lowest average combination of the three. Supply-price will be composed (under absolutely free competition) of these marginal expenses.

Differential expenses of production above this composite limit, whether they be rent, interest, or wages, will not enter into the market-price of the supply.

CHAPTER V.

PART I.

§ 1. Having indicated the changes in economic conceptions and terminology requisite to enable us to establish the general coördination of the three factors of production and the application in each case of the idea of a measurement of price from a no-pay margin of cultivation or employment, we may proceed to investigate with more particularity how far the marginal and differential grading admitted in the case of land is applicable to the other requisites, and how far the laws which govern the increase in supply of land for various markets operate in analogous fashion upon the supply of labour and capital.

First, let us take labour. How far can we apply to labour the system of grading which we have employed in the case of land?

The tendency of earlier economists, motived by theoretic considerations, was to impute too much fluidity to labour, too much choice of occupation to individual labourers, and (as an oft-quoted

passage of Adam Smith illustrates) to make in-
sufficient allowance for differences of natural
aptitude between man and man. The early theorists spoke too much of *the* labour-market, as
if to all intents and purposes it were one market,
as if each new-grown labourer had the whole field
of employment open to his choice, as if the removal
of certain legal barriers, such as the Law of Settlement or gild regulations, would enable labour,
already specialised in some occupation, to leave
that occupation easily and freely and seek another,
where the wages or net advantages were higher.
They failed to give adequate recognition to the
fact that there exists not one but many labour-
markets, marked off from one another not merely
and not chiefly by locality, but by many racial,
educational, industrial, and social demarcations.
Between many of these labour-markets, even in
England to-day, the passage is so narrow and so
slow that there can hardly be said to exist an
effective tendency to equalise the net advantages
of the various employments. The wide differences
of class wages, and even of local wages, for similar
work, is ample testimony to this truth.

How far the causes which prevent the forces
making for equalisation of the net advantages of
labour from being fully operative are to be spoken
of as "natural," in the same sense that the laws
which determine the contribution of land to different supplies are natural, we need not here dis-

cuss. What does concern us is the fact that, as a given kind of land in a given position is, partly from natural, partly from social-economic causes, confined to contributing toward a particular supply, so a given kind of labourer is by natural and social-economic circumstances similarly limited in the application of his labour-power. It may be and is easier to alter some of the circumstances which determine the application of labour than in the case of land, though agricultural science and machinery of transport have done much to impart greater adaptability to land. But though the freedom and adaptability of labour be greater than of land, if we take the existing supply of labour it must be regarded as subject, though in a weaker degree, to a gradation similar to that which we trace in land.

§ 2. As we have land which is good for nothing but rough grazing, the worst of which yields a merely nominal rent, so we have a mass of low-skilled, low-untrained labour, which earns in its worst sorts a wage of bare physical subsistence. In fact, the lowest wage is less than a bare subsistence wage, if by the subsistence of the individual we mean his maintenance during the full span of his natural life, or even through the whole term of his effective working life. Slave-labour, under an intelligent profit-monger, may require provision to be made for a full working life, though even under slavery it may sometimes pay to use up a slave by intense toil during a shorter period. An effective system of poor law, which guaranteed an adequate support to able-bodied labour out of employment, upon terms not degrading to the applicants, might, by offering an alternative to ordinary wage-labour, secure economic conditions which would raise the minimum wage of low-skilled labour to a level of life subsistence. The actual minimum wage under normal modern industrial conditions must be taken to be such a wage as enables a worker to go on working until he has provided through his family a substitute. Of course if there is an increasing demand for labour expected in the future, the minimum wage must be such as to evoke more than one substitute, *i.e.* to call for an increase of working population in this lowest grade.

This dependence of growth of working population upon wages is, of course, modified by the operation of poor laws, private charity, and public support of various kinds. It will therefore be the case that population may grow at a somewhat faster rate than would be brought about by the play of wage-forces alone.[1]

[1] Early economists overstated the directness and the exactitude of the influence of purely economic forces (wages) upon the supply of labour. The tendency at present is to underestimate it. In particular it has been pointed out that a higher standard of wages in a country like England does not cause a corresponding growth of the labouring population. On this point three things may be said. First, it is often forgotten that

I have spoken of a certain minimum wage as analogous to a depreciation or wear-and-tear fund of capital. This sum, varying somewhat, of course, with the various kinds of labour, as the depreciation fund varies for different forms of capital, I estimated at 15*s.* In a progressive industrial community, where an increase of labouring population with a sufficient margin of unemployed to be utilised in periods of booming trade was required, the minimum wage, or cost of subsistence, must of course be more than this 15*s.* required to keep a stable population in that grade; and this additional wage (say 3*s.*) required to raise the population must be regarded as analogous to a minimum interest required to call forth additional capital.

§ 3. If, then, in a community the lowest grade of labour was paid 18*s.* for its least efficient members, we should find rising above this grade various

one important effect of a higher standard of comfort is that a larger proportion of children grow to maturity. Secondly, with a higher standard of comfort, the effective supply of labour is increased, not only by the number of labourers, but also by the quantity of labour-power each labourer represents, *i.e.* the average working life is longer, and is capable of yielding in a given time a larger quantity of efficient labour-power. Lastly, the check which forethought and preventive methods have placed upon the growth of population in the more intelligent classes plays yet a very small part in the labour-markets of the world.

It is still true that rising wages evoke an increased supply of labour-power.

other grades paid upon higher scales. Speaking generally, we should be able to classify the workers by a sort of stratification beginning with the low-skilled worker at the bottom, proceeding through several strata of factory hands, the building trades, skilled mechanics, into the salaried, professional, and managing classes. The rate of payment will be higher, as we rise, for the least efficient labour actually employed at the various levels. In other words, we should find a number of class minimum wages analogous to the different specific marginal rents which mark off the margin of pasture land, wheat land, hop land, city lands, etc. This stratification of labour is now commonly admitted, though to some economic thinkers it seemed novel when Cairnes gave his vigorous indorsement to the idea. "What we find in effect is, not a whole population competing indiscriminately for all occupations, but a series of industrial layers superimposed on one another, within each of which the various candidates for employment possess a real and effective power of selection, while those occupying the several strata are, for all purposes of effective competition, practically isolated from each other."[1] It is not necessary to insist too strictly upon this "practical isolation." Individuals can pass from one stratum to another; new labour has some considerable choice. It is sufficient to recognise that at any given time we

[1] *The Slave Power*, p. 73.

do find a gradation of labour with different rates
of wage for the least efficient members of each
grade. Again, within each group will be found
a number of different qualities of labour earning
different rates of remuneration. These, too, we
may measure from the position of "the determinant
labourer" of each class.

The same correction of the position assigned to
the "marginal labourer" is required as in the case
of marginal cultivation of land. In the labour-
market what is really sold is not labour-time, but
units of labour-power; the determinant labourer,
therefore, need not be the least efficient labourer,
but may be a superior labourer, who is "determinant" in the sense that he is only just induced by
the class wage paid to contribute to supply. The
least efficient labourer might have no alternative
employment, and might be willing, therefore, to
accept a lower wage, if he were obliged; but a
superior labourer of the class might have an alternative employment so that the wage must be such
as to induce him to apply his labour-power to this
use. It is the economic position of this "determinant" labourer which from the cost side helps to
determine the value of a unit of labour-power and
so to fix not merely the wage he himself receives,
but also the wage of the various other labourers
in his labour-market, whose actual wages depend
upon the number of units of this labour-power
they can give out. Thus the efficiency of the

least efficient labourer in the class has no direct
determining power over the class wages, as is
sometimes suggested; it is the economic power of
the "determinant labourer" which fixes the pay
of the least efficient labourer.

The system of piece wages makes this easily intelligible. The least efficient worker in a trade
may be earning by piece wages 20*s.* a week; this
may be regarded as a marginal wage in this class
of labour, differential wages of superior individual
skill rising above it. The "determinant" labourer
may be a superior worker earning 30*s.*, 10*s.* being
a wage of individual ability within the class.
This labourer must receive 30*s.* in order that he
may do this kind of work in preference to some
other. He is the final seller in this labour-market,
whose action determines on the selling side the
price for the whole market.

But though this 30*s.* labourer may be accounted
the determinant labourer, it does not follow that
the whole of the 30*s.* is necessary to divert him
from his alternative employment. Just as in our
grading of land we found that in addition to the
marginal and differential rents there might be a
rent of sheer "scarcity," where demand pressed
upon a short supply, so here it might be that the
alternative employment open to the "determinant"
labourer would yield him a wage of only 27*s.*; but
although any wage above 27*s.* would secure his
contribution to the supply of labour under inves-

tigation, he is able in his capacity of determinant seller to exact 30*s.*, including a scarcity wage of 3*s.*, which last sum corresponds to the forced gain that accrued to the stronger member of the final pair of bargainers in our horse-market.

The term "rent of ability," frequently applied to the higher wages earned by a more competent worker, shows that the analogy of classification of land and labour has made some considerable way. The margin in both cases is not rigid, but is continually shifting, faster, no doubt, in labour than in land, but the same economic terminology applies.

§ 4. Moreover, the price of labour is seen to enter into the price of commodities upon precisely similar terms to the rent of land, when we exclude the bare subsistence wage, as we exclude the depreciation fund for land and capital.   The 15*s.* subsistence should rightly be regarded as a first mortgage upon the product, along with the corresponding provision of maintenance for capital and land.

Beyond that necessary provision no element of true wage (or labour profit) enters into the price of the product of the lowest labour.   But the minimum wage of a Lancashire weaver (say 21*s.*) will yield a marginal rent measured from 15*s.*, amounting to 6*s.*   This marginal or "class" wage will enter into price.   If a mason's minimum wage be 30*s.*, the excess of this sum over 15*s.* will similarly enter into price. But the individual wage earned by a more skilful weaver or mason will form no element in expenses of production, and will not enter into price. Modern economists often admit that only the wage of the least efficient labour counts in price of the product, but not clearly recognising the difference between the "determinant" labourer and the "marginal" labourer, they are often disposed to impute to the latter a determinant influence which really belongs to the former. All that we have to add is that there are a number of different marginal labourers for different labour-markets. There are marginal rents of labour (sometimes containing also a rent of scarcity) which are represented in "price," and there are differential rents which are not represented.

PART II.

§ 5. How far may capital be submitted to a similar process of marginal and differential grading? How far can we distinguish different classes of capital more or less profitable, and individual differences within a class?

How far does the alleged "fluidity of capital," making for a single supply and a common level of remuneration for its services, impugn this theory of stratification?

We have seen that this belief in an equality of

remuneration for capital arises partly from the fact that capital is commonly reduced to terms of its money-value — a process which assumes equality of remuneration as its starting-point. When we turn to the actual forms of concrete capital, we certainly find wide variation of remuneration. But can we regard these differences as analogous to the specific and differential rents or earnings of land and labour? It has been necessary to select the term "interest" to describe the remuneration of capital, but capital cannot earn interest of itself or even in conjunction with land and labour. Capital, in order to function in industry, must be handled by a business man, and it is always possible to claim that a part at least of the net gain, after all other deductions commonly named, is due to skill or economy of handling.[1] The extra gain which comes from handling a large quantity of capital, as compared with a small quantity, even though this handling requires no more skill or effort, is commonly assigned, not as payment for use of capital, but as wages of management.

But though in practice it is extremely difficult, perhaps impossible, to sever this interest, or pure

---

[1] This claim is, of course, not confined to the remuneration of capital; the productiveness of land and labour is also dependent upon skilful handling, and it is possible to claim as true earnings of management part of the results of increased productiveness of land and labour. In the case of labour, Mr. Mallock has pressed this claim, asserting that high wages really include earnings of management.

payment for use of capital, from other elements, an orderly scheme of economic theory requires us to do so. Now my suggestion is that if this severance were made, interest would certainly be shown not to be equal for the use of all equal quantities of capital. The different concrete shapes, which equal quantities of "saving" take, will most likely differ as widely in the profits they obtain for their owners, as one 10-acre field differs in rent from another 10-acre field, or one labourer differs from another labourer in wages.

There is no force in operation which would guarantee that the saving which went into a steam-engine would earn for its owner an "interest" identical in size with that for the same quantity of saving which went into a shop-building, or that one railway carriage is as remunerative as another railway carriage of equal quality.

In other words, some employments of capital are more remunerative than others, and, within a given employment, some pieces of capital are more remunerative than others.

If these differences were due to the difference of skill with which they were handled, they must of course not be reckoned as differences of interest in our sense.

But if there exist certain conditions which prevent absolute fluidity of investment, which limit and mark off certain fields of investment for certain owners of capital, and which give within a

field of investment special advantages to some
owners as compared to others, it will seem legitimate to grade capital, as we grade land and labour,
into a number of practically non-competing groups
with differential gains within each group.

§ 6. If it were open to all savers to have full,
equal knowledge of every field of investment, and
to have equal access to all fields, real interest, like
money interest, would be uniform. But is this
the case?

General Walker has explicitly denied the allegation that different classes of investment differ
in the rates of profit they yield, and even suggests
that the differences of "interests" derived from
different pieces of capital in the same class are not
true interest.

"That different bodies of capital do, in fact,
yield different rates of interest is too evident to
require proof; but this is due to many causes,
which are irrespective of the nature of the capital
itself."[1]

General Walker enumerates three chief causes
for these differing rates of remuneration: (*a*) Difference in risk; (*β*) miscalculation on the one
hand, or fortunate speculation on the other;
(*γ*) disguised rent, disguised profits, or commercial good-will.

Now, in the first place, it may be observed that
a and *β* are not different causes, but two ways of

---

[1] *Quarterly Journal of Economics*, July, 1891.

looking at the same cause. A "risky" investment is nothing else than an investment prone to
"miscalculation," or in which success is in large
measure the result of fortunate speculation; *a* is
the objective, *β* the subjective, view of the same
factor.

But does this fact meet the allegation that
different classes of investment differ in remunerativeness? Not at all. It only helps to explain
why, within the same class of investment, the rate
of interest upon some pieces of capital is higher
than for others. The allegation that the nature
of the capital has something to do with determining the rate of interest means, of course, that in
certain employments of capital there is a higher
average rate of interest than in others. It is certainly strange that General Walker should have
failed to perceive that while his last cause (*γ*)
refers to classes of investment, (*a*) and (*β*) refer
only to individual investments within a class.

Turning to (*γ*) it will be at once admitted that
disguised rent is a *vera causa* in determining what
seems to be the higher interest for certain classes
of investment. There are several ways in which
rent is liable to figure as interest.

Certain classes of business yield a higher rate
of interest because the capital invested in them is
protected from free and effective competition by
association with monopoly of land. Land-values
and capital-values are not always clearly distin-

guishable. If the term "capital" is confined to
its only logical use, to express production-goods
and plant, we shall see that those engaged in the
early steps of converting the raw material of the
soil into early forms of capital are, in part landowners, in part capitalists. The businesses of ex-
tracting ore, of raising cattle, and the whole
industry of agriculture are businesses in which
land-values are not easily distinguishable from
capital-values or rent from interest. Even where
these operations are conducted on rented lands,
the custom of leasing does not enable us to clearly
or precisely determine whether in a given year
some profit has not been returned as economic
rent and *vice versa.*

Where the owners of a business are also the
owners of ground upon which it is conducted, a
growing element of land-value will often show
itself as a rise in interest. No consideration of
the value of surrounding land can wholly guard
against this confusion. If this is the case in
ordinary businesses, where the use of land is for
machinery and other plant, warehouses, etc., much
more is it the case where the elements of the soil
or spatial qualities play a direct part in the business. Such a case is that of breweries. The
interest paid on capital engaged in gas or waterworks, or tramcars, is complicated, as we shall see
presently, by another monopoly influence; but it
is rarely possible to separate, in the dividends

paid to shareholders, the elements of economic rent and interest. Most important is the part placed by land limitation in transport industries. Professor Marshall is of opinion that "the dominant economic fact of our age is the development, not of the manufacturing, but of the transport industries."[1] Now the transport industries, so far as they are left in private hands, require a monopoly of earth surface. Between any two points of population there is only one shortest way. Whether it be a railroad, a telegraph road, or a tram line, the most advantageous route can only be in the possession of one company at the same time. Most transport companies obtain a more or less permanent possession of the most advantageous route, supporting this natural monopoly, in many cases, by a state privilege protecting them against competition, even beyond the limits of their natural monopoly. Here, again, it is impossible to say how far the higher rate of interest paid by a successful railway or tramcar company is really an economic rent of land, and how far land monopoly has assisted certain other monopoly powers inherent in certain uses of capital.

If it be the case that more and more capital and labour will be engaged in distributive than in extractive or manufacturing processes, the importance of this close alliance of land ownership with

[1] *Principles of Economics*, 2d ed., p. 724.

capitalism is a growing one. Where the effect
of land ownership is to restrict the competition of
capital in any given employment, it may fairly be
urged that any abnormal interest due to the restricted competition or the power of capital is
ultimately traceable to land-power. But inasmuch
as this "specific rent" appears as interest and
cannot conveniently be separated from genuine
interest, it is rightly regarded as an element in
the specific differences of forms of investment.

By "disguised profits," General Walker may
mean one of two things. It may signify the
higher interest paid upon certain capital owing to
superior skill of management. In this case "rent
of ability" figures as interest. The skill of an
able manager who is paid by a fixed salary may
for a time secure higher dividends for the share-
holder, just as the mismanagement of an incom-
petent manager may lower the dividends. But,
unless it can be shown that a particular class of
business, by its very nature, presents special
attractions to managing ability, this form of disguised profit is an individual affair and cannot be
placed on the same footing with disguised rent
as an explanation of specific differences in remunerativeness of capital.

But the term "disguised profits" may cover
a real form of class gain. Certain classes of
investment are, in fact, restricted to capital in
the possession of men who enjoy certain "class"

advantages of position, education, or trade connection. It is admittedly difficult for a poor man who has saved a little money to find a safe or remunerative investment. The spread of education and improved methods of coöperation may effect some change, but it is at present true that capital invested by persons of means, position, and intelligence is, on the average, more remunerative than the capital invested by the poorer and more ignorant. The restricted access to knowledge and skill, where the use of capital requires special skill, secures for certain classes a practical monopoly of certain forms of investment. Lawyers and bankers, it is generally held, possess certain opportunities of profitable investment not open to ordinary persons.

Any higher rate of interest secured by capital invested under these conditions may, of course, be regarded as a "marginal rent" due to special advantages of education or opportunities, and, as such, classed under the head of profit rather than of interest. The vagueness still attaching to the word "profit" as an economic term favours this interpretation. But if, on the other hand, we regard limitation of investment as a quality attaching to capital, the "marginal rent" of such form of capital may not unfairly be claimed as a "rent" of capital.

While the restricted access to land or opportunity serves to explain the higher rate of real interest for capital in certain forms of investment, there are other causes, political, social, and economic, which endow certain forms of capital with a remunerativeness which is rightly regarded as attaching to the nature of the species of investment.

First: privileges conferred or restrictions imposed by national or local authority limit the freedom of competition in certain employment of capital, *i.e.* endow certain capital with a power of monopoly. ˅

Sometimes a charter gives to a particular body of capitalists an absolute monopoly, with or without restrictions as to maximum price of the commodity they provide. No direct competition touches the monopoly of gas or waterworks established in a town and secured by charter for a given body of capitalists. In addition to the maximum price and to a maximum rate of interest, sometimes imposed but commonly evaded by watering the stock or other devices, there are two economic limitations to such monopolies. The first is that furnished by the Law of Substitution, the ability of the consumer to dispense with the article of monopoly and to use some other article in its stead. If the price of gas were raised beyond a certain point, the enlarged use of electricity, of oil, candles, or other illuminants would check the rise. Hence the monopoly of a water company is a stronger one; for it would be more difficult to obtain another supply or to substitute some other commodity than in the case of gas.

The second limit depends upon the complex relations existing between supply-price and demand in the particular case. Every rise in the price of gas above the competitive price of two rival companies would bring a certain shrinkage of demand. Hence it arises that the highest price does not necessarily yield the largest net profit. Generally, it may be stated that the most profitable price is high in proportion as the article of monopoly is indispensable.

Since neither of these qualifying conditions of "monopoly" is of the nature of that competition which tends to reduce to a common level ordinary classes of investment, we have clearly a specific interest which enables us to grade these protected classes of investment according to the various degrees of monopoly pressure which they possess.

The power vested in owners of valuable patents, and even in those who, without legal protection, have exclusive control of any market or of the sale of any class of goods, is of a similar economic character, and enables the capital invested in such businesses to get a specific interest.

Protective tariffs, or bounties, in so far as they succeed in restricting or limiting freedom of competition in certain employments of capital, help to maintain a special rate of interest in those businesses in which new capital cannot easily enter so as to share the advantage of the state-granted monopoly. The only economic reason which can induce any class of manufacturers to seek protection for the goods they make, is the desire to reap the marginal interest of capital which this protection secures.

But the most important cause of marginal rents (specific interests) of capital resides in the nature of capital itself as a factor of production in certain classes of business, independently of all social or political privileges or restrictions.

In whatever branches of industry the economic Law of Increasing Returns prevails, that is to say, where capital and labour are most advantageously employed in large quantities, the capital invested may obtain a special rate of interest. It is unnecessary to enumerate the particular economies which in most manufacturing and mercantile businesses give a net economic advantage to the big capital. But it should be kept in mind that these economies do not of themselves furnish any guarantee of a higher rate of interest. They operate indirectly, by reducing the number of competitors and abating the pressure of competition. If the competition between the smaller number of large capitals was as keen and constant as between the larger number of small capitals invested in other businesses, the advantage in higher interest which these economies might seem to justify would entirely disappear. But the size of the capitals

engaged prevents the competition from being so
keen and so constant. At certain periods, it is
true, competition may be as effective between two
or three competitors as between two or three
thousand. But where the competition is between
few, it is, on the average, less persistently effective. The different competitors exercise each a
certain practical monopoly over certain districts
or in certain lines of goods. Even where the competition with a big competitor is keen, its keen-
ness is abated when prices are driven down so low
as to yield only a common rate of interest. Above
all, the opportunities of suspending competition,
or of forming agreements for maintaining prices,
limiting supply, or keeping down wages, are
vastly greater in a trade given over to a few large
capitals than where there are many small competing capitals. The advantage given to capital in
controlling the price of labour in employments
most subject to the Law of Increasing Returns,
where a small number of large capitals is constantly narrowing to the apex of a Trust, is most
significant. Certain disadvantages common to
most forms of labour in bargaining with capital
are greatly enhanced where the competition of
capitals is restricted to a few large masters.
"Labour," writes Professor Marshall, "is often
sold under special disadvantages, arising from the
closely connected group of facts, that labour-power
is 'perishable,' that the sellers of it are commonly

poor and have no reserve fund, and that they cannot easily withhold it from the market." [1]   A position of vantage in bargaining with labour is one of the chief economic advantages in those industries where the action of the Law of Increasing Returns has thrown the business into the hands of a few large firms.

The net economic advantages which large capitals enjoy in industries where the Law of Increasing Returns is more powerfully operative than the Law of Diminishing Returns, secure to those capitals a position of limited monopoly, *i.e.* a monopoly limited by the consideration that a very high price would bring new competitors into the market. The gain which this limited monopoly secures is a "specific marginal interest." Industries where the monopoly is very limited draw a small specific interest; industries where the monopoly is of a prime necessary of life, a substitute for which cannot easily be found, where a supply from a more distant market cannot easily be procúred, where new capittal cannot easily be applied to the industry, and where a considerable reduction of consumption is impossible, are in a position to derive a very high marginal interest.   The Law of Increasing Returns forms the basis of economic grading of capital, just as the Law of Diminishing Returns forms the basis of grading in land-values. According to the varying pressure of this law in

[1] *Principles of Economics*, Vol. I, p. 600 (2d ed.).

different industries, the capital engaged therein
enjoys a greater or less degree of monopoly power
and draws a greater or less specific interest, in
addition to the minimum interest socially required
to induce the "saving" of capital. Where the
economies of large-scale production are biggest,
the tendency is to bring about an absolute or
limited suspension of competition among hitherto
competing capitals and to secure the "saving of
friction" which attends the establishment of a
ring or trust, where the present action of competition is reduced to a minimum.

The monopoly of a strong trust differs only in
degree, and not in kind, from the monopoly held,
in different proportions, by all large forms of capital protected against the competition of smaller
intruders by the advantage conferred by the operation of the Law of Increasing Returns. Of course
there are doubtless industries where this Law of
Increasing Returns ceases to be operative beyond
a certain point, or more strictly speaking, where
a decline in efficiency of management in a business
of ever growing magnitude would outweigh the
economies of a larger capital.[1]

But it is safe to say that in any industry within
the limits of the dominant operation of this Law

---

[1] Professor Marshall, who has worked out the operation of
the Law of Increasing Returns and its limitations, considers its
operation from the standpoint of individual firms, not of classes
of investment. Bk. V, Ch. XI.

of Increasing Returns, there is an element of economic monopoly yielding a specific marginal rent.

We are now able to recognise that, in economic theory at any rate, pieces of capital may be graded, just as pieces of land may be graded, according to their capacity of contributing to various supplies.

There are several reasons which explain why this conclusion, which seems to follow so clearly from the admitted operation of the Law of Increasing Returns, should have so generally escaped acknowledgment.

The great variety in forms of capital, its superior mobility as compared with land, its more rapid and intricate fluctuations of value, have materially contributed to conceal the gradation of capital. More important still is the fact that, since capital is measured in terms of money, actual forms of capital are being continually revalued according to their remunerativeness. This "marginal rent" of monopoly is constantly absorbed into the higher valuation which is given to the capital. The outside investor of £100 gets no more interest by purchasing a share in a business reaping a high marginal rent than in a business enjoying no such rent.

Lastly, the confused and illogical connotation given to the term "capital" by most English and American economists has helped to obscure the truth.[1]

---

[1] Professor Böhm-Bawerk expresses a natural astonishment that so many English economists, differing so widely in their

But, in addition to these causes which operate to hide the nature of capital-values, there are special reasons why marginal gains of capital have escaped recognition among many who have clearly grasped the conception of scarcity-value in land and in natural ability.

First, there is the difficulty, to which attention has been already called, of accurately distinguishing interest of capital from other special gains with which it coalesces. The interests of capital drawn by the firms of Bass or Guinness are not separable from the gains arising from certain forms of land and water monopoly which form part of the business "capital" of these companies. It is not possible to say precisely how much of the monopoly rent which falls to Messrs. Carnegie is due to monopoly of land, how much to the legal protection of the tariff, and how much to the competitive advantages of a large capital over a small one in the steel rail industry. The capital invested in a chemist's shop probably yields a higher average interest than that employed in a tobacconist's. It is not possible to say how much of this advantage is due to the fact that it is cheaper to stock a tobacconist's shop than a chemist's, and that competition is, therefore, keener among the former, and how much of the

definitions of capital, should agree in the inconsistency of including under capital consumption goods in the possession of labourers. (*Positive Theory of Capital*, p. 67.)

advantage should be regarded as rent of ability or as rent of a legal monopoly, because any one may purchase a license to sell tobacco, while certain personal qualifications are required in a chemist.

This difficulty involved in a separate estimate of capital is one of the chief reasons why the specific marginal interests of capital have escaped notice, and have generally been attributed to land, legal monopoly, or natural ability, with the rents of which they often coalesce.

Another reason why they escape notice is that they are hidden generally by the greater prominence of individual rents. Marginal rent is only an approximately accurate term, selected for certain purposes of convenience. If we apply to different employments of capital the Law of Increasing Returns, we see that it acts with varying force in various employments. It thus gives rise to a number of marginal rents of capital. But, within each species of employment, it also applies with varying force to various sizes of business.

If any evidence were required of the existence of marginal and individual interest of capital, it would be afforded by the persistent attempt which is constantly made by a number of owners of small capitals to obtain these special gains by massing their small capitals into a single large one. The starting of new joint-stock banks is strong evidence of a belief in the inherent advantage of a large capital over a small. One result of successful coöperation of a number of small capitals, in employments once monopolised by a few rich owners of large private capitals, is, of course, to introduce that very element of keen competition, the absence of which was the basis of the monopoly rent. Where coöperative small capitals can compete on equal terms with large private capitals, marginal and differential rents of capital alike tend to disappear. So far, however, as it is true that a particular class of business requires a capital of a given size in order that it may be conducted with an ordinary chance of success, this limitation is able to secure a marginal rent for the capital employed in it with average business ability, as within that business the advantage which a larger capital has over a smaller constitutes a basis of individual rent.

One further objection to the proposed grading of capital requires an answer. It will doubtless be urged that the differences upon which it is suggested capital should be graded are not differences inherent in the nature of capital, but rather differences in the conditions of its employment. The answer is that the conditions under which any given piece of capital are employed, the size in which it is massed, the place it occupies in the industrial machine, belong to the nature of this material *qua* capital just as the element of relative position belongs to the nature of land-values. The value of particular forms of capital, of so

many engines, or pianos, or sovereigns, depends
in large measure upon where they are situated,
and in what quantities they are collected; according as they are more or less advantageously situated in these respects, they help to earn a higher
or lower specific interest.

The other form this same objection takes, that
capital is inseparable from the guiding mind of
its employer, and that differences in rates of remuneration are entirely attributable to skill or
good fortune of the *entrepreneur*, needs no further
discussion. It has been already admitted that an
element of disguised profit is liable to figure as
interest, just as it may also figure as rent of land
when a rapacious landlord rack-rents the tenant of
a well-conducted shop. The intelligent activity
of man is requisite to the employment of capital
just as it is to the employment of land and labour-
power, if they are to be put to serviceable use
so as to yield a return in value. But the skill of
management is no more the cause of the rents of
capital which we are tracing than of the specific
rents of land.

In reckoning capital-values just as in reckoning land-values, we are entitled to assume that
average human intelligence is at work in their
employment. It is important to keep this in
mind, for it furnishes a complete refutation to
a view which is often held respecting the high
rates of interest in certain classes of investments.

Where successful firms obtain very high interest, it is alleged that these high returns are balanced by the low-interest, or the no-interest, or the minus-interest, *i.e.* failure, of less successful firms. In kinds of employment of capital where the prizes are high the blanks are more numerous.

Now it is only natural that the high monopoly rents obtained by successful firms should tempt foolish owners of capital to engage in rash speculation with the view of sharing these monopoly rents. But, in reckoning the specific rent or the total interest of capital employed in such an industry as gold-mining, we have no right to count in the sums which greenhorns hand over to the floaters of bogus companies. We do not assess good agricultural land at a minus rent because many a fool has squandered his money in bad farming. The specific rent of a given class of land is what it will pay in the hands of a tenant of average skill; so the specific rent of gold-mining or any other form of investment presupposes the application of ordinary business intelligence. When this is borne in mind, it will be seen that the rates of interest, set down in statistical reports of the conditions of railways, banking, mining, and other industries, generally conceal a portion or the whole of the specific rent, by including in the capital whose interest is averaged a great deal of capital not applied under the above-named condition. If we are to exclude, as is admittedly right, the element of disguised profit, due to special skill of management, we must also exclude the element of disguised loss, due to the folly of ignorant investors and incompetency of management.

§ 7. The greater facility of transferring forms of capital from place to place, the fact that a large proportion even of "fixed" capital can be transferred, though at a loss, from one employment to another, the large field of choice which an average saver has for the storage of his saving power in forms of capital,— these and other considerations perhaps impart a larger fluidity and freedom of competition to capital than to land, or even than to labour.

But none the less, the idea of practically non-competing groups with differential positions within each group seems conveniently applicable to the supply of all three factors of production. In none of the three cases must we regard the specific and individual status as a rigid one; there is a constant shifting of marginal and differential values. But at any given time only a certain quantity of land, of capital, of labour, is available for contribution to a class of supply: the worst of this land may pay a rent, and this rent will enter into price; the worst of the labour may earn a class wage above the unskilled labourers, this wage will enter into price; the least favourably situated mill or mine contributing to the supply may be able to earn an interest above the minimum, this interest will enter into price.

The individual superiorities enjoyed by special pieces of land, labour, capital, though they procure for their owners special rates of rent, wages, and interest, will not enter into price. Following this analysis, if we took the market-price of a supply of finished manufactured goods, we should find that price representing a complex of a large variety of marginal money-costs; these marginal costs would be the marginal rents of the land, capital, and labour required at each stage in the different processes of production. At some stages no-rent land might be used; at other stages the worst land in use would be rented; at other stages no-interest businesses might be competing, and profits would not figure in the costs at that stage; in other processes unskilled labour at a subsistence wage might be employed, and this "wear and tear" alone would cost.

It is, however, all-essential to perceive the need of a close coördination of the three factors of production. Every price must contain a provision against the wear and tear of the land, capital, and labour employed at each stage of production (whatever that wear-and-tear fund be called), and it must contain a variety of positive costs required to evoke the use of the "marginal" portion of the land, capital, and labour required. These costs may be merely nominal, as where no-rent land,

no-interest capital, no-wage (15*s.*) labour, be
used; or they may be positive, where the worst
portion of the land, capital, or labour in use
requires a positive marginal rent.

CHAPTER VI.

§ 1. The results of our reasoning have been
(1) to coördinate the several factors of production
with regard to the application of a Law of Rent;
(2) to amplify the Law of Rent by distinguishing
a number of margins of employment with differential rents measured from these margins, the marginal rents entering into price, the differential
rents being excluded from price; (3) to substitute
a composite margin for the land-margin in considering the effects of increased demand upon
production.

Now this restatement and expanded application
of the idea of rent throws· important light upon
two closely related matters: (1) the composition
of a price as an amalgam of payments for the use
of various factors of production; (2) the theory of
Distribution or of the proportion in which price is
divided as income among the owners of factors of
production.

An increased demand for a commodity which,

by raising its price, stimulates an increased rate of production, will in most cases lower the margin of employment of all three factors, calling into economic use inferior qualities of land, labour, and capital. The new use, not only of land, but of labour and of capital, will, considered as a separate unit, be more expensive to buy than the same quantity of the old use, for the same rent which was paid before for an acre of marginal land will now be paid for an acre of land below the former margin; and, since a larger number of acres will be required to furnish a given quantity of productive power, the price of a unit of land-use will be greater; so, likewise, an increased number of inferior labourers must be employed at the same wages previously paid to the marginal labourers formerly employed, in order to obtain a given increment of labour-power, and a higher price must be paid for a given quantity of use of new forms of capital. The case of capital should be clearly understood. If there are in actual existence unused forms of capital, plant, machinery, etc., somewhat inferior to those in previous use, these stand precisely in an analogous position to land which lies below the margin; in order to get out of them a given amount of productivity of capital, a larger number must be employed than of the superior forms, and the payment will be the same as in the case of these latter. This can only be done by increasing the payment for the use of each mill, machine, or other concrete piece of capital, which means a rise of price per unit of capital-power and a corresponding raising of the differential rent or interest of the better sorts of forms of capital which were formerly in use. The same result occurs if, instead of bringing into use inferior existing forms of capital, it is sought to work more fully existing forms of capital already in use; this is analogous to an attempt to get more land-power out of a given piece of land by intenser cultivation; in each case the added increment of productive power is obtained at a greater expense, which can only be defrayed on condition that forces of supply and demand have raised the price of a unit of productive power. Similarly, if no unused or half-used forms of capital exist, and the new use of capital now required must be supplied by new savings, these new savings can only be brought into economic existence by raising the rate of interest, so that the new forms of capital will be paid at a higher price for their use than the old forms were previously paid.

§ 2. At first sight this seems to indicate the universal dominance of the Law of Diminishing Returns over the whole field of industry. If the demand for an increased use of each factor calls into use an inferior quality of the factor, involving an increased expense for a given quantity of each sort of productive power, with every increase of supply the marginal cost would rise, and the price of the whole supply would be enhanced.

Indeed, so long as a purely mechanical character is accorded to the operation of productive forces, and each new unit of force is simply regarded as an addition to the old units, there is no escape from the Law of Diminishing Returns. Why, then, do we say that the Law of Diminishing Returns dominates agriculture and the extractive industries, and enters manufactures and other industries only in proportion as raw materials and productive powers of nature are expenses of production? Why do we trace a Law of Increasing Returns in many industries?

The explanation is this. When the margin of cultivation for land is lowered and inferior lands are brought into use, the addition of the new increments of land-use has no power to raise the productiveness of the earlier increments of land-use; no doubt the same causes which have lowered the margin of cultivation have raised the price of the productivity of the better lands, but they have not made them absolutely more productive; the different portions of land stand in no strong organic relation, so that what happens to one piece will affect the productivity of other pieces. To a certain extent it is true that the enlargement of a farm by taking on inferior outlying land might enable the farm to be more self-sustaining, by promoting a more advantageous division of uses in the other land, the new inferior land perhaps furnishing certain necessary accommodation which would set free a better piece of land for a more profitable use. But in every country for most sorts of farming there are well-recognised limits of size, and any further taking in of land beyond the economic limit will not recoup the farmer for the inferiority of the new land by any sufficient gain in the arrangement of his operations.

The economies of division of labour which often attend large farming as compared with small farming cannot of course be imputed to an increased productivity of land-use, as they are not attained by a mere addition of new increments of land.

Since the new units of inferior land-use, obtained by lowering the margin of cultivation, have no considerable or corresponding influence in raising the productivity of other productive force resident in other portions of land, we obtain a diminishing return from a given quantity of labour applied to agriculture where inferior lands are called into use.[1]

§ 3. With labour it is different. Though, if we treat the new increment of labour-power as a thing apart, it seems to give a diminishing return, that diminution may be more than compensated

---

[1] When agriculture has become chiefly a capitalist rather than a land enterprise, it may sometimes conform to a Law of Increasing Returns, as possibly in some forms of bonanza farming.

by its influence upon the aggregate of labour-power with which it is coöperating. We have here to consider a close organic structure of industry, so that a lowering of the margin of employment of labour may be followed by such improved efficiency of the whole coöperative mass of labour-power as shall enable the increased aggregate of supply of commodities to be produced less expensively in terms of labour-use than the former smaller aggregate.

This is no more than to say that the Law of Diminishing Returns is a law of matter, the Law of Increasing Returns a law of mind. Just in proportion as labour-power is low-skilled and physical, its efficiency depends less upon intelligent coöperation and is less amenable to specialisation. A lowering of the standard of employment in navvy labour or in the labour of fruit-pickers may easily show that the industry conforms to the Law of Diminishing Returns, *i.e.* that the inferiority of labour at the same pay is not compensated by improved division of labour or other organic economies of the particular business. It is just in proportion as we rise to those grades of labour in which physical power plays a relatively unimportant part, that we realise the operation of the Law of Increasing Returns.

It is the inelasticity, the inorganic character of the productive powers of nature, which Ricardo signified by applying the epithets "inherent and indestructible," that explains the operation of the Law of Diminishing Returns. The productive powers of man must be so ordered by intelligent coöperation that the addition of factors inferior to those in former use may raise the volume of productive power by a total larger than that represented by the numerical proportion which the new units of labour-power bear to the old aggregate supply.

§ 4. It is difficult to know whether we ought to classify capital with land or with labour in respect of increasing or diminishing returns. An addition to the stock of capital obtained by lowering the margin of employment may be represented as giving an increased efficiency to the capital in earlier use, by allowing more specialisation of capital. But since this increased efficiency or productivity would be inseparable from the employment of an increased volume and division of labour-power, such increasing return would best seem attributable to economy of increased labour-power.

The actual effect of a demand for increased capital is of course often to introduce improved forms of capital, which, so far from needing for their utilisation an increased supply of labour-power, cause a net displacement of direct employment, taking the business as a whole. But this case is not an illustration of a lowering of the margin of employment, for the new forms of capital called into use are not inferior to the old; it is parallel to the opening up of a new rich tract of land, which may for a time reverse the normal tendency whereby an increased demand calls inferior lands into use.

If, however, this analogy does not dispose of the case of improvements in quality of capital-forms, it will be necessary to refer this apparent application of a law of increasing returns for capital to the labour represented by the invention of the new forms taken by the increment of capital. The capitalist below the margin of employment is, *qua* capitalist, capable of putting in the field of industry only the customary form of capital; the interest paid him for this cost of saving is the price for producing an increment of the old forms of capital. These new copies of the old forms of capital cannot, I think, be rightly or conveniently regarded as giving such increased efficiency to the similar forms which have been functioning in industry as to afford an increasing return to the increased aggregate.

While, therefore, I claim that it is convenient to attribute direct productivity to forms of land and capital, an increased demand for their use, which compels recourse to inferior or more expensive portions, can exercise this compelling power only in conformity with the Law of Diminishing Returns, by raising the former price of each unit of land-use or capital-use. This is, of course, not inconsistent with the general tendency of the rate of profit or real interest to fall. Although there may be a growing willingness to save for a lower rate of remuneration, still, if we compare the actual saving which takes shape in capital with the potential saving which might take shape, we must regard the latter as lying below the margin of employment, and only capable of coming into actual existence on condition of a higher rate of interest than is paid for capital already in use.

Only when we take the productive prices of labour-power which function at the command of the human will, do we escape the limits set by the material world upon industry. So long as we persist in measuring labour-power in independent units, we fail to understand the vital law of industrial growth. The Law of Increasing Returns is simply the law of intelligent coöperation.

§ 5. This is nothing but a necessary theoretic preface to the study of progressive production in the several industries.

When we have grasped the idea that a composite margin of employment must be substituted for a land margin, we shall be obliged to work out in each case of increased supply the problem how far this new increment of supply lowers the margin, and how the lower margin is composed.

At this point we perceive the identity of the theory of the Composition of Price with the theory of Distribution.

In order to illustrate the operation of the Law of Rent as the determinant in distribution, it will be best to take the case of an increase in the product to be distributed. Our question then will be, What determines the proportion of the increased product which goes to the owners of the three requisites of production? or, in other words, reverting to our general application of the law of rent, What determines the rise of marginal and differential rents in the case of land, capital, and labour, respectively? Let us assume, for convenience, that the increased product requires for its production an additional quantity of land, capital, and labour, involving a proportionately equal increase in all three factors of production, *e.g.* a rise of 10% in the quantity of each factor industrially employed. How will this increased demand for the use of the factors of production affect the proportion in which the product shall be distributed?

If the demand for use of more land, capital, and labour can be met by the employment of a new supply of each, lying just below the margin of employment, but only nominally inferior to the supply in previous use, the prices of use of land, capital, and labour will not appreciably rise, and the new product will be divided among the three, in strict accordance with the previous proportions. In that case, the fall of the margin of employment and the rise in rental of each rent-paying portion

of the land, capital, and labour in previous use
will be very slight — just sufficient to call into
economic existence the required increase of supply. But if, while there is plenty of land and
capital available, of barely inferior quality to that
on the margin of employment, an equal addition
to the supply of labour is not so easily procurable,
the growth of demand for labour acting in relation
to a fixed supply will raise the price or rent of
labour above the margin of employment until that
margin is driven down low enough to include the
required new supply. That is to say, while in
the case of land and capital a merely nominal fall
of the margin involving a nominal rise of rent has
produced the new supply, in the case of labour a
considerable fall of the margin, attended by a considerable rise of rent, has been required to produce
a corresponding increase of supply. Thus, while
the rent of land and capital remain practically at
the same level as before, the rent of labour will
have risen greatly, and will absorb almost the
whole of the increased product, shifting the balance of proportion in the distribution of the aggregate product among the industrial community.

The advantageous position here accorded to
labour may with equal reason be assigned to land
or capital. In proportion to the difficulty of supplying each increased quantity of the several
requisites of production, will be the rise in price
of each unit of those factors already in use. The

mechanism by which this operates is very simple. The rise of price will be caused by the deficiency of available supply considered in relation to an increased demand reckoned at former prices; the new supply can only be brought into the same quantitative relation to the new demand by the maintenance of a new price per unit of productive power, the new price representing in relation to the old the greater difficulty of keeping in economic use the determinant portion of supply of that factor of production.

Thus we reach the law that the proportion of the aggregate product which is paid as rent of land, of capital, and of labour varies with the difficulty of keeping in economic use the quantity of each factor of production required to maintain the rate of current production. As there is vacant land below the margin of cultivation (*i.e.* yielding less productive power per acre than can be utilised at a given amount of expenses of cultivation per acre), so there is potential capital (*i.e.* capital containing powers of productivity too low to defray working expenses at formerly current remuneration, but which, given a sufficient motive, will become active forms of capital); and, lastly, there is vacant labour of inferior quality (*i.e.* a larger quantity of which is required to furnish a given amount of effective labour-power). In each case, the potential or unemployed factor is called into economic use by a sufficient rise in the rent of that which lies above the existing margin of employment.

This theory that changes in the proportionate payments to land, capital, and labour, are dependent upon the comparative ease or difficulty of increasing the supply of each, would seem so obvious a truth that it could not have failed to secure adequate recognition. That it has failed to do so must be attributed to the extreme reluctance which economists have shown to admit the truth, that the only *immediate* cause of a change of price is a previous change in the quantitative relation of supply and demand at current prices. If it were once clearly recognised that a restriction of supply at current prices were the only possible immediate cause of a rise of price, and if this were kept in mind in dealing with the prices of the use of land, capital, and labour, the main difficulty in forming a satisfactory theory of distribution would disappear.

It will perhaps be convenient to sum up the conclusions so far reached in the following three propositions: —

1. If there exists an indefinite quantity of each of the factors of production just below the margin of employment, of almost equal quality to that upon the margin, an increase in production will neither alter the proportion of distribution among the owners of the three factors nor appreciably raise the differential rent of each portion of a factor above the margin.

2. If there is not a sufficient quantity of any of the factors of production easily available for new supply, and the difficulty of procuring each piece of additional supply is equal in the case of each factor, the differential rent of each rent-paying piece of land, capital, and labour will rise, but the proportion of distribution of the aggregate product will remain unchanged.

3. If there is a difference in the amount of difficulty of procuring the increased supply of the three factors, that difference will be accurately measured by the relative rise in rent of the rent-paying portion of each factor, and by a corresponding alteration in the proportion of the aggregate product which falls to each, *i.e.* if it is desirable to increase by 20% the quantity of each factor of production in order to increase the product, and it is twice as difficult to procure the increased quantity of land as of capital and labour, one-half of the increased product will go as rent to land, one-quarter as rent to capital, one-quarter as rent to labour.

In applying the rule of measurement thus far, we have assumed the case where the increase of production acts as a call for an increase in the use of the three factors which is proportionately equal. But, in fact, it is of course seldom the case that the proportionate part played by the respective factors of production remains the same when there is an increase of production. It by no means follows that if in the old quantity of production the numbers 3, 2, 5, represent the respective contributions of land, capital, and labour, and the production be doubled, the same proportion will hold among the contributors. The Law of Substitution is constantly operative, enabling capital to displace labour, economising land by increased use of capital or labour.[1] We know, in fact, that every increase in the aggregate product will be attended by a change in the proportion of the contribution of the three factors. Hence the practical application of our rule of measurement is obviously no easy task. For every change in the distribution of the aggregate product will depend on the relative strength of two forces : first, the relative growth in the demand for each factor signified by the increased product ; second, the relative difficulty of supplying that increased demand. The frequent use of the word "relative" here is itself a proof of the complex nature of the problem. Before we can say in what degree an increase of 10% in the aggregate production of a community will affect the proportionate distribution, we should have first to ascertain two facts : (x) the precise amount of land, capital, and labour

---

[1] Böhm-Bawerk, in his treatment of *The Value of Complementary Goods*, clearly and accurately indicates the importance of the Law of Substitution among the requisites of production in determining the amount of remuneration which each of the several factors obtains. He first shows relative indispensability as the measure of economic force.

required to take part in the new production and
the proportion each addition bears to the quantity
in previous use ; and (y) the extent of the fall in
margin of employment necessary to furnish in the
case of each factor the desired increase. Now,
each of these two facts, x and y, is itself a resultant
of various conflicting forces, and can only be ascertained by an elaborate calculation.

A whole group of considerations affects the proportionate increase of each factor of production
required by each increase in the aggregate production.   Among them the following are most
prominent : —

1. Improvements in the industrial arts, and
application of labour-saving machinery, (a) enabling the same quantity of capital to suffice in
turning out an increased product, (b) enabling
capital to take the place of labour, so that what
might seem to be an equal demand for more capital and more labour, will act as a demand for a
large quantity of new capital and a small quantity
of new labour.

2. Social and industrial reforms, improving the
organisation of labour, or inducing greater care and
economy in the use of material and of machinery,
will, by adding to the average effectiveness of both
capital and labour, enable an increase in the aggregate product to be achieved by a less than corresponding increase of capital and labour. Even here
the movement is not simple, but complex. *E.g.*

in the case of economy effected by coöperation or
profit-sharing, so far as the economy consists in
greater care of machinery and less waste of material, it might operate as an equal check upon the
increased quantity of both capital and labour required to furnish an increased product. So far
as it acted merely as a stimulus to greater working activity, it would figure chiefly as economy of
labour, so that an increased product might be
wrought by the same quantity of labour acting in
conjunction with an increased quantity of capital.

3. Every improvement of physique, morale, intelligence, and technical skill among the workers
will enable a demand for more labour-power to be
satisfied by a less than corresponding increase in
the number of workers.

4. Improvement in agricultural arts may enable a larger product to be obtained without a
corresponding fall in the margin of cultivation,
i.e. without a correspondingly increased employment of land.

These are some of the determining forces which
would require study before we could reach the
resultant *x*. Another set of forces and circumstances affect the ease or difficulty of procuring
increased supplies of the respective factors of
production. Such are the following: —

1. The effect of growing improvements in
communication, and the breaking down of international barriers for trading purposes, in their

respective bearing upon (*a*) the increase of the effective land supply for a given community, (*b*) the increased " fluidity " of capital, (*c*) the easier migration of labour.

2. The effect of war, political insecurity, national commercial restrictions, and the like, as affecting (*a*) the available quantity of each requisite of production, (*b*) the relative fluidity of each factor of production.

3. Effects of the growth of prudential motives, increased sense of security, and fluidity of capital, as affecting the ease with which an increased demand for capital may be supplied.

4. Complicated effects of rising standard of comfort, education, artificial checks on population, and the like, in determining the increased supply of labor at different degrees of availability.

It is not too much to say that each of these considerations opens up a large field for speculation and involves special difficulties of its own. Each of them has an importance in assisting to determine the resultants x and y. But, unfortunately, this is not all. x, representing the amount of land, labour, and capital required for an increased production of commodities, or any single commodity, is not the simple composite we have assumed it to be. The land it represents is itself composed of a great variety of land-uses entering into the different processes of production, some with differential rents measured from a no-rent margin, others with differential rents measured from positive margins. In some of these cases the increased demand for commodities will greatly lower the margin, raising largely the differential rents; in other cases the increased supply can be afforded by a very small fall of the margin; in other cases, maybe, the fall of margin may be obviated by a change of method of production which will economise land-use by increasing uses of capital and labour in conformity with the Law of Substitution. Thus the effect of increased demand for land-use will affect differently the land-use employed in all the processes. The same will apply to capital and labour, various specific and individual forms of which will contribute to the production of supply at different points. When, therefore, we consider what would be the effect of an increase of supply of 10 % of any commodity in affecting the proportion of the price which will be paid to the owners of the different factors, we are evidently faced by a very complex computation. The determination of both x and y has to be made first separately at each point in production. But even that will not suffice. Not only should we have to measure the relative pressure with which these two forces act at each several point in the increase of production, in order to reach the change in the proportionate distribution. For alas! x and y cannot be determined as entirely different forces. These are not merely

two varying forces, but varying forces which act
upon one another with a force which likewise
varies.   What we mean is this: it is impossible to
state accurately how much new land capital and
labour would be used to furnish an increased
product, unless we know already the amount of
difficulty there would be in procuring that increased supply; for we cannot without that knowledge determine how far labour-saving machinery
may be introduced instead of an increased quantity
of labourers, nor can we determine how far the
increased demand for land will operate in intenser
or more efficient culture of the land already above
the line of occupation, instead of stimulating the
enclosure of hitherto unused land.   On the other
hand, it will be evident that we cannot ascertain exactly the amount of fall in the margin
of employment of the three factors of production, unless we know, not merely what increased
product is required, but also to what extent
this increased demand will act upon the three
factors of production respectively,—in fact, until
we know the resultant x.   As the two main
forces, which for convenience we regarded as
distinct, are thus seen to modify one another, the
full nature of the complexity of the problem of
distribution begins to dawn upon us.   In order
accurately to ascertain the disturbance in proportionate distribution of the product between land,
labour, and capital caused by an increase or de-

crease of production, we have in effect to measure
the varying pressure of a number of industrial
forces (which pressure also varies in the rate of
its variation), each of which affects a number
of other forces with different degrees and varying
rates of attraction. We have u, v, w, x, y, z, etc.,
all moving at different rates, and all affecting one
another to a different degree in proportion to the
force of their respective motions.

Such is the intricate theoretic setting of the
problems which have to be worked out by the
managers of businesses and by the organisers of
labour. In each trade, at each time, in each
country, the problem will be different. Indeed,
if we take the standpoint of nationalism in economics, and ask what the effect upon the demand
for the several factors for the different processes
in a particular country will be, arising from an
increased demand for a class of commodities, we
have to consider not merely the purely economic,
but also the political considerations which move
nations in this trade competition.

Those whose business it is to work out the
probable influence upon profits or wages of an
assumed increase or decrease of production in a
particular trade, are compelled to consider the
coöperation of all these forces, so far as they are
ascertainable. The success of a particular capitalist enterprise or of a labour movement will
ever more largely depend upon the skill and

experience of those responsible for such computation.

We have now discussed the changes in terminology and in point of view requisite to coördinate land, labour, and capital, so as to measure their influence upon price and their respective strength as claimants upon the general product. We have seen that the conception of a margin of employment with differential rents for more productive forms is equally applicable to all three factors, while a right regard for the Law of Substitution involves the application of a composite margin of employment in considering the effect of an increased or a decreased demand for productive energy upon the distribution of the product among the owners of the factors.

It has also appeared that the process of determining the price of a supply of land, labour, or capital is substantially the same as the process of determining the price of a supply of commodities, when acres, labourers, and £100's of capital are reduced to some standard measure of the productive power which, underneath the irregularities of form, is the real object of sale. The price-point for the sale of a unit of land-power, capital-power, labour-power, is determined by the stronger of a final pair of bargainers within limits reached by competition of buyers and sellers of these factors of production. The wide external differences between a market for goods and a market for sale of the several factors, where competition is often extremely slow, indirect, and incomplete, must not blind us to the substantial identity of the economic processes. When the competition is slight and imperfect, the result is that the upper and lower limits of price are wider apart than in a freely competitive market for goods, so that the economic force of the stronger of the final bargainers has fuller scope. The contrast between the money-market or the wool-market under normal conditions, and the market for sale of land-uses in a growing city, is no doubt a striking one; but though competition lapses at a far earlier point in the latter than in the former cases, the difference is one of degree and not of kind. In both cases, competition between buyers and sellers, in both cases, economic force are determinants of price, though to different extents.

To those who are lovers of simplicity this may not seem a very satisfactory result, but a large part of the disrepute from which the science of economics suffers among "practical" men is due, not, as is often alleged, to an inherent distaste for theoretic treatment, but to the hasty fabrication of economic laws which are so delightfully simple that an attempt is made to use them as "rules of thumb" in the actual movements of industry. They are then found to be inapplicable, and the practical man is not satisfied with the scientific economist's elaborate explanations of the difficulties involved in applying economic laws to details of economic fact.

These intricate considerations teach caution. They are often used to suggest inertia. Many of the forces involved are quite incapable of accurate measurement, and it may easily be shown that it is impossible to predict with any degree of certainty the effect upon profits or employment of a particular industrial action involving a change in demand for the several factors of production. But this does not justify inaction. Human conduct is always speculative; the future never admits of exact prophecy; risk and faith are at all points essential to progress. A reasonable man is prepared to take ordinary chances, his calculations are confined to a comparatively small number of factors, and these not exactly measured; after a reasonable computation of certain large issues he can often afford to ignore smaller ones. Wide experience produces a capacity of judgment which is apparently intuitive, though strictly ratiocinative in its secret working.

Hence large industrial movements affecting the production and the distribution of wealth are often rigidly guided by a clear grasp of certain leading facts or generalisations. For example, large organisations of labourers may be quite incapable of working out all the intricate effects upon each trade, of a general policy of higher wages or shorter hours; but they may have a right knowledge that the conditions of bargaining between labourers and employers are on the average so favourable to the latter as to place in their hands a large surplus of wealth, the diversion of which into higher wages or more leisure is economically feasible. Possessing such knowledge, they will not rightly be deterred from action by the real risks involved by the pressure of other unknown or incalculable forces upon certain sections of labourers. It is sufficient if they make good use of such knowledge as they can get. Human conduct is notoriously enfeebled, or even sterilised, by the growing conviction of risk and uncertainty which weighs upon the student who comes to realise the infinity of knowledge in any department of inquiry. The practical man has to decide for himself how much he may safely leave unknown, though he can never know exactly how much this is, and what risks he must be prepared to run, though the precise size and nature of these very risks must always baffle him.

CHAPTER VII.

§ 1. There are certain special considerations affecting the sale of labour-power which make the sellers of that commodity normally weaker than the buyers.

This normal condition of inferior strength is often summed up by saying that it is more important or more pressing for the individual owner of labour-power to effect a sale than for the employer to effect a purchase.

This is evidently and particularly the case where there exists an excess of any kind of labour-power beyond the amount required at a price which would enable minimum business profits to be earned. A supply of goods or of land which, if it is placed upon the market, would bring down prices to an unprofitable level, can in most cases be withheld from the market without sustaining irreparable damage. This is not the case with labour-power. It must be sold; if not sold for a week, not only is the week's supply wasted, but the aggregate of labour-power, the labour-capital, the labourer himself, perishes. This labour-power must be sold continuously; it must be sold in small quantities, commonly measured by the day or week; finally, it must be sold to a buyer who knows the necessity under which the seller stands to effect a sale. In a word, the labourer is selling his labour-power under the conditions of a forced sale. In a labour-market the bargain of the marginal pair (which directly rules the price) will be that of a seller whose inability to refuse a bargain is known all the time, to the buyer with whom he is "higgling for a price." Under such circumstances the superior force of the buyer is so well recognised that he is commonly able to avoid the necessity of higgling, and to dictate a customary price of labour. Again, the organic continuity of an individual's labour-power, the fact that one week's energy is vitally connected with the next week's, makes his weakness in bargaining a cumulative disadvantage.[1] A bad sale for a number of weeks or months, a failure to obtain regular and proper employment at reasonable wages, brings about a deterioration of working efficiency for the following weeks, and perhaps a permanent injury to physique and morale.

These weaknesses of bargaining attach to labour-power, as distinct from other things that are sold, because labour-power cannot be detached from the vitality of which it is a function.

Putting this peculiarity in another form, we

[1] Cf. Marshall, *Principles*, 2d ed., Vol. I, p. 602.

may say it resides in the fact that, while the
worker is selling a portion of his labour-power,
he is also buying the permission to live, and the
future production of his labour-power depends
upon the terms of this purchase. Hence, while
the employer is directly concerned only with the
purchase of labour-power, the inevitable terms of
such a purchase give him power over other vital
functions which he does not buy, but which are
"thrown in for nothing." What I mean is ad-
mirably summed up by Mrs. Webb: "The wage-
earner does not, like the shopkeeper, merely sell
a piece of goods which is carried away; it is his
whole life, which, for the stated term, he places
at the disposal of his employer. What hours he
shall work, when and where he shall get his
meals, the sanitary conditions of his employment, the safety of the machinery and tempera-
ture to which he is subjected, the fatigues or
strains which he endures, the risks of accident or
disease which he has to incur, — all these are matters no less important to the workman than his
wages. Yet about the majority of these vital
conditions he cannot bargain at all."[1]

Even if he can bargain, he bargains at a grave
normal disadvantage. Even where collective bargaining has largely taken the place of individual
bargaining, the power of labourers to get adequate
safeguards against the abuse of these individual

[1] *Commonwealth*, February, 1896.

risks and hardships has been small, and as they are no proper part of what is offered in the sale of labour-power, no monetary compensation is appropriate and no monetary valuation possible. "All that a man hath will he give for his life." The necrosis of the phosphorus match-maker, the phthisis of the Belfast linen-spinner, are not part of any bargain and are not paid for.

§ 2. How far the process of collective bargaining improves the relative position of the sellers of labour-power, so far as the price is concerned, it is difficult to judge. Bearing in mind that capital is generally far more advanced in collective organisation than labour (each large employer bringing a large number of closely welded units of joint-stock capital to confront the much more loosely and imperfectly welded units of labour-power), it is difficult to believe that the substitution of the labour-group for the single labourer can redress the balance of advantage on the side of the employer. This involves no depreciation of trade-unionism ; a group of labourers bargaining for a sale of labour-power over a long period of time, through skilled agents, is absolutely in a far stronger case than a single labourer, higgling like an ignorant amateur. But where organisation of capital has made similar advances, the relative advantage of the employer may be as great as ever. For any modern struggle between equally developed organisations of manual workers

and employers, so far as it is left to economic
might, untempered by legal or charitable interference, exhibits the superior power of the employer
resting on the fact that the sale of labour-power
involves the purchase of the right to live; the
power to starve labour into submission still sur-
vives as the final economic arbiter.   So far as
organisations of labourers can modify or postpone
this superiority of the employer, it is not by the
mere substitution of collective for individual bargains in sales of labour-power, but by amassing a
fund of capital so that they may no longer contend as mere proletariat.   The attempt of a trade-
union with accumulated funds to fight a body of
employers is a fight of capital against capital.

.§ 3.   The ordinary process by which the wage is
immediately determined is sometimes regarded as a
separate disadvantage to the labourer.   Whereas
the employer may have before him a number of
applicants for employment who will closely compete and underbid one another, it does not often
happen that employers meet face to face and directly compete to buy the services of a labourer.
Thus it appears that the levelling tendency of
competition is less operative among the buyers
of labour than among the sellers.   The immediate
position which faces an unorganised worker applying for a job is one which offers hunger and
possible starvation as the alternative to accepting
the offer of an employer; for though there may

be other employers who will each separately be willing to make an offer, he cannot rely upon this being the case, nor can he make these several employers bid directly against one another. Where, as is the case in many trades, the supply of available labour is normally in excess of the demand at the standard wage, the economic weakness of the seller of labour is aggravated by this mode of conducting the sale.

"The art of bargaining," observed Jevons, "mainly consists in the buyer ascertaining the lowest price at which the seller is willing to part with his object, without disclosing, if possible, the highest price which he, the buyer, is willing to give. . . . The power of reading another man's thoughts is of high importance in business." "Now the essential economic weakness of the isolated workman's position is necessarily known to the employer and his foreman. The isolated workman, on the other hand, is ignorant of his employer's position. Even in the rare cases in which the absence of a single workman is really inconvenient to the capitalist employer, this is unknown to any one outside the office. What is more important, the employer, knowing the state of the market for his product, can form a clear opinion of how much it is worth his while to give, rather than go without the labour altogether, or rather than postpone it for a few weeks. But the isolated workman, unaided by any trade-union official, and unable to communicate even with the workmen in other towns, is wholly in the dark as to how much he might ask." [1]

The condition of bargaining for sale of labour-power which I have described, applies in its fulness to low-skilled labour. Of such labour we may say that the normal wage is one of bare subsistence, unless some alternative of squatting, stealing, begging, or public charity is able to qualify it. To place the "marginal labourer" of such a class upon a footing of equal power to bargain with the marginal employer who buys his labour, it would be necessary: —

(*a*) To guarantee him and his family a full wage of economic efficiency as an alternative to the acceptance of competitive employment.

(*b*) To safeguard him in his giving out of labour-power, against conditions of work which can impair his efficiency for future work.

Just in so far as certain individuals and classes have practically obtained these securities, the terms upon which they bargain for the sale of their labour-power are superior to those above described.

Bodies of skilled manual workers with a firm hold on an important labour-market, where capital is in genuine competition, are often able to maintain a standard wage for the marginal labour, considerably higher than the wage of low-skilled

labour. Possessing a "corner" of some highly
serviceable skill, and perhaps some resource of
capital, they can reduce considerably the advantage which the capitalist-employer must naturally
possess in bargaining with a proletarian. As we
rise to the professions and other grades of skilled
mental workers, we are dealing with persons who,
by reason of some assistance of capital, their own
or others, or from legitimate confidence in some
alternative employment, are often able to enter
on a bargain for sale of this skill, upon terms of
equal or even superior advantage with the buyer.

The marginal lawyer or the marginal doctor in
the West-end market is probably able at least to
hold his own in the slow and indirect forms of
bargaining which fix the price of his professional
skill.

In each labour-market there will be many individuals who can take high differential rents,
marking their superior value over the marginal
seller. These differential rents seem to become
both absolutely and relatively larger as we ascend
to the higher grades of labour. Indeed, it would
be straining the system of gradation too far to
apply it with rigidity to the most highly remunerated forms of personal or professional service,
where what is sold is not so much advice, so
much acting or singing, but where each individual more or less constitutes a market of his
own, drawing monopoly rents rather than the

differential rents which arise where industrial services of a more routine or impersonal order are sold.

§ 4. Socialism and labour-movements in general are chiefly motived by a more or less clear perception that bargains for the sale of labour-power differ from other kinds of bargains in that there is a considerable normal balance of economic strength on the side of the buyers. An application to a labour-market of the analysis applied in Chapter I will show that true competition gives way at a point which leaves a marginal labourer face to face with a marginal employer, under conditions which enable the latter to fix the price close to the lower limit, thus assigning a "forced gain" to each buyer of labour-power.

It is the perception of this inequality which places in the forefront of social questions the rectification of methods of selling labour-power. "In any given state of industrial morality," writes Mr. Charles Booth, "the social value of competition is measured by its equality — by the possession of equal powers both mental and material by both sides to a contract or a bargain."[1] No such equality exists, or can exist, until equal access to all economic and intellectual opportunities is open to all.

[1] *Life and Labour of the People*, Vol. IV, p. 214.

CHAPTER VIII.

§ 1. Some special mystery has been often supposed to attach to bargains for the use of capital.
This has arisen partly from people failing to
understand what was actually sold in a loan,
what it was that interest was paid to buy, and
partly from certain circumstances historically associated with lending and borrowing.

I have held a number of sovereigns in my
strong-box for some time past, and they lie there
neither increasing nor diminishing in number.
You come and entreat the loan of them, I let you
have them, and they begin to breed and return to
me in a year's time with added sovereigns. How
can this be?

Money does not breed; the wisest of men—Solo-
mon, Aristotle, Bacon — are sure of that, and they
are convinced that I have come by the extra
sovereigns wrongfully, by some process of extor-
tion.

If I plead that you, after taking my sovereigns,
circulated them in commerce, buying goods with
them, taking these goods to other people and sell-

227

ing them, and that by processes of this kind you obtained a considerable increase of sovereigns and had some over, even after returning my original stock with increase, the above-named worthies would not be appeased. For just as I had made no increase of sovereigns by lending them to you, so you have made no rightful increase by circulating them in commerce. If I plead that you have not been a loser, then you must have used my sovereigns in cheating sovereigns out of others. The process of lending money could give no rightful increase, for it' cost me nothing to lend my idle cash to you, and sovereigns cannot make anything, but only pass from hand to hand.

There was to the ancient mind no ground for payment of interest upon money lent;[1] no valuable service was rendered, whatever origin you give to value; there was no apparent cost and no apparent utility. Or if there was an obvious utility, if I lent to you in your dire necessity, I

[1] It seems, however, pretty clear that in Babylonia as in China, and probably in other ancient societies, a distinction was early made between loans for need and loans for business. This reasonable distinction would easily make itself manifest even in the most primitive forms of lending. "Among the primitive progressive peoples who cultivated the wild wheat of Babylonia, we may feel sure that the primitive instincts of hospitality never sank so low, as for one man to ask another to give him back with interest, the corn borrowed and eaten in a day of need. But the case is quite different as regards corn to be used, not for food but for seed, capable of bringing forth a hundred fold." (Simcox, *Primitive Civilisation*, Vol. I, p. 194.)

was able to trade upon your weakness, and exact terms which were cruel and inequitable. . There was very little fixed capital used, and comparatively little lending for trade; most loans were made by the rich to the poor to purchase for the latter current necessaries of life. Wherever interest is especially associated with such loans, as in Russia to-day, the condemnation alike of the theory and the practice of interest is quite intelligible.

§ 2. But even when we come to the conditions of a modern industrial community, where loans are quite as often made to the rich as to the poor, where some lenders plainly deprive themselves of certain present opportunities of satisfaction, and where it is quite clearly seen that what is borrowed is not really money, but plant, machinery, and goods, — though the necessity and even the abstract justice of paying interest is generally admitted, — there is no clear apprehension of what it is that is really bought and paid for by interest.

"The use of capital," it has been said; but that answer does not carry us far. For what is that use? Capital performs a service in production. Even Karl Marx allows that. But what service, and why should it be paid in interest? If the service of a piece of capital, (say) a machine, consists in helping to work up raw materials into finished goods, as it seems, then this machine will wear itself out in a few years,

or, if one prefers, it will itself be worked up or
consumed in the goods it helps to produce. Put
it on a par with the labour that tends it, secure
the machine against its wear and tear, procure for
it continuity of existence, by providing against
depreciation. But whence comes the interest?
You say "it is productive," but what it has produced is clearly the goods which have been sold:
how has it produced the interest actually paid its
owner, who, even after the actual machine is dead
and is replaced by another one, continues to receive this interest just the same?

§ 3. Just as the interest does not clearly seem
to correspond to any productivity, so again the
cost represented by its use is not so patent as in
the case of labour. Earlier economists of this
century, including Ricardo, inclined to resolve the
"cost" incurred by capital into the labour of making the forms of capital. But this treatment of
capital as accumulated labour gives no explanation
and no justification of interest. McCulloch's assertion, "that profits of stock are only another name
for the wages of accumulated labour," is simply a
denial of the validity of interest. Take the case of
the earliest form of capital, which we may assume
to be entirely made by labour. If the labourers
who made it sold it, when made, in a free market,
we should be obliged to say they obtained its full
value as the wages of their labour; if, on the
other hand, they kept possession of it, and either

used it to assist them in their labour, or loaned it
to others for a similar purpose, at the end of the
year they would obtain an added value which was,
ex hypothesi, not payment for the original labour
which went into making it, but was what we call
interest. In such a simple case it is easy to perceive that, not the labour-cost of making it, but
some cost connected with the use of it either by
themselves or others during the year, was the
cause why interest comes to them. To the "some
cost," Senior gave the name of abstinence. These
men received the extra value as a reward for their
postponement of their immediate gratification.
But it was difficult for Senior to explain how
this cost of abstinence was the efficient cause of
any increase of wealth, analogous to the increase
of wealth due to the cost of an output of labour-
power. "How could mere abstinence, the nega-
tion of activity," he was asked, "possibly cause
an increase of wealth which went as interest?" and
he had no valid answer.

How is the cost of abstinence productive? It
is quite plain that the taker of interest need do
nothing but abstain; that is, in fact, the only
"cost" he undergoes. This was perhaps not
clearly seen when most capital was owned by
workers, who used it to assist their labour. But
when we turn to the normal use of capital for
investment, we see that all the owner need do to
earn the interest he receives is to abstain from

immediate consumption, to postpone satisfaction. How can this negative action be productive of the wealth returned as interest?

For the answer to this question (there is an answer), we must turn to another school of economists, who have, I think, unconsciously furnished a clew to the mystery.

We have already seen the trouble caused by the antagonism of two theories of Value — the "cost" and the "utility" theories. I have shown how, by approaching value through price, we reach a true statement of value as the resultant of forces operating from both sides, the relations of cost to utility. Now it is worthy of remark that although the question of capital and interest has commonly been severed from the general theory of value and submitted to separate investigation, the same divergency of conflicting explanations has arisen. One set of thinkers explains interest by abstinence — a cost theory ; another by productivity — a utility theory.

It is not curious that this conflict should arise in connection with an imperfect theory of value. It is, however, of the utmost importance to recognise that the question of interest is nothing else than a particular case of price.

The Law of Price stated above applies to the price of service of capital as to all other prices. The loan market is subject to the same forces which determine prices in other markets; there is the same competition of bargaining pairs, the same narrowing of the competitive price toward a point finally determined by the will of the stronger member of the final pair ; final cost and final utility are represented here as in other markets by the final pair.

The final pair in the loan market will, as in other markets, consist of the lender who, among those who conclude a loan, sets the highest valuation upon the services he is selling, and the borrower who, among actual borrowers, sets the lowest valuation upon the service he is buying. The former, in accordance with our general analysis of value, will be the marginal saver (the person incurring the largest " cost," or requiring the largest inducement to " abstain " or " wait "), the latter the marginal borrower (the person who imputes the smallest utility to a loan).

§ 4. But the root questions still await an answer : " How is the cost of abstinence the cause of the utility of capital? " " What is the ' utility ' of a concrete piece of capital which yields a continuous interest to its owner ? "

I build a house, let it to you, you pay me £80 a year and undertake to keep it in repair at a cost of £20 a year. You are paying £100 a year, £80 of which comes to me as rent or interest. What does that interest and insurance buy for you? Clearly the shelter and other conveniences furnished by the house. May we not say that the house is engaged in producing a continuous supply of shelter? You say the house is only dead matter and cannot produce. This begs the question that conscious human effort alone produces. This again is only a question of convenience of terminology. I suggest that it is convenient to regard both land and capital as productive factors, and their rent and interest as analogous to wages. Land is not dead, but yields a recurrent supply of natural forces analogous to the recurrent supply of labour-power put forth by man, and upon similar conditions, viz. that she is recouped artificially or is allowed to recoup herself for the drains to which she is subjected. Is it altogether fanciful to suggest that the repairs done to the house correspond to the subsistence wage paid to labour and to land to maintain their continuous economic existence, and that the interest paid the owner is for continuous services rendered by the natural powers of the materials of which the house is constructed, the powers to resist rain, atmospheric influences, and animal intruders? Do not these, in fact, constitute the utility for which you pay £100?

There are those who would make a mystery of the fact that capital can yield interest in perpetuity. "A house or a machine or other piece of capital is not," they say, "eternally productive; even allowing it is productive in the way you claim, it wears out in time, and yet after it is worn out and gone and is replaced by a different house or machine you will continue to receive the interest just the same."

Yet this difficulty disappears if we look more closely at our example. My interest on my house, the rent you pay me, is £80, but you value the utility you get at £100, for you are willing not only to pay me £80, but to spend £20 a year in repairs. Now this arrangement about repairs is not inherent to the theory of interest. I can arrange that you shall pay me £100 a year instead of £80, and I will do the repairs myself. Now in either case provision is made that my capital, my house, is eternally productive. The £80 I receive will continue indefinitely as the payment for the shelter furnished by my house; this continuity or preservation I furnish myself by additional labour put into repairs. I may make you pay for these repairs, but none the less they are to be deemed my repairs, for the house is worth—for an indefinite time—£100 to you, and I only take £80 as profit. The case is perhaps still clearer if I occupy my own house, enjoying the same shelter, and doing the repairs with my own hands. Here it matters little whether I speak of the house as capital producing a profit of £100 or regard £20 as my wages for current repairs.

Continuous external existence of capital and interest is only obtained by consenting to forego a portion of a higher profit which could be taken for a limited time. This interest foregone represents a continual repair, and since this repair can (in theory at any rate) secure eternity for the form of capital, there is no reason why the price of a utility which still continues should cease to be paid.[1]

Or take the case of a machine. If wear and tear is provided for, as in the case of the house, the objection against perpetuity of interest, on the ground that the machine is worked up in a limited time into a given quantity of goods, falls to the ground. This machine has its continuity secured, and it has a yearly productivity consisting of the service it renders by coöperating with labour, which brings in interest to its owner. This productivity and interest will not, however, disappear if, instead of fully providing against wear and tear of this particular machine, it is allowed to wear itself out and is replaced by another. For it cannot matter either in the case of the house or the machine whether the £20, which measures the yearly contribution to depreciation, is put into repairs of the old structure or the gradual provision of a new fabric which shall take its place.

---

[1] Böhm-Bawerk begs the whole question when he asserts (*Capital and Interest*, p. 249) that a house rented is "a store of energies to be released bit by bit." Böhm-Bawerk confuses the "waste" of the material fabric of a form of capital with the "use" of which that waste is one among other conditions. That waste made good, as it is made good, the "use" becomes perpetual.

The continuous existence of the house or the machine does not really obscure or impair our understanding of the origin or the legitimacy of interest.

If the owner hired out the machine, he could get as rent or interest, say, £100, if he made no stipulation as to the wear and tear; or he can let it at £80, on the understanding that it shall be kept in repair or replaced when worn out. Some people let out machines (*e.g.* bicycles) upon the former terms, others on the latter; the former yields a higher interest for a limited time, the latter a lower interest without the limit. The eternity of the capital is secured by what may be regarded as a payment out of gross interest, which accurately corresponds to a fund for maintenance of economic efficiency and payment of rent and wages in the case of labour and of land.

In order that labour may command a price for its use, three conditions are admittedly essential: first, there must be objective or technical productivity, an actual increase of " goods " due to the use of the labour; secondly, there must be a subjective cost or painful expenditure of effort; thirdly, there must be a subjective utility or fund of enjoyment afforded by the result of the labour.

All three conditions we have shown are present in the case of the functioning of forms of fixed capital. ‚ A house or a machine when economically used gives out a continuous supply of objective economic goods to which value is attached, and a "price" affixed by consideration of the relation between the marginal "cost" of that abstinence which is essential to secure their economic existence, and that marginal "utility" which directly measures the economic importance attached to them by borrowers.

The case of fixed capital is thus plainly seen to be on all fours with the other factors of production with regard to the conditions of value, and the determination of price.

The case of loans which take shape as circulating capital, or as commodities for present consumption, present at first sight a somewhat different aspect, and have misled many economists into adopting a special explanation of value and price of the use of capital.

Instead of taking the loan of a house or a machine, let us now consider the loan of capital which takes shape in material of manufacture, fuel for generating manufacturing power, or goods which form the stock in trade of a business. Do these conform to the same conditions as fixed capital? Do they possess, as capital, continuous existence, and can objective net productivity be imputed to them? At first sight one is disposed to give a negative answer to both these questions. "Circulating" capital, in the very terms of its most common definitions, ceases to exist after a single use; the raw cotton once spun is no longer

raw cotton but yarn; the coal once burnt ceases to
function as coal; the shop goods once bought by a
customer now only possess economic existence as
consumptive wealth. But this superficial view disappears before a more exact conception of industrial order. In the case of the labourer, the mere
fact that the material fabric of his body is continuously worn out in the course of his working
life, each particle of tissue being wasted and
replaced by another particle, does not impair our
conception of the identity and the continuous
existence of this fund of labour-power. In the
case of a building or a machine we are ready to
admit that the conservation of its identity does
not depend upon the fact that all or any of its
original material structure remains intact; in the
long course of wear and repair every particle of
the original house or machine may disappear, and
yet we rightly recognise the continuous existence
of the capital it embodies. Now there is no real
or essential difference in this respect between
fixed and circulating capital: in the latter case
the change of the matter which represents the
capital is more rapid and more regular, that is all.
Just as a loan of capital, which takes shape as
a machine or a house, is kept in continuous
economic existence by replacement and repair of
wasted matter, so in the case of the capital which
takes shape as coal to food an engine or to heat a
house. In the case of the latter as of the former,

there is continuous waste (or "consumption" if this ambiguous term be preferred), and continuous replacement : the particular matter which represents the capital is in incessant flux.

This is the true explanation of the mystery which Böhm-Bawerk affects to find in the attribution of "continuous use" to perishable goods. " It had to be discovered that a hundredweight of coal can be burnt to cinders on January 1, 1888, and yet be 'used' uninterruptedly throughout the whole year, and, perhaps, for five, ten, or a hundred years to come; and what is best of all, that this lasting use can always be bought for a particular price, although and after the coal itself, and the right to consume it to the last atom, has been given away for another and a different price." [1] The "fiction" which Böhm-Bawerk claims to be the animating principle of this theory is only a "fiction" if continuous existence and continuous use were claimed for the same material embodiment of a hundredweight of coal. But no such claim is preferred. The economic continuity achieved by replacement shifts the "capital" contained in the hundredweight of coal to a second, and a third, and an indefinite number of hundredweights of coal, which are the legitimate economic representatives and successors of the first hundredweight and may well survive for ten or a hundred years. So long as the owner of the original hundredweight of

---

[1] *Positive Theory*, p. 287.

coal which was loaned stands out of his property, his abstention is a legitimate economic cost, which force preserves in economic existence and use a hundredweight of coal or some other industrial representative of it.

This is no fiction, but an important fact, the understanding of which is essential to a comprehension of the working of modern industry. A manufacturer maintains his stock of raw materials or of fuel in the same way in which he maintains his fixed capital, though his mode of book-keeping may suggest a difference. Out of the gross receipts from his sales he replaces the one as he replaces and repairs the other. Or take the stock of a retail store which does a regular trade, the same quantity of the same kinds of wares will constantly be there. The tobacconist's furnisher who supplies on credit a small retail store, has precisely the same claim to receive continuous interest for that part of the capital which is in cigars and pipes, as for that which takes the shape of shop furniture and fixtures: the one is just as permanent as the other, as cigars and pipes are sold they are replaced by fresh orders just as the fittings or furniture are replaced when they are damaged or worn out. The claims of objective capital to continuity of existence depends not upon continuity of substance, but of economic form. This continuous existence of so-called circulating capital also implies a continuous objec-

tive productivity which corresponds to that which
we discerned in fixed forms of capital. As a
machine continuously working is continuously
productive, so with the fuel which furnishes its
mechanical energy: when we recognise that the
existence of the fuel, as capital, is not dependent
on the permanence of any particular particles of
coal, we perceive that its use is continuously productive of wealth, taking shape in the goods that
are manufactured by the machine. The same
must be said of the raw materials themselves
which, by the operation of machinery, are taking
serviceable shapes; they, too, are functioning
productively in industry, and that productivity
is continuous so long as the supply of materials
which represents that form of circulating capital
is maintained.

Loans of commodities for which interest is paid
are often instanced in triumphant refutation of
the alleged need of objective productivity of
capital.[1] A loan of corn for purposes of present
food, a loan of wine drunk as soon as it is borrowed — these things may form sources of the
payment of continuous interest, though continuous
existence and productivity cannot be imputed to
them. What are we to say of such cases? We
do not need to evade the issue by urging, as Böhm-
Bawerk, who raised the difficulty, enables us to

----

[1] Cf. Böhm-Bawerk, *Capital and Interest*, pp. 214-259.

do, that such loans are not loans of capital[1] and that what is paid for their use is not true interest. The fact is that, if the corn lent is used to sustain productive energy of labourers, so as to enable them to produce more corn and out of this produce to repay capital and interest, the case is on all fours with that of capital which functions as fuel or as raw material, though it may for convenience be best to exclude consumptive goods from ranking as economic capital; the real source and justification of interest is identical in the two cases.

But what of the loan of wine which is drunk as soon as borrowed, and cannot be regarded as " consumed productively "? Whence comes the continuous interest that must be paid for this loan so long as it remains an undischarged debt? No continuous use and no objective productivity appears here. How, then, can interest arise? The answer is that, if this case be taken by itself, interest cannot arise at all, and the fact that it cannot be paid is seen to rest upon the non-productivity of this loan. Böhm-Bawerk, who adduces this instance to refute the supporters of use and productivity as the source of interest, is really hoist with his own petard, for he cannot show

---

[1] " Consumptive goods are not means of production; they are therefore not capital; and the advantages which they confer do not proceed from any productive power they possess." (*Positive Theory of Capital*, p. 272.)

in such a case that the interest paid for the drunk
wine arises from a "ripening of future into present
goods" as his theory demands. In point of fact
the instance is invalid. No true interest can be
paid for such a loan; if money interest is paid, it
is derived from the productivity of some other
factor of production. The case has no bearing
whatever on the theory of interest. The rent of
a piece of land must be paid even by a farmer who
is losing money, but we cannot on such a ground
deny that productivity of nature is a necessary
condition of payment of rent. If a borrower misapplies his capital, or converts it into wasteful
forms, he must pay that rate of interest which is
determined by the condition of its most effective
and productive economic use. If a piece of capital
is squandered, the interest must be paid out of the
productivity of some other piece of capital or some
other factor of production. If none such is available, *cadit quæstio*, the interest cannot be paid at
all.

§ 5. I have found it necessary to dwell at length
upon this matter and to illustrate from the several
kinds of capital, because it appears to be thought
by many that modern representatives of the Austrian School, Böhm-Bawerk in particular, have
destroyed the theory which would rank interest
with other payments, and have established a separate origin and nature for this source of income.
Böhm-Bawerk has, at the close of his "Positive

Theory of Capital," [1] challenged economists to prove the existence of an " ' enduring ' use of perishable goods, for which interest is supposed to be paid."

I claim, here, to have met this challenge and to establish the " enduring use " and the enduring objective productivity of the various forms of capital as the source and the fundamental condition of the payment of interest. By showing the economic provision for continuous replacement of the matter in which a stock of " perishable goods " is at any given moment embodied, I have removed the difficulty which beset most of the older theories of dependence of interest upon productivity.[2]

---

[1] p. 295.

[2] Böhm-Bawerk, in dealing with the arguments by which Knies defends the view that interest arises from a durable use in perishable goods, attempts to turn his opponent's position by *argumenta ad ridiculum* which utterly evade the issue. Admitting (p. 289) that " in a certain point of view the individual goods replaced may be looked upon as if they were actually the same individual goods which were given away in the loan ; they have identically the same effect on the economical position of the lender who receives them," he affects to deny that herein is any evidence of " continuous use " or " productivity." One might, he thinks, " as well use the identity of perishable goods to prove that oysters will keep fresh for ten years." It is, he insists, really " a question which must find its answer in considering the nature of the perishable good and the nature of the use." But " the nature of the use " is precisely what Böhm-Bawerk does not consider. Had he done so he would have perceived that the " nature of the use " is such that the economic consumption of a perishable form of capital replaces it

Interest is paid out of an increased product whose existence requires the presence and services of capital. But this increased product does not necessarily constitute interest, nor does it provide a measure of the value of the use of capital. A new machine introduced into a trade might double the output, but of course it by no means follows that the profit obtained by the owner of the machine corresponds to the value of half the increased output, still less to the value of the whole of the earlier output. If the machine were an absolute monopoly, its owner could hold, against the encroachments of labour on the one hand and the consumer on the other

by another form, and in addition yields a surplus which is destined to figure as interest. This surplus (a net Nutzung) arises from that productivity of use of capital which Böhm-Bawerk simply denies, but the non-existence of which he fails to prove. He boldly asserts (p. 291) in following up Knies that " the enjoyment of effects indirectly obtained from the consumption of goods is not in the least a utility which we get in addition to the consumption, it is just the utility we get *from* the consumption," *i.e.* the consumption of a ton of coal cannot be productive in the sense that it not only yields a value enabling another ton of coal to replace it, but a surplus value which figures as interest. Whether Knies is technically right or wrong in his account of the indirect services arising from this consumption, we have seen that the economic consumption of a ton does yield a surplus over and above the ton which shall replace it. Without such surplus we shall presently see there exists no objective fund for payment of interest which is thus thrown back upon a subjective fund that is impotent to explain real interest.

hand, the whole of the increased product, at a value only lower than the value of the former output by such fall of price as he deemed desirable to allow, in order to increase the sale of goods to the point which would yield the maximum aggregate of net profits. But where the machine is no monopoly, the competition of other capitalists may oblige him to hand over part of the increased productivity to consumers in large reductions of price, or to labour in much higher wages, receiving only a minimum profit which has no fixed or directly assignable relation to the increased productivity.

§ 6. The amount of the profit or the value of this use of capital will, according to utility theorists, be dependent, not upon the productivity of each separate machine, but upon the subjective utility imputed to the "marginal" machine, that which is least effectively applied.

Needless to say, I reject this assertion that the price and value of the use of capital is determined by final utility. Utility and productivity are essential conditions of interest, and interest may be rightly regarded as paid out of increased productivity; but the amount or proportion of the added productivity required for profit is not to be determined by confining attention to the utility of capital.[1]

But a complete presentment of interest as a

[1] This is Von Wieser's mistake in *Natural Value.*

case of the general law of price requires not
only that the capital shall be coördinated with
other factors of production in relation to utility
and productivity, but also in relation to cost. If
the use of capital is what is sold and paid for by
interest, how are we to describe the "cost" from
which a price proceeds helping to determine that
price?

§ 7. No novel answer is required. Abstinence
still seems to me the best term to describe the
human effort which enables capital to be productive. Misunderstanding upon this theory of abstinence as a cost arises from two sources: first,
as to the nature of the abstinence; second, as to
the economic position of those who practise it.

Upon the nature of abstinence early economists
expressed themselves ambiguously. The abstinence which enables capital to function does not
consist in the original determination which leads
a saving person to abstain from making what he
can enjoy at once, in order to make something
which cannot be at once consumed, but which is
of service in production. That initial act is only
the beginning of the effort of abstinence. That
effort, or "cost," must be considered to be going
on all the time that capital is utilized; the owner
of this capital must be conceived as exercising
a self-restraint which enables him to resist the
temptation to substitute for his capital a fund of
present enjoyment. This effort, moreover, need

not be regarded as a purely negative action; the effort of self-restraint is as positive as any other effort, and indeed has its psychical and physical measurements, like the efforts which go out in present labour-power. This effort of abstinence is not, indeed, to be regarded as the efficient cause of the productivity of capital; we cannot say in so many words that abstinence is productive, but this continued effort is plainly to be regarded as keeping capital in continuous economic life. If that abstinence fail and owners demand instant enjoyment, capital lapses, and its services are withdrawn. Professor Marshall, I think, does wrong to compromise the view by substituting "waiting" for "abstinence." The human subjective cost is the self-restraint implied by abstinence; the self-restraint as a psychical process involves waiting, and waiting is but the immediate condition which enables capital to operate productively.

Precisely the same relation exists between abstinence and the utility of capital which exists between labour and the utility of commodities. Philosophically, abstinence is to be regarded as a form of human economic "cost" referable to some common denominator with labour-power, and paid for its sacrifice upon the same scale. Interest from this point of view must be regarded as a wage of abstinence. Abstinence must be regarded as a form of painful effort voluntarily incurred by individuals, paid for in interest out of a product which owes its existence to the incurring of the effort.

To some this is a "hard saying," which they seek to deny, either by pointing to a possible order of society in which individuals would not be called upon to practise abstinence, or by allusions to the Duke of Westminster and others whose abstinence involves no effort, but consists in a refusal to incur the positive discomfort of increasing their consumption after all felt wants are fully satisfied.

But neither of these objections is really substantial. The substitution of collective for individual saving would not really do away with abstinence or even with the painful cost of it; it would always be more pleasant, and perhaps more immediately profitable, to a society to convert an undue proportion of its energy into immediately consumable goods, and so to make inadequate provision for the future. A rational society resisting the temptation and making due provision for future production must be held to practise abstinence and self-sacrifice analogous to that practised by the individual now. In the administration of such a collectivist society, no particular portion of the increased wealth due to this provision might be classed as interest; the need of the old terminology might have passed, but the thing itself, the "interest," would be there.

So also, under an individualist dispensation, as long as the abstinence or postponement of gratification on the part of any of those required to contribute to the supply of capital involves a sacrifice, interest must remain. If, as some suppose, a time might come when a sufficient number of savers might consent to abstain in order to consume more serviceably in the future the same quantity or even a less quantity of goods, interest in any positive shape might indeed be abolished; for if abstinence involved no painful effort, however much it might be serviceable in producing wealth, it would receive no pay; it would be among the bounties of nature which have no value.[1]

The fact that the Duke of Westminster suffers no painful effort in saving, of course is beside the point for all who have considered that waiting, like all other " costs," must be measured from the marginal saver, and not from the saver whose saving comes easiest. A large, an unduly large, proportion of saving is performed by those whose abstinence involves no pain or appreciable loss of present enjoyment. Even the self-restraint of the ordinary well-to-do saver may not greatly reduce his current rate of enjoyment. But the total supply of capital employed in industry certainly con-

---

[1] Subjective interest even then would not disappear. For a discussion of the question, "Is objective interest necessary?" see Appendix at the close of this chapter.

tains some portions which are the result of a real considerable sacrifice of present comfort. Not only the superfluous income of the Duke of Westminster, but some of the hard-won earnings of John Smith of Oldham, are required to contribute to the aggregate supply of capital. Now, while the Duke might, and probably would, consent to do his saving even if no interest was paid for its use, John Smith probably would not consent. So long as John Smith must receive $2\frac{1}{2}\%$ in order to evoke the genuine effort of abstinence, the Duke must get the same payment for his formal abstinence. It is economically necessary to pay the Duke at the same rate at which we pay John Smith, because, in the investment market, as in any other market, there can only be one price for the whole supply, that price measuring either the cost of producing that portion of supply which is produced most expensively, or the utility afforded by that portion of supply. The relation between the cost of production to John Smith, and the utility of the portion of capital which he furnishes, determines the rate of profit. If it seems unjust that the Duke of Westminster should be paid for no actual effort or sacrifice incurred, we must bear in mind two facts. First, our analysis of the operation of bargaining has shown that the distribution of gain in a bargain is not based on any moral principle of distributive justice. The injustice apparent in the payment of interest is

also found in the payment of wages. A strong-
bodied labourer, who finds his work easy to per-
form, is paid as much as a weak-limbed labourer
who gives out a far more painful effort in the
performance of the same task. The first hour
of the working day, which may be nothing else
than a pleasurable exercise, is paid for at the same
rate as the last hour, which is exhausting and
injurious. So with saving, the effort of the marginal saver, not of the other savers, is the determinant of profit from the cost side of the equation.

§ 8. "But," it may be further pressed, "the
analogy with labour is not complete, the labourer
whose labour is easiest at any rate gives out some
personal exertion; but the capitalist whose savings are only the self-accumulation of excessive income does nothing at all." Now this statement is
indisputable, but the attack it suggests is misdi-
rected when it is applied to impugn the principle
of interest. The real gravamen of the charge,
against those whose interest is unattended by any
"cost" of abstinence, has reference, not to the
payment of interest, but to the modes by which
they have come into possession of the capital. In
other words, the frequent assertion that "the real
abstinence is of the worker and not of the capitalist," does not meet the point at issue. Supposing it be true that the capitalist steals from the
worker a portion of the product and uses it for
capital, receiving interest for its use, a true bill of

indictment against him would rest, not upon the wrongful receipt of interest, but upon the prior act of stealing the product of labour. If the injustice of paying interest to those who have earned it by no effort be admitted, that injustice has no special reference to bargains for the use of capital, but must be located chiefly in prior bargains for the sale of labour-power, or in other bargains where the capitalist enjoys a superior power of bargaining. Those who hold that capitalist employers forcibly extort from their workers a surplus value, weaken their case when they enter a specific attack against the payment of interest for this surplus value after it has taken the form of capital.

The economic necessity of interest and the law of its payment is not really affected by the fact that some of the capital for which interest is received may have come wrongfully into possession of its owners.

§ 9. I claim by this argument to have shown that the price of the use of capital, called interest, is determined in the same way as the price of a commodity in a market, *i.e.* by the establishment of a relation between two bargainers, one representing final or marginal cost, the other final or marginal utility. Abstinence and productivity must be admitted each to contribute toward determining the economic importance attached to the use of a piece of capital.

§ 10. According to this treatment, interest, the price of capital-use, is determined like every other market-price. There are, however, certain reasons, other than those already named, which have helped to remove the consideration of interest from the general treatment of prices, and to apply to its determination special laws and special terminology. Both economists and moralists have treated interest as a payment distinct in kind from other payments. And it must be admitted that certain conditions which apply to capital seem to sever it naturally from other articles, the use of which is bought and sold.

In the first place, until quite recent times in all countries, and even now in all save the most developed countries, most loans of capital were not for industrial purposes, but for consumption or for some pressing temporary emergency. The conditions of such loans have generally been far removed from market competition of the kind with which we have been dealing. The negotiations of the money-lender with his client give to the element of force or monopoly power a far larger place than is commonly accorded in bargaining. The practice of usury has thus been strongly dissociated from ordinary dealings, and still yields, even in advanced industrial communities, the most striking instances of forced gains in the determination of a price. The lender has, from the very nature of the case, so powerful an advantage over the borrower, that both economics and ethics have been habituated to treat such bargains as a thing apart. But though the balance is commonly so ill-adjusted for these bargains, they are not intrinsically different from other bargains where competition among sellers is closely restricted.

Again, when we turn to industrial capital, we find that in most countries the great bulk of this capital is used by its owners, and its profit is not reckoned apart from the wages or the earnings of management of a worker or an employer. The proportion of savings which have been used for investment outside the business of the owner has been quite small until recent times, and many such investments are determined by other than purely competitive conditions.

Thus the conception of a fluid-market for the investment of money in which two-sided competition exists, and where the lender cannot be deemed to have any natural advantage over the borrower, is of quite modern growth, and has not yet displaced the conception of capital and interest associated with the old order of things.

But in so far as the use of capital is the object of a sale, whether on the older terms of usury or in modern investments, the price is determined, like the price of commodities, by the bargainers, who represent final cost and final utility: the supply of the use of a particular form of capital is subject to the same laws determining its increase or decrease as the supply of land, or of labour, or of goods.

APPENDIX TO CHAPTER VIII.

Is Objective Interest Necessary ?

There are those who think that even at the present time objective interest is unnecessary as a stimulus to saving, or, in other words, that there is no economic cost in saving which requires a reward represented by an objective increase in the quantity of goods returned by the borrower. According to these thinkers, interest is maintained by the option which an investor has of buying land and drawing rent (H. George), or by the further option of getting hold of a limited and legalised "monopoly," money, and extorting usury for its loan (M. Flürscheim). If land and money were removed from the field of investment, interest, they maintain, would disappear. Those who hold this view seem to me to weaken their case by limiting to land-owning and money-lending the forms of investment which support a positive interest. All other industries which, by reason of the enjoyment of legal protection, dependence upon land-use, or restricted competition, due to purely economic forces, are enabled to tax the consuming public, will, in as far as they are open to investment, stand in the same position to support interest as land and money. But if these forms of protected industry were withdrawn from the field of private investment, would interest disappear, or, in other words, would the marginal saver lend without a larger return?

No direct or general answer can be given. The question of the influence of reduced interest on saving is often discussed as if the motives of the saver were the only determinant. This is not so. The relation of the motives of the saver to the amount of savings socially required is the problem. It is a particular case of " value," involving, as does every other case, consideration of the relation of marginal cost to marginal utility.

Saving is due (1) partly to the self-accumulation of surplus incomes not needed to satisfy any demand for current satisfaction. A fall of interest, even to zero, or below, might not appreciably affect this saving; (2) partly to a desire to provide against old age, or other infirmities, or to support a family. Saving for such purposes is probably stimulated by a fall of interest. If it is intended to expend the capital sum of the savings for these purposes, the rate of interest will not have an important influence as motive, but so far as it operates, a high rate will check saving by enabling a somewhat smaller amount of saving, accumulating at interest, to achieve the desired result. If, on the other hand, it is intended to make provision, not by expending the capital, but by using the income from that capital, a low rate of interest is likely to evoke more saving because a larger capital will be required to yield the necessary income. Against this, however, must be set the consideration that, if interest is so low that the task of accumulating by saving sufficient capital to furnish it becomes too difficult, or quite impossible, such saving will not be undertaken. But when we remember how much saving is often done in primitive industrial societies for these purposes, and how much more would be done if political and social conditions were such as to protect these savings effectively, we shall be inclined to conclude that a fall of interest is more likely to increase than to reduce the aggregate of savings for purposes of definite future expenditure.

(3) Savings are made by men of substance engaged in industry, in order to extend their business, or generally to improve their financial position. In such cases it is reasonable to hold that a high rate of interest will stimulate saving. For, in the first place, the interest upon capital, already in existence, must be regarded as the portion of income out of which the largest proportion of savings can be most easily made. Where interest is high, the proportion of the general income, which admits easily of saving, will be large. In spite of the maxim "lightly earned, lightly spent," it is reasonable to expect that a rise in the aggregate of interest, or of any portion of income not earned by direct labour, will be attended by an increase of saving. When a temporary rise of interest takes place during some industrial boom, most careful business men will try to reap a golden harvest while they can, by using their abnormally high profits to extend their businesses. A temporary, and even a normal and gradual, fall of interest will reduce this sort of saving.

Most economists,[1] admitting the contrariety of mo-

[1] This was not true of early economists, cf. Webb, *Industrial Democracy*, Vol. II, p. 622, etc. Mr. and Mrs. Webb, however, are wrong in their interpretation of the view of Senior

tives, incline to the belief that on the whole a fall of interest checks saving.   But is this true ?

If the Duke of Westminster, who saves because he has a superfluous income, would save no less if interest fell, while John Smith of Oldham, who saves in order to provide against a rainy day, might save more, is it certain that those who save with the more general object of making· money would so far reduce their savings as to bring down the aggregate savings of a community below what was needed to furnish the industrial capital required to maintain current consumption, and to provide against increased consumption in the future ?

Is it not possible that the automatic saving of surplus elements of income, and such other saving as was stimulated by a fall of interest, would suffice to furnish the socially necessary capital ; in other words, that the marginal saver might consent to save without positive interest?   It is at least conceivable.   Much would depend upon (*a*) the absolute amount of income, (*b*) the distribution of wealth, (*c*) the condition of the industrial arts, and (*d*) the nature of consumption. (*a*)· Where the income of the community is large, a relatively large portion of this income may be taken to be applicable to the satisfaction of weaker or less urgent current desires.   This portion of the income of an individual or a class may, it is generally admitted, be saved at a low rate of interest.   It is not so readily admitted that it may be saved at zero or minus interest.   Professor Marshall writes as if some

and McCulloch.   (Cf. N. Senior, *Pol. Econ.* 5th ed., p. 140, and McCulloch, *Pol. Econ.*, Pt. I, Ch. II, § 8.)

objective interest were essential because "the future pleasure to be got in return for giving up a present one could not be expected to be greater than it, but rather to be less" (IV, Ch. VII, par. 8). But this is by no means true in cases where the present pleasure given up is a little-valued luxury, and the future pleasure placed in its stead is a necessary or an important comfort. Professor Marshall here does not exhibit the essentially subjective character of the problem. A person who has just eaten a loaf will consent to postpone the consumption of a second loaf which he has in his possession, on condition that a loaf or even less is given back to him at a future time when he has no bread. For although the utility as a future one is discounted, the satisfaction of the future consumption of a necessary, when discounted, will be greater than the present satisfaction of consuming a superfluity. This is why, even in uneducated communities, money and treasure are laid up in a stocking. If a man found that he had ten years to live, and that his income, £1000 for the first year, would be £900 for the second, £800 for the third, and so on, he would, assuming his capacity of enjoyment and his tastes to be steady, save at zero interest some of his higher income in the earlier years when it would have been spent in luxuries, in order to spend it in comforts during the later years. He would not absolutely equalise his expenditure over the period, for such a course would imply that he did not discount future pleasures. The truth is, that, though he values a present comfort higher than a similar future comfort, he values a future comfort higher than a present

luxury. It is evident from such a case that not merely
a zero but a negative objective interest is possible,
because it is consistent with a positive interest which
forms the human motive of saving.

(*b*) The amount and the proportion of a community's
income which would be saved from such a motive at
zero interest or less would probably depend upon the
distribution of wealth, though it is not easy to assign
any general law for the influence of distribution upon
saving. At first sight, it would appear as if inequality
favoured saving, since it would set a larger total income
free for the purchase of superfluities or such luxuries
as had but a small hold upon the desires of consumers;
in other words, a larger proportion of the income of
the rich might transcend their standard of comfort
and accumulate as savings. But further reflection
makes this position doubtful; for though the existence of a rich class may thus lead to the saving which
consists in self-accumulation of superfluous income,
equality of income would seem to favour deliberate
saving for old age and other emergencies. For in so
far as large incomes are drawn from the rent of land
or profits on investments, such incomes do not lapse
with old age or personal inability, and there is little
need for such a man to provide against special emergencies. On the other hand, in a working community,
where an approximate equality of incomes existed, the
largest proportion of the people would be both enabled
and inclined to save. For the maintenance of a sound
standard of · comfort for themselves throughout life
and for their family will involve an abstinence from
present luxuries for the sake of future necessaries or

prime comforts—that kind of saving which, as we have seen, least requires an objective interest.

The total subjective interest of saving is greater when the saving is applied to the future provision of necessaries, smallest when it is applied to the future provision of luxuries. Therefore the aggregate subjective interest attending a given amount of saving would be greater where a larger proportion of it was done by poorer persons than where a smaller proportion was theirs. Thus it would appear that motived saving should be larger where distribution was more equal. How far this would be offset by the larger unmotived saving of a wealthy class is of course doubtful.

(c) Whether the quantity of saving which can be induced without objective interest will suffice must, however, largely depend upon the character of the industry that is practised, or, in other words, upon the relative importance of capital as compared with the other factors of production. In a simple community, where abundant material wealth might be drawn by simple processes from rich natural resources, the requisite amount of capital might be evoked without interest; whereas in a country with highly developed machine-production, the same quantity of wealth might require a much larger capital, some part of which would not be brought into economic existence without objective interest.

(d) The importance of capital as compared with other factors is not, however, merely a question of the development of the productive arts, though it is sometimes assumed that as civilisation advances, capitalism and machine-production must occupy a part of ever growing prominence. Much will depend upon the character of a progressive nation as expressed in modes of consumption. A nation, which is dominated by a constant craving for increased quantities of certain common forms of material goods, will indeed assign an ever increasing relative importance to machine-processes and will exercise a correspondingly increased demand for saving to be stored in material forms of capital. A nation, on the other hand, whose consumption, beyond a certain standard of common material consumption, grows more qualitative and demands the satisfaction of the taste and special needs of its individual members, while it employs an ever larger proportion of its income in demand for intellectual goods, personal services, and other non-material forms of wealth, may assign a place of relatively diminishing importance to material capital, so that the requisite saving might be done by those who do not require the incentive of objective interest.

The problem is a highly speculative one, and no adequate data exist for attempting a solution, but the considerations above stated entitle us to question the generally accepted view that the marginal saving always requires the stimulus of objective interest. In a truly progressive society, where growing foresight and precaution reduce the discount of future utilities, where increased equalisation of incomes enables a larger proportion of members to lay aside for definite future uses, and where a coördinate improvement in the arts of production and consumption enables the production of routine material goods to be more easily achieved, and consequently a larger proportion of purchasing power to be directed to the demand for consumables which lie outside of capitalist industry, it is quite conceivable, perhaps even probable, that the requisite amount of saving could be induced by the stimulus of subjective interest alone.

The question whether private saving can be evoked in sufficient quantity without objective interest has too often been discussed with exclusive attention to the "cost" side, the motives which actuate savers; the influences operative upon demand are often ignored. But the economic importance or value of the marginal capital will be equally affected by forces proceeding from both sides, as is the case in any other market.

CHAPTER IX.

§ 1. The coördination of capital with nature and labour as a factor of production, and of interest with rent and wages as a price of a use of a factor of production, differs so widely from a recent theory of interest which has gained much acceptance among economists, that it seems only fair that I should make a formal investigation of that theory and set forth the grounds for denying its validity.

My rejection of the one-sided interpretation of the general phenomena of value and price pressed by disciples of the "marginal utility" school, would necessarily involve a rejection of a theory of interest which claims to be an application of that same theory of value. The "Positive Theory of Capital," however, if it were merely an application of the marginal utility theory of value to capital, treated as a productive factor along with nature and labour, would require no separate consideration ; its strength and weakness would be merely those of the general theory.

But the theory most closely associated with the name of Böhm-Bawerk, by refusing at the outset the position of a productive agent to capital, involves an application of "marginal utility" which differs widely in its results from its application in the case of labour and nature. The "subjective" elements in determination of value and price will be found to be accorded a part essentially different from and more important than that accorded them in other cases of value and price.

§ 2. It will be best to begin by a short presentation of the cases by which Böhm-Bawerk unfolds his theory in his work, the "Positive Theory of Capital."

The simplest case is that of A, the owner of £100, who, instead of using it now to buy consumption goods, lends it to B, with the view of receiving it again in a year's time and then using it to buy consumption goods. £100 regarded in terms of present consumption goods is more highly esteemed than £100 in terms of consumption goods a year hence. Look at £100 worth of goods a year off — they look smaller. They look perhaps only as large as £96 worth of present goods. Yet as the year passes to its close this quantity of utility esteemed at £96 rises to the full £100. Thus the lapse of time, bringing future into present goods, appears as a natural source of interest, estimated in this case at nearly £4. Interest arises because £100 in our hands now is not the same as £100 regarded a year hence.

So again the owner of a house or other durable form of capital possesses "a sum of future uses discounted according to their futurity" (XII). Productive goods (*i.e.* raw material of manufacture, machinery, land) are endowed at the beginning of the year with a value imputed from the utility of the consumption goods they are going to make; but since these goods are not existing at the beginning of the year, their value is discounted in our estimate of the machinery, etc. During the year "future goods" ripen into "present goods," and their increased value recoups the original expenditure on capital and yields an interest.

Take the case of a machine thus endowed with a six years' life. At the opening of the first year, the first year's utility is reckoned at 100. But the total utility of the machine does not stand at 600, because its utility for the subsequent years is estimated lower than for the first year. Let the discount for the second year be 5% on the estimate of the first year, and let the same rate of discount be applicable to each following year. Then the total utility viewed from the beginning of the first year will be $100 + 95.23 + 90.70 + 86.38 + 82.27 + 78.35 = 532.93$.

At the beginning of the second year, each year's valuation according to the first year's estimate will have moved one step forward; the second year upon last year's estimate, which was worth 95.23, has now become the first year and is worth 100; similarly with each succeeding year.

The total utility at the beginning of the second year will therefore be $100+95.22+90.70+86.38+82.27 = 454.58$. In other words, the valuation of the sixth year is knocked out, there being now no sixth year. At the beginning of the third year a similar forward movement of each year's value takes place, the former fifth year having disappeared. The total utility is now $100+95.22+90.70+86.3 = 372.31$. Similarly in the three succeeding years, while he enjoys a current utility of 100, the estimate of the total utility of the machine is reduced by a less amount.

In other words, during the first year he has realised a service worth 100, but taking stock at the end finds he has lost only 78.35, because the value represented by all the remaining years has advanced.

At the beginning of the fifth year he has left $100 + 95.23$, during the year he gets a service worth 100, but at the end finds he still possesses 100, and so has only lost 95.23.

For simplicity, a definite life has been here assigned to the machine, and so the amount of what may be called "gross interest" is different in the different years. If, however, a perpetuity of life be secured for the machine, by means of a fund for depreciation, it will easily appear that, while the sum of the series of valuations now reaches infinity, the net interest for each year will be the same.

In Böhm-Bawerk's words, " The cause of net interest " is " an increase of value of the future services, which were previously of less value, but during the period of the goods' use have pressed forward into or toward the present." [1]

§ 3. This brief statement embodies the essence of Böhm-Bawerk's teaching set forth at length in his work, the " Positive Theory of Capital." His chief points of divergence from the treatment given in the last chapter may be stated in three propositions, which I will first explain and afterward discuss.

1. Interest is not the price of the use of capital, but the price of the purchase of present goods in terms of future goods. [2] The underlying fact is this, that " present goods are, as a rule, worth more than future goods of like kind and number " because, other things equal, present satisfaction is valued higher than future satisfaction. A man who has not present goods may buy them from another man who has them, but he must pay for them in a larger quantity of future goods. If the loan is of money, " the borrower will purchase the

[1] *Positive Theory of Capital*, p. 346.
[2] pp. 285, 286.   Introduction, p. xx.

money which he receives now by a larger sum of money which he gives later. He must thus pay an 'agio' or præmium, and this 'agio' is interest. Interest then comes in the most direct way, from the difference in value between present and future goods."[1] What is sold, *i.e.* present goods, forms the subject of a single act of purchase, though the future goods paid for it are usually paid in instalments at regular intervals over a term of time. The annual interest, together with the principal repaid at the end of the term of borrowing, forms the single price of the present goods.

2. Böhm-Bawerk denies that the objective or "technical" productivity of capital is essential to the emergence of interest: the subjective "productivity" which consists in the ripening of future into present goods is deemed sufficient to provide a fund for the payment of interest.

In the elaboration of his "Positive Theory," Böhm-Bawerk has given so much space and skill to proving and illustrating the nature of the technical productivity of capitalism that it is likely that many of his readers do not clearly understand that his technical productivity is not essential to his theory of interest. The most serviceable portion of his work consists in the analysis and explanation of the processes of "roundabout production" with the object of proving the technical productivity of these processes.

[1] p. 281.

This objective productivity — the increased quantity of forms of wealth due to "roundabout" methods — is both an incentive and a reward of saving. It is one reason for postponing present consumption that you are thereby enabled to have more goods to consume in the future.

But from the examples we have given above, and from the express statements of Böhm-Bawerk himself, it is made manifest that interest does not depend upon or require such objective productivity. The one essential feature, according to his teaching, is the undervaluation of future as compared with present goods. Objective or technical productivity is only one factor of this undervaluation, and it is not indispensable. There are three factors of this undervaluation, each of which is, according to Böhm-Bawerk, by itself sufficient cause for a difference in the value of present and future goods, and an adequate reason why interest should be paid. These factors are " the difference in the circumstances of provision between present and future, the underestimate due to perspective, and, finally, the greater fruitfulness of lengthy methods of production."[1]

§ 4. The first factor has reference to the real services or satisfaction which the same goods would yield now as compared with what they would yield at some future time, and is concerned with comparative capacity of enjoyment

[1] *Positive Theory,* p. 272.

and comparative wealth at the two periods. The second refers to the rate at which the same amount of real services will be discounted by forethought or intelligence. The third factor corresponds to what is generally called "productivity of capital." It is, however, right to record the fact that Böhm-Bawerk persistently repudiates the expression "productivity of capital" and refuses to identify with it the factor which he denominates "the greater fruitfulness of lengthy methods of production." The significance of this "greater fruitfulness" of capitalism consists, according to him, in "the technical superiority of present goods" rather than in the greater quantity of products which arises from the productive use of "present goods." The chapter in which this "technical superiority of present goods" is unfolded is the most difficult portion of his treatment, not from any obscurity in the texture of the reasoning, but from the perversity with which he labours to assign to time the productive power commonly attributed to capital. He proposes at the outset to substitute for "productivity of capital" what he terms "the facts." "These facts are as follows : that, as a rule, present goods are, on technical grounds, preferable instruments for the satisfaction of human wants, and assure us, therefore, a higher marginal utility than future goods."[1] From the elaborate explanation which

[1] p. 260.

follows, this sentence appears to mean that a given quantity of forms of capital or other productive means in our possession now is superior both in marginal utility and in value to the same quantity to be possessed a year hence, because the productivity of long-period production begins earlier and is represented at any given time in the future by a larger quantity of goods. This, of course, is quite consistent with the ordinary view of productivity of capital; capital which begins now to be applied productively will be represented by a larger amount and a larger aggregate value of goods in five years' time than the same amount of capital which only begins to function one year hence. The difference, however, between Böhm-Bawerk and the ordinary "productivity" economist is, that the former seems to insist that the increased quantity of goods and of value is due to a priority of time and not to a productive use of the material forms of capital. To this issue I shall presently return. It is here, however, enough to point out that the third factor to which Böhm-Bawerk alludes is virtually a productivity of capital, though his explanation of "the greater productiveness of lengthy methods of production" assigns the efficient causality to the length of time rather than to the "use" or the "productive consumption" of the forms of capital. However we explain it, this third factor does yield an objective fund of wealth from which objective interest can be paid. If, then, this third factor were essential to all functioning of capital and all payment of interest, Böhm-Bawerk's theory would at any rate contain an objective fund of productivity. But he denies explicitly that this third faculty is essential, for he affirms that "each of the three factors, independently of the others, is adequate to account for a difference in value between present and future goods in favour of the former;"[1] and this undervaluation of future goods is continually put forward as the essence of the problem of interest. In other words, the change in human subjective valuations, which takes place when the passage of time ripens future goods into present goods, is assigned as in itself a sufficient explanation of the payment of a sum of objective goods in interest.

That Böhm-Bawerk does not deem the productive use of capital to be essential to the emergence of interest is further attested by his treatment of saving and abstinence. Of "saving," he says that "it has its place, not among the means of production, but among the *motives* of production — the motives which decide the direction of production."[2] Now, if our reasoning in the last chapter is correct, we have shown that saving not only determines the direction but the amount of production, in that it enables an increased productive power to function in industry. This denial of sav-

[1] p. 273.   [2] p. 128.

ing as a means of production is implicitly and necessarily a denial of the productivity of capital.

The plainest denial of the productivity of capital, however, is conveyed in Chapter III where, putting the question " whether capital is a third and independent 'factor of production' alongside of labour and nature," he says "the answer must be a most distinct negative."[1] " Capital has, first, a symptomatic importance. Its presence is always the symptom of a profitable roundabout production. I say, deliberately, 'symptom,' and not 'cause' or 'condition' of profitable methods of production; for as a fact, its presence is rather the result than the cause."[2] From the context it is evident this means not merely that some production can be carried on without capital, and that in this sense capital cannot rank on an equality with nature and labour, but that in so-called "capitalist production" capital is not a factor or cause of production. A certain sort of "productivity" is admitted of capital. " It is first 'productive' because it finds its destination in the production of goods ; it is further productive because it is an effectual tool in completing the roundabout and profitable methods of production once they are entered on; finally, it is productive indirectly because it makes the adoption of new and profitable methods possible."[3] But it is not an "independent factor of production" along with nature

[1] p. 95.　　　[2] p. 92.　　　[3] p. 99.

and labour, but only "the medium through which the two original productive powers exert their instrumentality."

§ 5. It is not easy to deal with the mixed thought embodied in these judgments. It is true that capital cannot operate as an "independent factor," but neither can nature or labour; it is true that these two latter factors have a claim to be deemed "original" in a sense to which capital cannot lay claim, but for all that, as soon as capital exists and functions as an integral part of a more productive method, it is possible and perhaps even necessary to treat it as a joint cause, or at any rate "condition," of the increased productivity. It is of course possible to force language so as to insist that capital is only a "tool" by the use of which the two original powers, nature and labour, attain greater productivity, and to attribute the whole of this increased productivity either to labour and nature, as Böhm-Bawerk appears to do, or to labour alone, as socialism, following early English economists, does, or to nature alone as did the physiocrats. But nothing is gained by drawing such hairbreadth distinctions between a cause and a condition, a condition and a tool. If it is convenient, as it is generally admitted to be, to separate capital from labour and nature in tracing the organic operations of industry, and if, moreover, capital is admitted to be necessary to the operation of the more productive methods, no object is served by denying direct productivity to capital ; the question whether it is an "independent" factor is entirely beside the point. The description of the actual place filled by capital, which Böhm-Bawerk gives here and elsewhere, amply justifies and even requires the attribution of direct productivity to it, and so provides a fund for the payment of real interest corresponding to the fund which the admitted productivity of nature and labour furnishes for the payment of rent and wages. There is, of course, neither "independent productivity" nor an independent product, for the organic nature of coöperation of the factors renders this impossible. But the account of the actual functioning of forms of capital given by Böhm-Bawerk does not justify him in placing capital on any different footing from nature and labour in a theory of distribution.

§ 6. But while Böhm-Bawerk, as we see, admits that capital as an instrument does assist to increase objective productivity, he denies that such objective productivity is essential to explain the payment of interest. The "subjective productivity," the ripening of future into present goods by the passage of time, is deemed a sufficient source of interest. Thus, time itself is given as a sufficient explanation of the origin and payment of interest.

Professor Smart puts this in unmistakable terms : "The simplest case of interest is that in which it appears in the loan for consumption. Here we have a real and true *exchange* of a smaller sum of present money or present goods for a larger amount of future money or goods. The sum returned principal plus interest is the market valuation and *equivalent* of the principal lent. The apparent difference in value is simply due to our forgetting that £100 in our hands now is not the same thing as £100 a year hence. This agio on present goods is interest. In other words, interest is a complementary part of the price — a part equivalent of the principal lent. Apart altogether from an organised system of production this agio would emerge, and has emerged, as something claimed by the saving from the unthrifty." [1]

§ 7. This passage summarising the extreme claim of Böhm-Bawerk's theory will serve to bring home to our minds its deficiencies. My first criticism is that a theory which explains interest by the rise of subjective valuation taking place when future goods become present goods, is inadequate, because it provides no fund for the payment of real or objective interest. I have already shown that the instance of a loan of consumption goods to an unthrifty person shirks the issue, because either the payment of interest is impossible or it proceeds from the abnormal productivity of some other factor : such payment is no more a

[1] Preface to *Positive Theory*, p. xi.

case of normal interest than the advance obtained
by a farmer to pay "rent" which his land has not
justified, is a normal instance of rent.   An "agio"
of the kind Professor Smart describes, a mere rise
of subjective valuation, cannot of itself explain
how a quantity of goods with an objective exchange value is paid as interest.   A change of
estimate cannot of itself be capable of yielding an
increase of objectively measured values.   The undervaluation of a future as compared with a present satisfaction provides in itself no economic
means of enlarging the objective source of the
future satisfaction when it comes.   The lapse of
time cannot be held to cause forms of capital to
breed or grow so as to furnish an increased number for future enjoyment.   Yet it is evident that
this objective interest is what we require to explain.   If I lend goods represented by 100 pieces
and receive back at the end of the year goods represented by 105, no change of subjective valuation
will account for the existence of the extra 5.
Neither the lapse of time nor my change of view
will explain this origin.   They must arise from
some industrial power to which the term "productivity" may be given.   Since it is admitted
that the service of capital as a tool is to lengthen
the processes of production, and that "every
lengthening of the process is accompanied by a
further increase of the technical result,"[1] in other

_____

[1] p. 84.

words that "every extension of the productive
process leads to some surplus result,"[1] it is
surely wise to regard this surplus result as the
true source of objective interest. We have here
an objective productivity as a basis of interest.
If Böhm-Bawerk and Professor Smart had confined their view to these cases of loans of capital
for productive purposes, they could at any rate
have supported the theory of "Undervaluation" of
Future Goods as the source of "interest" by falling
back upon an objective product which should furnish the goods to pay this interest. But the
hardihood of these instances in which this objective productivity is directly and purposely excluded invalidates this theory. Referring to
Professor Smart's statement, I cannot for one
moment admit that " apart altogether from an
organised system of production this agio would
emerge." If there were no organised system of
production, the subjective undervaluation of future
goods by a lender would in no wise enable him to
receive any material representative of this " agio "
in interest. Böhm-Bawerk's theory of production
does not require him to dispense with this " sur-
plus· product " of long-period production, and by
doing so he wrecks his theory. In a word, the
problem which appears to Böhm-Bawerk an essentially "subjective" one is also objective.
Böhm-Bawerk and Professor Smart think that

---

[1] p. 86.

they have only to prove an emergence of subjective values, whereas they must prove an emergence of objective values, or, other things equal, an increase of products. Treatment of the problem of loans in terms of money sometimes enables them to evade this fact. The simple essential setting of the problem of interest is not that of a loan of £100, but the case where A lends B a saw and receives back a saw plus a plank. Required to explain the existence and payment of the plank.

§ 8. The truth seems to be that the part played by time, and its treatment as a sort of agent of production of value, is altogether misconceived by Böhm-Bawerk.   In his treatment of what he terms, in a phrase which itself begs the question, "the technical superiority of present goods," he asserts, "It is an elementary fact of experience that methods of production which take time are more productive.   That is to say, given the same quantity of productive instruments, the lengthier the productive method employed, the greater the quantity of productivity that can be obtained."[1]   Here he would make it appear that the lengthiness of method is the cause of productivity.   He affects to have proved this, but he has done no such thing.   He has only proved that time or "lengthiness" is one condition of those roundabout processes which are technically more productive.

[1] p. 260.

The effort to attribute to lapse of time a causal efficiency due really to the nature of the processes which require time is most plainly manifested in the following instance. "Suppose that, in the year 1888, we have command of a definite quantity of productive instruments, say, thirty days of labour, we may assume something like the following. The months of labour, employed in methods that give a return immediately, and are, therefore, very unrenumerative, will yield only 100 units of product, but of course yields them only for the year 1889 ; employed in a two years' process it yields 280 units for the year 1890, and so on in increasing progression ; say 350 units for 1891, 400 for 1892, 440 for 1893, 470 for 1894, and 500 for 1895." [1]

Here time is made to appear a cause of objective productivity. But what are the facts? It is not the duration of the process which gives the increased yield, but the nature of the processes which take a longer time, *i.e.* the employment of concrete forms of capital which are more productive instead of concrete forms which are less productive. Böhm-Bawerk shirks the issue by taking for his example " 30 days of labour," a thing which is not capital, and which is expressed in terms of time. Let him take concrete forms of capital and he will have difficulty in evading the conclusion that " the technical superiority " consists

[1] p. 261.

not in duration, but in the industrial character of these forms.[1]

When Böhm-Bawerk proceeds to claim [2] for duration of time increased value as well as increased technical productivity, he falls into another error. In a contribution to a theory of interest he is required to prove that this time process yields objective or exchange value. What he actually claims for it is an increase of subjective value, or, to quote his words, "If it puts more means of satisfaction at our disposal, it must have a greater importance for our well being." But this greater "satisfaction" is only one factor in the attribution of greater exchange or objective value to goods.

The confusion of thought, which is involved in this whole attempt to make time do something which it cannot do, is most curiously illustrated in the final paragraph in which Böhm-Bawerk summarises the "positive result" of his argument. "The relation between want and provision for want in present and future, the undervaluation of future pleasures and pains, and the technical advantage residing in present goods, have the effect that, to the overwhelming majority of men, the subjective use value of present goods is higher than that of similar future goods. From this relation of subjective valuation there follows, in the market

---

[1] The tabular illustration on p. 262 only makes the same assumption more elaborate.

[2] p. 263.

generally, a higher objective exchange value and market-price for present goods."[1] Passing over the assumption contained in the last sentence, that objective values are determined by the subjective valuation of one of the two parties to an exchange (the root fallacy of the Marginal Utility School), I wish to call attention to the astonishing "argument" of the earlier sentence in which "the undervaluation of future pleasures and pain" is made a cause of the fact that "the subjective use value of present goods is higher than that of similar future goods," *i.e.* undervaluation is the cause of undervaluation.

The involved reasoning which arises in the vain effort to impute objective results to purely subjective causes almost inevitably lands its author in patent absurdities like this.

By stating the problem of interest as consisting in the undervaluation of future goods, time is represented as a producer of values by undoing this undervaluation. The point of view which the familiar process of discount presents lends itself not unnaturally to this subjective view of interest which assigns to time itself a productive power. But the attribution of such power to time is quite erroneous. The change of subjective valuation which comes with time indisputably plays a part in determining the price of the use of capital, or, in other words, how much of the total

[1] p. 281.

increase of objective productivity due to the
coöperation of capital with the other factors shall
be paid to the owner of the capital; but the part it
plays is entirely different from that assigned to it
by Böhm-Bawerk. In the pages of the "Positive Theory" itself are expressions which might
have put its author on the right track. "The
disadvantage connected with the capitalist method
is its sacrifice of time "[1] surely suggests that
time is a cost of capitalist production rather than
a creative force. So, again, we are told that capitalism "demands a sacrifice of time, but it has
an advantage in the quantity of product," which
surely suggests the entire truth that this "advantage in the quantity of product," affords a
fund out of which payment of interest is made for
the "cost" involved in "sacrifice of time."

§ 9. Not merely are we not justified in regarding time as capable of the technical productivity
required to explain real interest, but we cannot
regard it as creative of a rise of subjective values.
Because my valuation of a house is £100 for this
year, £95 4s. for next, and because in a year's
time I shall value at £100 what I had valued at
£95 4s., Böhm-Bawerk insists that by lapse of
time a piece of goods, value £95 4s., has added
5 % to its value.

We have already noted the fallaciousness attending the treatment of interest as payment for
the use of capital as valued in money. Since the

[1] p. 82.

money value of capital is only obtained by capitalising the interest, this process assumes the very point at issue, namely, the growth of value. For if I receive for the use of forms of wealth, during the past year, the sum of £5, I proceed to do a little sum which enables me to say that what I lent was worth £100 at the beginning of the year and £105 including the interest at the end. But by saying this, I beg the question of a growth of value by my method of reaching the £100. I only know that what I lent has been returned with an addition of $\frac{1}{20}$; I cannot, however, assume that the increased quantity of goods returned has $\frac{1}{20}$ greater value, either subjective or objective, than the smaller quantity originally loaned, for this is to assume an absolute stability or inherency of value in material forms. I am not logically entitled to assert that the bargain by which I get £105 goods instead of £100 is a growth of value from £100 to £105, for if instead of getting back £105 I only get back £102, I should be obliged to say that what I lent was not worth £100, but a smaller sum of money. In other words, the value of the capital is not a prime *datum*, but is calculated from the interest by a method which assumes that an increase of value has been brought about by the process of lending. This increase of value I suggest is due to the greater technical productivity which Böhm-Bawerk himself admits of capitalism.

§ 10. In other words, the "ripening of future into present goods" by process of time is really a *cost* theory of interest. The positive and even the productive complexion it puts upon the familiar phenomenon of discount or undervaluation must not deceive us. The statement of undervaluation is simply the quantitative statement of the cost of abstinence which involves time as a condition of its operation. If I value the services of a house at £100 for this year, my preference of present to future enjoyment may lead me to value next year's services at £95 4*s.* But when next year actually comes my £95 4*s.* valuation has risen to £100. But to say that I now esteem the current year's services at £5 more than I esteem the prospective services of next year is only another and a less obvious way of saying that I estimate the loss or pain of a year's postponement of satisfaction at £5. If I could take out the whole satisfaction at once, the man who shall persuade me to postpone it must pay me what the market determines to be the price of this effort of abstinence or postponement. It is evident what time does here, and what it does not do. It does not create either increased product or increased value, but does constitute a condition of the *cost* which, by affecting the supply of capital, helps to determine the price of the use of that capital, or from the standpoint of the capitalist the price of the effort of abstinence. I have already shown that this abstinence is not a merely negative force, but one which must be ranked as positive and productive, at any rate in the sense that it is essential to the existence and so to the technical productivity of capital.

Undervaluation, or discounting of future values, is simply one way in which the cost of abstinence presents itself to the mind of the person who saves or lends. It is not a source of interest, it affords no explanation of the possibility of objective interest, it is simply one determinant of the amount or rate of interest. As an economic factor in the determination of price it ranks as a subjective cost with the subjective cost of labour, and as an expense of production must be defrayed out of the extra product due to the productive coöperation of the capital and labour.

§ 11. It is to be clearly understood that I do not dispute any of the facts of Böhm-Bawerk's statement of undervaluation, or that they have a true bearing upon the problem of interest. Where I join issue with him is that while he admits the productive services of forms of capital, he refuses to regard these services as the root and indispensable condition of interest and finds instead a purely subjective cause.

Let me briefly rehearse my objection to his argument as to the payment of interest for use of durable goods. He says, " If the current year's use of a machine is worth 100, and the machine is capable

of doing work of equal quality for five years more,
the machine is not worth 6 × 100, but 100 + 95.23
+ 90.70 + 82.27 + 78.35 = 532.93."[1]   The capital valuation of the machine at the beginning will
be 532.93 ; but, during the six years it lasts, the
total use or " consumption " of the machine will
work out at an aggregate value of 600.   The
difference between the two sums affords a fund
out of which interest is payable.   This fund appears to arise from the ripening process of time.
Now I dispute none of the facts in this statement,
but I assert that they do not furnish the required
explanation of the economic phenomena which
actually occur when a loan of durable goods is
made.   As a matter of fact, when a loan of a
machine or other durable goods is made, the terms
are such as to secure a permanent life for the
machine ; interest does not fructify during six
years, but for a perpetuity.   According to Böhm-
Bawerk's setting, it is possible to obtain the exact
value of the capital by adding up the value of the
services of six years ; in actual industry, though
the capital possesses an exact known value at the
outset, its value for purposes of loan or investment is not calculated by consideration of its gross
services during the time it lasts, but by capitalisa-
tion on the basis of the value of the net interest,
after provision for its continuous existence has
been made.   If A rents to B a house or a machine,

[1] p. 343.

he reckons the capital value of this loan by capitalising the rent or net interest, provision being made to repair or replace the house or machine. Now, since an indefinite or eternal life is thus secured to the house or machine, it cannot be pretended that the capital value can be obtained by adding the yearly· values, for these would come out as infinity. Böhm-Bawerk's explanation of interest· ignores, in the first place, the actual industrial services or "productivity" of the capital forms which are used, and whose use or consumption do actually furnish the goods whose "value" is returned as yearly interest to the owner, and finds the cause of interest in what is really a condition of this productivity. In the second place, it posits a fixed duration to the functioning of form of capital which is discordant with industrial facts. For the actual phenomenon which seeks explanation is the eternity of interest paid for the loan of a material form whose existence appears to be perishable. I have tendered an explanation of this phenomenon by showing that the economic existence of a material form of capital is not really terminable, but that it exerts a productive force which can secure for it a perpetuity of existence, and leave a margin of product from which perpetual interest may be paid. By ignoring the "productivity" of the services of capital, which he yet generally admits to exist, and confining his attention to a merely subjective phenomenon, — the change in the mind of the lender, — Böhn-Bawerk cuts himself off from all possibility of explaining the real problem of a perpetuity of net interest.

He rightly insists that, in order to support this theory of interest derived from productivity, it is necessary to prove a net surplus product after provision against wear and tear of capital, what he terms a " net Nutzung." I claim to have shown, by illustration from each of the several classes of capital forms, that this surplus product or "net Nutzung " does exist.

Thus, and thus alone, is it possible to place capital on the same footing with nature and labour. In the case of these two factors, a net surplus product, after replacement of wear and tear, is admitted. The ordinary finance of the business world enables us to attribute to capital a direct productivity analogous to that of nature and labour, of such size that, after similar provision for replacement has been made, a positive surplus may exist for payment of net interest.

Time is a condition, on the one hand, of the effort of abstinence which keeps as productive goods a value which would otherwise be consumed as consumption goods; and, on the other hand, of the productivity of the forms of capital which this abstinence supports. The productivity thus obtained furnishes a net product which forms a material economic fund out of which real interest may be paid; the amount of this real interest is determined directly by the relation between the marginal cost of the abstinence, and the marginal utility of the "use of capital," which is the effect of that abstinence.

§ 12. In thus repudiating the explanation of Böhm-Bawerk, we do not return to a mere "productivity" theory of interest. Productivity is not to be termed the efficient cause, but only the essential material condition of interest. Productivity of capital is consistent with the non-emergence of interest. The *value* and *price* of use of capital emerge, as do all values and prices, from the interaction of marginal cost and marginal utility of that which is bought and sold.

The representation of the problem of interest, as residing in an exchange of present against future goods, does not accord with the facts of commercial life, and throwing the whole issue upon conditions of subjective valuations, or differences in the mental vision of buyers and sellers, it furnishes no fund for the payment of objective interest. What is actually bought and paid for by net interest is use of capital, and, in order that payment may be made, that use must find expression in perpetual productivity.

I may, in conclusion, sum up my objections against Böhm-Bawerk's theory of Interest, in these four sentences : —

1. By denying the necessity of attributing ob-

jective productivity to capital, he provides no fund for the payment of objective interest.

2. He furnishes no explanation of the actual phenomenon of the eternity of interest.

3. He misrepresents the transaction as an exchange of present against future goods, making the issue one of subjective valuation alone.

4. The undervaluation of future goods assigned as the economic cause of interest is in reality a " cost " of the functioning of capital, and furnishes one side of the forces which determine the value and the price of use of capital.

CHAPTER X.

§ 1. If the analysis of economic bargaining given in the preceding chapters is correct, it cannot fail to have an important corrective influence upon the theory and the practice of Distribution.

Although the direct treatment of ethical considerations is still commonly ruled out of economic theory, it has always been tacitly assumed by *laissez-faire* economists that the laws regulating distribution normally assign to each owner of a factor of production that portion of the product which is economically necessary to evoke and maintain the efficient operation of his factor, and nothing more.

It is claimed that competition, or the free play of enlightened self-interest, among the owners of capital, organising ability, and labour-power, prevents the capitalist undertaker or the labourer from receiving any more than the minimum socially necessary under existing circumstances to secure the service he is capable of rendering. Any interference with the operation of this natural law has been represented as slight and transitory — a necessary friction for which special allowance is to be made. There are no powerful or enduring economic forces which enable the owners of any class of land, labour, capital, or business ability to secure more than the necessary minimum. The freedom of competition among the owners of the several factors, if not absolute, is such as to provide a process of filtration by which the whole advantage of improvements in methods of production of wealth passes into the hands of the consumer. "It is the consumer who is the residual claimant in the results of modern industry." [1]

Each producer gets his minimum; the rest goes to the consumer, and as all are consumers, the operation of the Law of Distribution is even conformable to a general sense of justice or of social expediency. Some little hitch rises in the matter of economic rent of land; from Adam Smith downward the *laissez-faire* economists felt that the power of the landowner to reap where he had not sown failed to harmonise with the moral symmetry which, in spite of occasional disclaimers, they really esteemed as a buttress of economic doctrine.

But, after all, rent did not affect directly the consumer; it did not enter into price, nor did it defraud labourer or capitalist, who got their due wage and profit.

Taxes levied upon the agricultural classes and

1 Hadley, *Economics*, p. 318.

more or less upon manufactures and commerce tended to settle upon rent, and an extension of this policy might enable the community to remedy what might seem to be a natural injustice.

It is curious to note how seldom economists since Ricardo have taken the trouble to probe the loose and flabby notion which represents the consumer as a fourth party in the act of distribution, in whose interests the antagonisms of land, labour, capital, find an ultimate harmony. Professor Hadley speaks of the consumer as "the residual element," seeming to imply that all consumers must be equally able to hold and to enjoy the benefits of improved industry which reach them in the shape of lower prices.

Now if the labourer, in his capacity of consumer, is able to hold all the advantages of falling prices, then his real wages, the only source of the money income which he spends, are capable of rising indefinitely above the necessary minimum. The same holds of the interest of the capitalist. Again, if classes of labourers and capitalists are necessarily able to maintain rates of real wages and real interests beyond the minimum, they will exert their power as producers, and this rise of real wages and interests would prevent prices from falling, for it would imply a stability in those expenses of production which admittedly enter into price. The forces upon which the *laissez-faire* economist relies to prevent capital and labour from taking more than minimum profits and wages, will seem to prevent labourer or capitalist from holding the advantage assigned to them as consumers.

The theory of the incidence of taxation suffers from this same confusion. It is often urged that a tax laid upon some product or some factor of production will be shifted on to the consumer through a rise of prices. But this, though often true, is no ultimate analysis. For it will be admitted that consumers can in some cases throw back the tax upon some body of producers. The only consumers who must be deemed taxable, *qua* consumers, are those in receipt of a guaranteed money income; those whose income is derived from and fluctuates with the value of some factor of production will be liable to have their income affected by a tax which is imposed upon them in an enhanced price of commodities. It would be necessary to investigate the sources of income of each consumer closely in order to ascertain how far he ultimately bore a tax which raised the price of the commodities he consumed. The ability to throw back a tax upon producers and the rapidity of such rejection are matters for detailed practical inquiry. But in a theory of Taxation every part of a tax must in its ultimate incidence be traced to some class of producers, if we are to understand its effect upon the distribution of wealth.

In a word, for purposes of the theory of Distribution, the antithesis of producer and consumer is a false one. The problem of distribution is that of the payment of owners of factors of production, and whatever advantage may actually accrue to each or any of the producers, by reason of a fall of prices to consumers, must be reckoned as a part of the real rent, wages, or interest which they receive.

We are entitled to dismiss altogether the consideration of the consumer in dealing with the theory of distribution, provided that we deal with real payments for the use of factors of production.

§ 2. It is, however, the consideration of the composition of a price which brings out the difference between our theory and the ordinary theory of English text-books. According to the latter, the price of a consumption good is entirely resolvable into a number of expenses of production at the several stages of production which represent the marginal cost of the labour and capital there employed. Now the whole tenor of our analysis has gone to show that the price of a commodity is not exhausted by the payment of these various minimum money-costs of production.

Let me briefly rehearse the method of reasoning adopted.

First, by analysis of the process of determining a price of commodities in a market, we recognise the existence of an element of price which was not explained by competition, which was not necessary to induce the final pair of bargainers to complete that bargain whose terms set the price for the market. In other words, we recognised the actual existence of an element of "forced gain," something not paid for as a "cost" of production, but yet forming an expense.

Next, resolving the price of a commodity into the several prices of uses of factors of production which entered into it, we investigated the conditions of determining the price of the use of land. Here we saw that while differential rents of land did not enter into price, the worst land in use for most specific purposes yielded a positive rent, that this marginal rent being necessary to evoke the use of land for this purpose must enter into price, and that the price of a consumption good will contain various marginal rents of land.

Investigating in similar fashion the determination of the prices for use of capital and labour, we found that they did not differ essentially from land in yielding marginal rents ; that both capital and labour could rightly be divided into practically non-competing groups, from which emerged a number of marginal class interests and wages, which entered into price.

Under the logical system of *laissez-faire* economics, there was properly no social problem of distribution to be solved, unless it were the question of the advisability of permitting private ownership of land ; the complete harmony of capital and labour was secured by the competition of owners of capital and labour-power, which would prevent the existence of any surplus beyond the necessary payments to the capital and the labour employed under the least favourable circumstances. Even allowing that the operation of the law of increasing returns would yield to the larger businesses a gain over and above this minimum interest, it would be difficult to regard this differential gain as a cause of discord between capital and labour, for it would not be possible for the labourers employed in these more profitable businesses to obtain a higher price for the sale of their labour-power than those employed in the least profitable businesses. So long as it is held that only the bare money costs of marginal capital and labour enter into price, while rent of land is altogether excluded, the problem of distribution is of a mechanical and business nature which cannot rightly engage the feelings or activities of the owners of factors of production.

The analysis offered here entirely changes the character of the problem. The prime distinction is no longer interest, wages, and rent, but between costs of 'subsistence of various factors of production on the one hand, and a variety of marginal and differential "rents" supported by various degrees of economic necessity upon the other.

It is of the first importance to understand what is respectively comprised under these two heads.

Distribution is achieved, excepting the cases of annuitants, officials with fixed salaries, etc., by a series of variable payments for the use of labour-power,[1] forms of capital, or land. These payments are made at each stage in the processes of production out of moneys received from the sales of goods or services.

The money paid as the price of retail goods is partly used by the shopkeeper to maintain his reduced stock and his premises, etc., partly to pay wages, profit, rent for the factors of production he employs. The merchant from whom he purchases goods effects a similar distribution, and so does the manufacturer, the farmer, and the other responsible managers of the earlier processes of production. Thus the circulation of the money said to be " spent " is achieved: the money which, being " saved," is used by the saver to buy new forms of capital, undergoes a similar process of distribution.

Thus the aggregate payment for a supply of commodities is resolvable into a number of separate payments for the use of the factors that are engaged in the several processes of production. Now the central problem of distribution consists

---

[1] In this general setting of the *Theory of Distribution*, I have thought it best to include under wages all kinds of payment for industrial work, including earnings of management, and much, if not most, of what is commonly included under profit, because no different principle is involved in the determination of these earnings.

in the varying degrees and conditions of necessity
attaching to the different parts of these payments
for use of factors of production.

In restating this problem a simple diagram
will help to mark the distinctions. AI represents
the total supply of a factor, either land, labour,

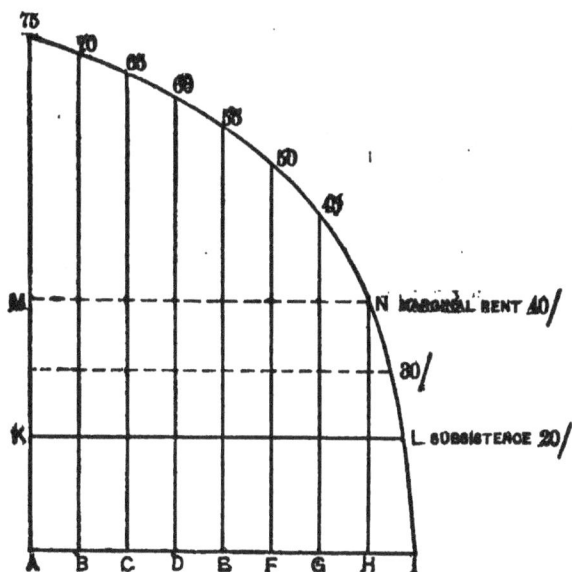

or capital, toward a specific market, comprised of
units AB, BC, CD, etc., with varying degrees of
value, HI being the marginal or least valuable
unit of supply. The total payment for the use
of this factor of production is the figure on the
base AI. Following our analysis we may represent this payment as divisible into the following
parts : the lowest portion will be a payment of
subsistence or maintenance, the sum just sufficient

to secure the economic use of the unit in default of any alternative use. This amounts in the present case to 20*s.* per unit of supply. In the case of labour we posited a subsistence wage of 15*s.* for labour of lowest skill ; in the case of capital a minimum interest of 2½ %. In the case of land a payment infinitesimally small would, in theory, be able to secure the use, so that here the line KL would fall so as to stand only just above AI.

In the case set forth in our diagram the worst or "marginal" portion of supply gets something more than this "rent" of bare subsistence. The "rent" it actually receives, the "marginal rent," is 40*s.* instead of 20*s.* It can obtain the additional 20*s.* chiefly because one or more of the units of supply have an alternative use open to them from which they could earn a high differential rent. Say that AB has such alternative use open to it. In order to secure AB for the supply in question it may be necessary to pay it at the rate of 65*s.*, because its alternative use would yield 64*s.*

This explains the major part of what figures on the diagram as marginal rent, but not the whole. For if AB only got 65*s.*, HI, the marginal unit of supply, would only get a marginal rent of 30*s.* instead of 40*s.*, for we have seen that the actual margin is determined (other things equal) by the necessary price of that portion of supply with an alternative use, which we call the "determinant portion of supply." Now if AB could only get

65*s*. and HI 30*s*., the dotted line would represent the margin.

But we have seen that although AB could be induced to contribute to supply at 65*s*., he may for all that be able to claim 75*s*., if in the bargaining for a price he is the stronger party, and can claim a "forced gain." The actual margin of 40*s*. in our diagram supposes that AB is in a position to take this forced gain of 10*s*., being able to secure for his services not 65*s*. but 75*s*. If he has this power, each of the other contributors to supply will profit by it, since their payment is determined by his. If he can take 75*s*., the next productive unit can get 70*s*., although he may have no alternative use open to him and would therefore, if necessary, have been willing to accept a far lower price. The determinant portion of supply fixes the marginal rent or price. In our present case the marginal rent is 40*s*., of which 20*s*. is payment of subsistence, 10*s*. dependent upon an alternative use of some portion of supply, and 10*s*. a "forced gain." In addition to the 40*s*. at the margin, superior units of supply can take differential rents marking the degrees of their superiority.

Now we have seen that all these payments are "necessary" in the sense that they issue naturally from processes of competition and bargain in which each competitor and bargainer seeks to get the maximum gain for himself.

But they are not equally necessary in the sense that they are payments essential as economic motives to the application of the productive force for which they are paid, and cannot be refused or diverted without interference with the present course of industry.

The issue is fraught both with theoretical and practical importance. It can be best approached from the standpoint of taxation. Power to resist taxation is the most efficacious test of economic necessity. Let us therefore inquire what is the relative ability of subsistence payment, marginal rents (comprising forced gain and a differential rent), and differential rents to resist direct and indirect taxation.

The taxability of subsistence payments need not detain us long. True wages of subsistence for labour or for capital cannot be taxed : non-taxibility is in reality implied in the very nature of a subsistence payment. It may, however, be briefly illustrated thus. Let us suppose that the marginal wage of unskilled labour in a town stands at a 15*s*. subsistence wage, and that an attempt is made under an old-age pension scheme to stop 1*s*. per week out of wages as a tax contributory to a pension. What happens? There exist *ex hypothesi* unskilled labourers who, if the real wages represented by 15*s*. are reduced, will refuse to contribute to the supply of labour. These "determinant owners of supply" would go

on tramp, cadge, beg, or steal, if 15*s.* is not
guaranteed to them. If employers, therefore,
were empowered to stop 1*s.* out of the 15*s.*
wages, the refusal of these men to work would
reduce the supply of labour, and, since the effective demand must be presumed to be constant, the
price or wages will rise and the 1*s.* per week will
be stopped out of 16*s.* instead of out of 15*s.*, this
rise of money wage preventing the withdrawal of
labour from assuming any considerable proportions. At this stage it appears as if the employer
must pay an extra shilling, representing the tax,
out of his own pocket. If his business is earning
for him a higher rate of profit than is economically
necessary to support the capital and skill engaged
in it, the tax will probably be defrayed, in large
part at any rate, out of these surplus profits, as it
will probably not pay him to raise prices which
are not fixed by conditions of close competition.
If, however, the employer's profits are already cut
down to a "subsistence" rate, the tax cannot be
defrayed by him. If the trade is one into which
scarcity rents of land enter as an expense of production, a portion, at any rate, of the tax may at
this stage be shifted on to the landowner through
a pressure by tenants operating through reduction
in demand for land-use. But it is safer to assume
that an increased wage-bill, shared by all the
employers in a trade, will oblige them to raise the
prices of the goods they sell, and pass the tax on

to the consumer through enhanced prices. But we have already seen that the consumer is a purely fictitious halting-place in the theory of Distribution. Making the consumer pay is no final policy. Our 16*s.* low-skilled labourer is a consumer. It appears therefore, that though he has thrown off the tax imposed upon him as producer, he must take up his share as consumer, by paying higher prices for the goods he buys. But this is not the case. He must have guaranteed to him as a condition of contributing to the labour-market such weekly sum of commodities as 16*s.* would have bought for him. If owing to the rise of prices a net wage of 16*s.* will no longer buy these commodities, his money wage must undergo a further increase by virtue of the same economic prices which raised his normal wage from 15*s.* to 16*s.* to meet the stoppage of 1*s.* from his wages. This rise of wage is in effect another tax, which will pass on a similar journey to the first, seeking some "surplus" or unnecessary element of income upon which to lie. What holds of the subsistence wage of unskilled labour can equally be shown to hold of all other subsistence payments. If it were necessary to evoke the savings of the "determinant saver" by paying $2\frac{1}{2}\%$ interest, it will not be possible to tax this element of income in the form of an income tax or indirectly through the prices of commodities.

This argument assumes, of course, that subsist-

ence wages are based upon natural necessities
and not on conventional necessities. The latter,
though possessing a strong power of resisting
taxation when firmly embedded in a customary
standard of life, may be defeated and rendered
taxable by a steady prolonged attack. Moreover,
though true subsistence payments are not really
amenable to taxation, attempts to tax them,
especially when levelled at skilled labour whose
true subsistence is more expensive, may be fraught
with grave injury by degrading the standard alike
of working efficiency and life of a class of workers. Taxation has been commonly directed so as
to prevent a rise of efficiency in work and life of
the working classes in a country. None the less
it is true that true subsistence wages, *i.e.* such
wages as a really enlightened employer will find
it profitable to pay, resist taxation.

§ 3. Turning next to marginal and differential
rents, it is convenient first to deal with the element in marginal rents called "forced gain."
These forced gains issue, as our analysis discloses, in the determination of a price where one
of the final pair is able to force the price up,
beyond what he would be willing to take, to
the utmost that his opponent is willing to give.
When markets are small and competition very
slight and ineffective, we saw that these forced
gains made a large element in prices. Their distinctive character is that they are not earned by

any effort of production, but constitute a gratuitous surplus which is obtained by the stronger bargainer. Forming no economic motive to any bargains, they cannot, in theory at any rate, resist taxation. A tax imposed upon them as an element of income could not be transferred to any other element of income.

But these "forced gains," forming, as we have seen, a part of "marginal rents," enter into the prices of commodities as portions of the marginal expenses of production. It is therefore important to consider whether a tax levied upon the price of commodities with which they enter will fall upon them.

The commonly accepted theory that taxes upon commodities generally fall upon the consumer is based upon the supposition that their prices only measure the necessary money-costs of producing the portion of supply produced under the least favourable circumstances. Taxes upon commodities, in conformity with this supposition, must normally fall upon the consumer who pays the tax in enhanced prices. Are these "forced gains" *necessary* money-costs in this sense?

Mill, in his formulation of the principle that a tax upon commodities falls upon the consumer, admits an exception in cases where "the article is a strict monopoly and at a scarcity price."[1]

" The price in this case being only limited by

[1] *Principles*, p. 515.

the desires of the buyer; the sum obtained for the restricted supply being the utmost which the buyers would consent to give rather than go without it; if the treasury intercepts a part of this, the price cannot be further raised to compensate for the tax, and it must be paid from the monopoly profits." Now it will be evident, if our analysis of price is correct, that every commodity will be sold at a price, which, however subject to the keenest competition in its final retail market, will contain monopoly elements derived from the scarcity of one or other of the requisites of production at different stages. Now a tax imposed upon commodities will not be represented by a rise of prices until these forced gains have been absorbed. We must admit that the prices of these commodities, however keen the competition of retailers in the final stage, are scarcity prices, and are therefore squeezable by taxation to the extent of the forced element they embody. Mill admits "that a tax on rare and high-priced wines will fall wholly on the owners of the vineyards." Why? Not because the owners of some vineyards can extort a high rent for differential advantages over the other vineyards contributing to the same market. If the worst vineyards contributing to this supply paid no rent, the tax would not lie upon the owners of better vineyards, for the first effect of the tax in making unprofitable the production of wine upon the worst vineyards, and so raising the margin of cultivation and lowering differential rents, will be checked and counteracted by the rise of price which would follow such a reduction of supply. This counteracting rise of price would prevent the worst vineyards from passing out of cultivation: differential rents would remain as before, enhanced prices would be paid by consumers, if we accept for the nonce the conventional view of the consumer as a possible ultimate object of taxation. So far as this enhanced price reduced demand for the wine, it might operate upon supply and raise somewhat the margin of cultivation, but even then the tax would only partially — not wholly — fall upon the owners of the vineyards. What Mill is really looking to is the case of vineyards producing a rare wine under conditions in which the worst lands yield a high rent. Here a tax upon the price of the wine must fall wholly upon the "forced gain" or scarcity rent until that is exhausted. For if the scarcity rent amounted to £2 an acre, no tax upon wine which did not eat up the £2 for the produce of an acre would make either the land or the capital and labour employed no longer profitable: so long as the labour and capital received subsistence wages and interest and anything was left for rent above the rent which could be got from converting the "determinant" vineland into other uses, the supply would not be reduced. If the supply remained as before, and the demand be assumed to stand unchanged, the price of the wine could not rise.

We have, therefore, in this case a crucial test of the allegation that a tax upon commodities will settle upon a rent of land which is represented by a monopoly price.

If, therefore, similar rents emerge from the employment of certain species of capital and labour entering into prices like the monopoly rents of land, these two will be amenable to taxation. Take once more the case of beer : if public-house property and breweries yield to their owners a rate of real interest (not interest on watered capital) higher than is necessary to remunerate the necessary amount of capital employed in these processes, the price of beer must be so high as to pay this monopoly element of interest, as well as to pay the specific rent of lands employed in growing hops and barley. A tax upon beer would then fall upon the interest of brewing and public-house property, as well as upon monopoly rents of hop-lands.

Although the special conditions of the production and distribution of beer give peculiar force and emphasis to the application of this principle, the difference between beer and other commodities is only a matter of degree, so far as the presence of the forced or scarcity element in price is concerned. If we took the price of bread or boots or any ordinary commodity and traced it back to its constituent parts through the various processes from the raw materials, we should find the different market-prices containing some element, however small, of the same superiority of bargaining power which we have styled "forced gain." If this theory of Determination of Market-prices is correct, there must in every commodity price be a certain portion which, representing monopoly or scarcity, is thus amenable to taxation. It would therefore not be true that "every tax on a commodity tends to raise its price," save in so far as such tax exceeded the aggregate of "forced gains" which entered into the price. That a tax on the rent of land or upon house-rents containing a large element of land-rent cannot be shifted, but must be borne by the landowner, is a generally received doctrine of economists. It is also frequently admitted that a tax on wages, so far as it relates to the higher grades of mental or educated labour, which enjoy some monopoly of opportunities, must be borne by these classes and cannot be shifted on to other members of the community.[1] If the same admission is not made regarding interest of monopolies in capital, it is only because these are regarded either as abnormal things or as the products of fortuitous and passing circumstances. There is, however, ample evidence to show that economists are quite aware that certain kinds of taxes upon articles sold at scarcity or

[1] Mill, Bk. V, Ch. III, par. 4.

monopoly prices will settle upon and be borne by
the owners of these monopolies. If, then, we can
discover similar elements of unnecessary gain inherent in all prices, we shall recognise a large
surplus which is represented in prices and which
forms a fund upon which taxation must naturally
settle.

§ 4. The conclusion suggested by this kind of
reasoning is that a tax imposed upon any class of
commodities will percolate through the various
channels of production, will be rejected from all
necessary or subsistence payments of capital and
labour, and will, either directly or through the
agency of consumers, settle upon " forced gains "
or unearned income.

This conclusion may appear at first sight to be
opposed to certain well-grounded judgments concerning the taxation of monopolies. It is a correct and generally admitted fact that a tax upon
the price of monopolised commodities may have
the effect of raising their price, and it appears as
if the monopolist, in this way, could exercise a
power to resist completely the taxation of his
rents of monopoly. A closer investigation of the
matter will, however, show that everything depends upon the kind of tax which is imposed.

A monopolist fixes his price so as to obtain for
himself the largest net revenue from sales. He
may sell a smaller quantity at a higher price, or a
larger quantity at a lower price. The price at

which it will be most profitable for him to sell will, in default of any tax or other external interference, depend upon the elasticity of demand on the one hand, and the elasticity of supply upon the other.

It can easily be shown that the effect of a fixed tax upon monopolised commodities may be the sale of a smaller quantity at a higher price. The simplest test is that of a monopoly which in its expenses of production conforms to the Law of Constant Returns, each new increment of product being produced at the same expense as each past increment.

Take the case of a coal monopoly, where the mines are so rich that a virtually unlimited amount of coal can be produced at a selling price of 12 shillings per ton, which will include under expenses of production ordinary interest upon capital and earnings of management.

The line XY represents possible supply, divided into increments of 1 million tons. While the cost per ton is constant with every increase of supply, the selling price falls. The perpendicular AB represents the selling price of 20 shillings per ton where 1 million tons are sold. If 2 millions are sold, the price is 19 shillings; if 3 millions, 18 shillings. So the selling price falls 1 shilling on each increment of 1 million tons, until we reach 9 million tons, which can only be sold at 12 shillings, or just enough to defray expenses of production.

Now, in order to ascertain what quantity of production and sales will yield the largest net revenue of monopoly rents, let us compare the different quantities of supply.

If 1 million tons were sold, the receipts would be 20 million shillings; deduct expenses of production, 12 million shillings, at 12 shillings per

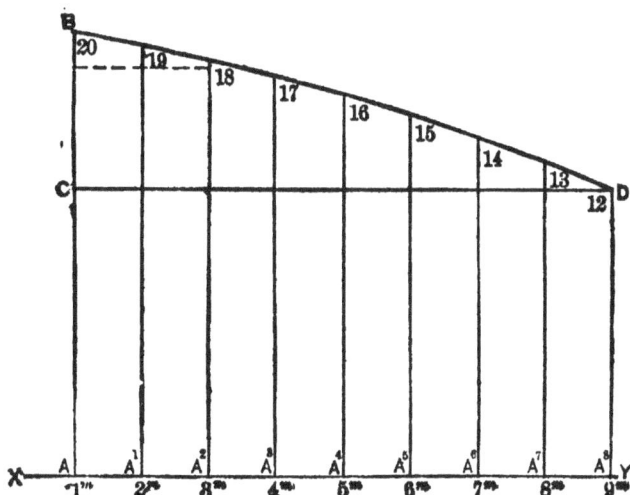

ton, and the monopoly revenue stands at 8 million shillings. If 2 millions were sold, receipts would be 38 million shillings (19 × 2) and expenses 24 millions, yielding a monopoly revenue of 14 million shillings. By similar calculation the net revenue of 3 millions is found to amount to 18 million shillings, of 4 millions to be 20 million shillings; 5 millions yields the same net revenue as 4 millions. After 5 millions a decline of net revenue appears; 6 million tons only yielding 18 million shillings and 7 million tons only 14 million shillings.

It is evident that a monopolist unhampered by taxation will produce 4 or 5 million tons, selling them at a price of 17 shillings or 16 shillings per ton, and taking on each ton a monopoly rent of 4 or 5 shillings.

Now what would be the effect of imposing a fixed tax upon a ton of coal, with the view of forcing rents of monopoly? Let us suppose a tax of 6 shillings per ton to be imposed. The effects are obvious. In the first place, since from the standpoint of the producer, expenses of production are now raised from 12 shillings per ton to 18 shillings, no sale is possible at a less price than 18 shillings. Instead of selling 4 or 5 million tons at 16 shillings or 17 shillings per ton, he is economically forced to raise his price to 18 shillings and sell 3 millions at that price. But at 18 shillings, though he pays the enlarged expenses of production, he earns no monopoly revenue. Has the tax then succeeded in taking the monopoly rents? No. Just as it was not to his interest at the lower level of expenses, 12 shillings, to sell 8 million tons at that figure, so at the artificially heightened level of expenses, 18 shillings, it is not his interest to sell 3 million tons at that price. It is his interest to sell some smaller quantity at a higher price so as to earn monopoly rents. In the case we have taken, the new net maximum revenue of monopoly will be obtained by selling 2 million tons at 19 shillings per ton.

A fixed tax upon monopolised commodities will not succeed then in taking the whole of the monopoly revenue, and will succeed in restricting production so as to force consumers to pay a higher price, which shall remain a monopoly price, for their commodities.[1]

If, instead of a production conforming to the Law of Constant Returns, the production were subject to the law either of diminishing or increasing returns, the calculation would be far more intricate, but the same general law would hold. Unless the curve of expenses happened to vary directly in exact proportion and for an indefinite extent with the curve of demand, so that the monopoly element in price per ton did not fall with the fall of selling price, a fixed tax on monopolies must have the effect assigned to it in the instance above taken.

If we were able to take into accurate account the eccentricities of both demand and supply curves in any actual trade, we should perceive, as Professor Marshall has shown, that there may be a number of equilibria between supply and demand, the prices at which yield an equal net

---

[1] See Professor Edgeworth's note in the *Economic Journal*, June, 1898 (pp. 235–6), for the mathematical proof of the effect of a specific tax on monopolised articles.

revenue to the seller. In such case a fixed tax upon commodities would in many cases be evaded in large measure by a monopolist choosing the equilibrium where the most restricted supply was sold at the highest price. The tendency of such a tax must always be to produce a restriction of supply and a rise of prices. Professor Marshall sums up the matter with admirable lucidity : " A tax proportional to the amount produced causes a greater total loss of monopoly revenue when the amount produced is large than when it is small, and we shall find it causes the sales which afford the maximum revenue to be somewhat smaller than before, and offers an inducement to the monopolist to raise his prices and contract his sales."[1] A fixed tax upon commodities is a "tax proportional to the amount produced."

But it must be borne in mind that the partial ability of a monopolist to resist such a tax, and the injury such tax inflicts upon consumers by restricting supply and enhancing prices, by no means justifies a general condemnation of a tax upon monopolised commodities, but only of the fixed tax.

The failure of a fixed tax upon each unit of supply is due to the fact that while the value of the tax is fixed, the value of the commodity on which it falls is variable.

A tax upon monopolised commodities so regu-

[1] *Principles*, 2d ed. p. 517.

lated as to take the same proportion, or even the whole, of the monopoly rent at each price, would not be open to valid criticism on grounds of theory. But the application of such a tax would imply the possibility of an accurate assessment of the relations between monopoly rents, expenses of production, and selling prices. An *ad valorem* tax upon the selling price of commodities would be open to the same objection, though in a less degree, as that which applies to a fixed tax upon each unit of supply. Since we could not presume the monopoly rent to vary directly and proportionately with the selling price, an *ad valorem* tax upon selling prices might make it more profitable for a monopolist to restrict production and raise prices.

The scientific basis of taxation of monopolies is an *ad valorem* tax upon the monopoly element in prices. Theoretically, this might be levied upon each unit of commodity; practically, it can only be safely and conveniently levied upon net revenues of monopoly as represented in annual incomes.

We saw how a tax placed upon subsistence wages of labour was shifted directly and indirectly upon those elements of income which, not being payments necessary to evoke the use of the factor of production for which they were paid, had no power to resist the tax. What is true with regard to subsistence wages of labour, is equally true of any other element in expenses of production.

Subsistence payments cannot be taxed; forced gains, of which the monopoly element in price of commodities is one plain instance, cannot resist taxation properly directed against it, whether the taxation be of net revenue, or an *ad valorem* tax levied upon the monopoly gains in each act of sale.

§ 5. But forced gains or scarcity rents only form one part of " marginal rents " ; it remains to consider the taxability of the other part of marginal rents, and of the individual differential rents.

A reference to the diagram on p. 303 will make it clear that when we remove from a marginal rent any element of " forced gain " that may inhere in it, the rest of that marginal rent is imposed by the determinant owner of supply, and measures the pecuniary inducement which causes him to abandon a differential rent he might have earned in some other supply. For example, if the marginal rent of 20*s*. for wheat land is determined by the fact that some of this wheat land above the margin, drawing (say) 25*s*., as wheat land, has an alternative use for pasture land which would afford a rent of 24*s*. 6*d*., it is evident that the marginal rent of wheat land depends upon a differential rent of pasture land, and that any cause which raised differential pasture rents would disturb this margin of wheat land. Under such circumstances we have a clear answer to the question, Can marginal rent (apart from the forced gain it contains) be taxed? A tax levied on marginal rent will fall also upon the units of supply earning differential rents. If the marginal rent of wheat land, 20*s.*, is taxed 1*s.* per acre, the determinant portion of supply, land earning previously a rent of 25*s.*, is now reduced to 24*s.* This land, *ex hypothesi*, possesses an alternative use for which it can earn 24*s.* 6*d.* ; it will therefore cease to contribute to the supply of wheat land, and convert itself into pasture at 24*s.* 6*d.*, thus reducing the total supply of wheat land, and raising the margin to a nominal rent of 21*s.* by the action of some other portion of supply which now becomes the determinant. An attempt thus to tax the marginal rent for some specific supply, will have the necessary effect of driving some portion of supply into an alternative use, and, by reducing the specific supply, will enable the whole of the contributors to that supply to evade the tax.

What holds of specific margins of land, holds similarly of specific margins of capital and labour. A tax upon " marginal rents " can only lie on condition that the alternative employment is similarly taxed. A tax upon the rent of marginal wheat land cannot be resisted if a similar tax falls upon pasture rents and rents for other uses of land.

The fact that the marginal rent for one specific use of land depends upon the rents for other uses, proves that the markets for land-uses, though conveniently separated for certain purposes, are organically related at certain points, forming a single supply of land.

So far then, as taxability is concerned, the marginal rent (forced gains excepted) may be treated as differential rents, and the real issue relates to the taxability of these differential rents.

§ 6. It is generally agreed by economists that differential rents of land cannot resist taxation. A tax of 10*s*. or 19*s*. in the pound upon all rent of land could not be transferred by the landowner to his tenant in rise of rent or to any other person with whom he has dealings.

How far is this economic precept applicable to capital and labour? In so far as our gradation of investments is valid, an *ad valorem* tax upon differential and marginal interests could not be resisted, for these are not necessary motives to the application of capital in the directions to which it is actually applied. Looking to the real and not the money forms of capital, we must place it upon precisely the same footing with land as regards taxability. Of land it has been said that differential rents cannot resist taxation, if the tax be levied upon all rents for all uses of land. For so long as any rent remains, no land will be withdrawn from supply. The whole, however, of these differential rents of land could not advantageously be taken, because some minimum differential rent is necessary to induce the landowner to put his land to its best economic use. It is necessary to preserve some inducement sufficient to persuade the owner of good vine-land to apply his land to this purpose rather than to wheat growing or some other less productive use.

Similarly with differential and marginal rents of capital. If an attack was made upon a specific kind of capital drawing high marginal and differential rents, by imposing a tax either upon the estimated forced element of price or upon the net surplus revenue, this tax might be evaded, supposing that some of this capital could be diverted without much waste to an alternative use nearly as profitable where it would not be taxed. If the capital engaged in brewing earned a rate of profit 5% higher than any of the owners could get in alternative investments open to them, almost the whole of that surplus rent could be taken by taxation. But if some portion of that capital were capable of being transferred with inconsiderable loss to another use almost as profitable, a special tax on brewing profits would not lie.

In a progressive condition of industry this taxability would not generally depend upon the adaptability of existing forms of capital to some other use, but upon the alternative employment open to the new savings which might be engaged in increasing the real capital of the brewing trade.

In capital, as in land, differential rents can only be safely taken by taxation, applied, not specifically, but generally. A general tax imposed upon

all interest above subsistence rate will lie without
disturbance of industry, provided it is imposed in
accordance with the principle evolved in our investigation of taxation of monopoly prices. The
whole of differential rents of capital could not,
however, be taken by taxation. If the special
profits of a particular brewery were derived from
a closer monopoly of "tied houses," this extra gain
could doubtless be taxed; such gain, however,
would not properly be a differential rent but
rather a "forced gain" or "scarcity rent" made
in a restricted market by means of monopoly
prices for beer. If the brewery was really competing in a market with other breweries, its higher
profit, or differential rent (if not disguised earnings of superior management), would be derived
from economics of large-scale production with the
use of the best plant and labour. An attempt to
take by taxation the whole of this advantage would
diminish the incentive of capitalists to make the
most productive use of their capital. In a word,
the superior differential productivity of capital,
though not of necessity rightly attributed to skill
of management (which is but one factor in productivity), is conditioned by such skill; unless the
capital has some element of differential interest
secured to it, there is danger it may not be fully
utilised. This consideration involves no general
denial of the taxability of differential interest of
capital, but merely enforces the retention of what-

ever minimum inducement in the shape of higher interest (or profit) may be found necessary to promote the most economical use of capital.

A tax rightly adjusted so as to take even 99% of the net revenue derived from such differential rents could not be resisted, and would have no effect in disturbing the application of existing capital, or the saving for the establishment of new capital. Differential rents are no necessary economic motive to saving; they do not enter into the market-price of saving, which is measured from the cost or the utility of the marginal saver, who is willing to-day to save for some $2\frac{1}{2}\%$.

§ 7. Now let us turn to wages of labour. Marginal class wages, so far as they do not consist of "forced gains" or "scarcity rents" artificially maintained, depend upon the option which some labourers possess to take a differential rent in some other trade. The transferability of some part of a given labour-market from one employment to another, is positively easier and freer than in the case of land and existing forms of capital, so that the question easily appears to resolve itself into that of a general power to tax differential wages over the whole field of labour; in other words, an income tax on wages above subsistence margin.

So far as a differential wage is really a wage of superior skill or productivity, and not a scarcity wage maintained by some artificial ordering of

the market, it appears to stand on a different footing from other differential rents with regard to
the power to resist taxation.

It is even commonly supposed that such a tax
would be defeated by a refusal of labourers to
apply their full productive power unless the full
rent of individual productivity were secured to
them. But closer scrutiny indicates that no such
general judgment can be pronounced. At first
sight, it doubtless seems as if a man, who gives out
twice as much productive power in a day's work as
another, must have twice as much secured to him.
in real wages, and that he can keep these wages
against all attempts to tax them. But is this necessarily true? Suppose A, B, C are three workers in a trade, and A produces a product 30, B 20,
and C 15; if a tax amounting to the value of 2
were placed on B's wage, and one of 6 on A's
wage, would they necessarily withhold part of
their labour-power? To argue that they necessarily would withhold, is to make productivity the
sole determinant of value and price, and to ignore
effort. The subjective basis of endurance enters
in as a chief determinant of supply, and requires
that certain units of labour-power, even in the
same market, shall be remunerated at a higher rate
than others. This does not contravene the principle of an equal price for an equal quantity in a market. What is really bought in the labour-market,
is not the objective units of labour-power for which

the wage is nominally paid, — the piece work or the hour, — but the subjective or vital effort which underlies it. The subjective effort of the determinant owner of labour-power in a given supply really determines, from the supply side, the price per unit of the whole supply, the supply price being the result of his bargaining with the representative of marginal utility on the demand side.

In the case taken above, the subjective effort of C may be the determinant on the supply side, and his bargaining with the marginal buyer may have fixed a price per unit of labour. If, now, B can produce one-third more units of labour in a day, and A twice as many, with the same amount of subjective effort as C gave out in producing 15, they take a differential rent of 5 and 15 respectively. But it by no means follows that they could resist a tax which reduced this rent by 2 and 6; for 5 and 15 are not necessarily the sums they insist upon receiving as conditions of giving out the same subjective effort as C gave out. Something more than C receives they must receive, or they will reduce their objective productivity to the level of C, but the "how much" is a problem separately determinable in each case.

In some kinds of work it might be the case that a man will consent to give out his superior energy or skill for a wage which is not proportionately higher than the wage of the marginal worker in his trade. In other cases, the greater intensity or

skill can only be evoked by a fully proportionate
increase of wage. No general principle could
therefore be applied in taxation of differential
wages. The taxability would vary, not only with
the varying character and conditions of the work,
but even with the individual nature of thé worker,
and with the character of the wants he used the
later increments of his income to satisfy. In many
kinds of work the utmost intensity of exertion can
only be evoked by a rate of payment even higher
than what is paid for an equal product achieved
by slower and less intense exertion, — a fact recognised in various schemes of task or piece wages, as
also in special rates for overtime. In other kinds
of work less disagreeable or exhausting, a capable
worker might consent to express his capability,
even if he could not reap the'full advantage of his
superiority over the least effective labourer by a
correspondingly higher wage.

We must always keep clearly in mind the real
nature of these "rents of ability." It is only
when we take the individual man or a portion of
his labour-time for our standard of measurement,
that the rate of remuneration seems differential.
If we regard the worker as a seller of productive
efficiency, the one who sells more than another of
his commodity, or who sells a better quality, naturally gets a correspondingly larger amount of pay.
If, however, we retain the idea of differential rents
of labour, we must admit that they are not amen-

able to taxation in the same way and to the same
degree as differential rents of land.

§ 8. The difference which manifests itself in the
· taxability of differential rents of labour on the one
hand, and of land and capital on the other, is not
difficult to understand.

Differential rents, beyond a bare minimum, are
not economic inducements to owners of land and
capital to apply these factors of production; for
existing forms of land and capital a minimum rent
and profit suffices to retain their economic service,
and though new capital is only brought into existence by a certain subsistence rate of interest, no
higher rate for any special purpose is an economic
motive of saving.

But labourers will withhold part of their productive power unless some differential wage of
ability is secured for them. Inanimate nature has
no ability to withhold its continuous output of
productive powers; the owner of a more fertile
field, who withheld its use because its differential
rent was taxed, would be cutting his own throat,
unless the tax swallowed the entire economic rent.
The value of such supply is determined on the supply side by natural scarcity. Where the supply
depends upon voluntary effort, as in the supply of
labour-power, the option to withhold enables the
owner to make conditions which shall secure for
him a differential rent, some indeterminate proportion of which must be even secure against taxation.

§ 9. Our analysis of the taxability of the various payments made out of money spent on commodities, resolves these payments into necessary expenses of production, subsistence payments for use of labour and capital, which cannot be taxed, and marginal and differential rents which are in various degrees and to various extents amenable to taxation. Forced gains or scarcity rents together with differential rents of land and capital have no power to resist direct taxation imposed upon them as elements in income. Forced or scarcity rents of labour, together with certain portions of differential rents of labour, are also in theory directly taxable.

The general tendency of this analysis is to justify the economic superiority of taxation upon incomes or net revenues over taxation imposed upon special classes of commodities or upon special classes of rents or profits.

A general income tax, graduated upon the supposition that the proportion of unearned and therefore economically taxable income varies directly with the absolute size of incomes, on the one hand, escapes the supreme difficulty of discrimination of the origins of special forms of gain, and, on the other hand, can be shown to have a genuine, rapid, and accurate tendency to discover and settle upon the various portions of incomes which are unearned in the sense that they furnish no necessary inducement to owners of factors of production to put these factors to their best economic use.

But while our investigation of the incidence of taxation exhibits the superior economy of direct taxes upon monopoly revenues or other unearned elements in income wherever they can be ascertained and measured, and approved a general graduated income tax upon the ground that it will discover and settle upon such elements of income, the condemnation of specific or even of *ad valorem* taxes upon commodities must not be misunderstood. We have seen that a monopolist appears to exercise a power to resist both these latter forms of taxation of monopolised commodities by restricting production and raising prices. By raising prices he appears to shift a portion, if not the whole, of the tax he nominally pays, on to consumers. But following the line of reasoning laid down in our discussion of the attempt to tax subsistence wages for an old age pension scheme, we perceive that such enhanced prices paid by consumers living on subsistence wages or subsistence rate of interest, have the effect of raising the money payments for subsistence, and thus of transferring the tax up to other persons who must eventually pay it out of unearned elements of income. To shift a tax upon to "the consumer," as we have seen, is no final determinant of incidence : a tax must always be deemed to settle upon some element of income ; the power of subsistence payments to resist taxation we have seen is absolute so long as there exist unearned elements of income upon which they can be placed. The particular monopolist, therefore, can only resist specific or *ad valorem* taxation of his monopolised articles by imposing the tax upon the unearned incomes of certain classes of consumers, and not by distributing it over all classes of consumers. The same general principle applies to all taxation of commodities, monopolised or free : no such tax can settle upon incomes which are subsistence payments for factors of production, until all forms of unearned income have been exhausted.

The chief condemnation of such forms of indirect taxation is not that they are liable to be paid indiscriminately by rich and poor, by those who can and those who cannot bear them, but that they tend in many cases by checking production to restrict the most efficient use of factors of production, and so to decrease the general output of commodities.

If this analysis be correct, the practical importance of its conclusions is very great. By indicating the existence of a vast "surplus" of rents analogous to the economic rent of land in its taxability, it strengthens immensely the economic means of social progress. By exploding two fallacious notions, that taxes are paid by the poorer classes of the working population, and that high taxation is injurious to trade, our analysis removes chief barriers to that increase of taxation and of wise public expenditure which are essential to a sound progressive social policy.

§ 10. Differential rents play so considerable a part in determining the inequality of incomes in an industrial society that it may be well to append to this discussion of their taxability some considerations of a more general character.

A progressive social economy is by no means confined to the difficult, sometimes hazardous, and always wasteful processes of taxation in order to procure for society some of these differential payments which are shown not to be necessary inducements to their recipients to take part in production. More enlightened methods of production, increased equality of economic opportunities, organisation of employers or of workers, will often succeed in effecting large reductions of differential rents. In respect of land this was seen by Ricardo and explicitly stated by J. S. Mill,[1] who argued that improvements of agricultural science or of means of carriage which increased or rendered more available the output of more fertile farms would, by rendering it no longer profitable to work farms on the margin of cultivation, raise that margin and so reduce differential rents. In similar fashion the differential rents or interests of capital may be reduced by such organisation of employers or of workers

[1] *Principles*, Bk. IV, Ch. III, § 4.

as throws a larger proportion or the whole of a trade into the hands of the largest, best-equipped, and most profitable firms.

Where an organisation of employers by organising a syndicate or a trust achieves this result by weeding out the weaker mills, it commonly succeeds in preventing this economy of differential rents from passing to the consuming public in the shape of lower prices, and, instead, substitutes a monopoly or scarcity rent for these differential rents. But none the less is it true that this "weeding out" or "crushing out" of feebler competing firms signifies a reduction of the differential rents which were formerly necessary to keep the requisite supply of capital in operation. The more far-sighted labour leaders are quite aware that their true interests lie in promoting this same improvement of trade organisation, provided that they can maintain among employers such competition as will enable them to take in a rise of wages the reduction of differential rents.

This policy, indeed, forms one of the stoutest arguments in favour of that attempt to acquire by legislation, or by trade unionism, a recognised standard of subsistence, of hours of labour, and of other terms of employment. This movement for better conditions of employment, implying a rise in current expenses of production which seems to press unendurably upon the weaker employers, is thus seen to be a positive instrument of economic progress. Upon this topic Mr. and Mrs. Webb thus write : "It is obviously to the interest of the trade union so to fix the common rule as to be constantly 'weeding out' the old-fashioned or stupid firms, and to concentrate the whole production in the hands of the more efficient 'captains of industry,' who, however, have to lower the cost of the product without lowering the wage. Thus, so long as the more advantageously worked establishments in the trade are not working up to their full capacity, or can, without losing this advantage, be further enlarged, the trade union could theoretically raise its common rule, to the successive exclusion, one after another, of the worst employers, without affecting price or the consumers' demand, and therefore without diminishing the area of employment. By thus 'raising the margin of cultivation,' and simultaneously increasing the output of the more advantageously situated establishments, this device of the common rule may accordingly shift the boundary of that part of the produce which is economically of the nature of rents, and put some of it into the pockets of the workmen." [1]

The failure of most economists to recognise the large proportion of "forced gains" and scarcity, or differential rents, which are included in the net profits of a trade, is chiefly responsible for the tone of disparagement in which even the most liberal

[1] *Industrial Democracy*, Vol. II, pp. 729–30.

minded amongst them speak of the economic efficacy of trade-union efforts to raise wages. That
wages at any given time are fixed absolutely by
the operation of economic laws which are immutable, few would now contend, but even Jevons and
Professor Marshall, while generally favourable to
trade unionism, are apt to deny its validity when
they come to apply economic reasoning. " The
power of unions to raise general wages by direct
means is never great," writes Professor Marshall,[1]
while Jevons boldly affirmed that, though organisation might enable one class of workers to increase
this wage, this increase was paid for by other
classes in their capacity of consumers.[2] The general tendency is to insist that trade unionism is
confined, so far as efficacy in raising wages is concerned, to securing rises that are already justified
by increased prices and profits, and to obtaining
such rises as are attended by a correspondent increase of productivity of labour, such increase, for
example, as is sometimes claimed to follow a raising of the standard of comfort.

Our analysis, if it be correct, involves the recognition of a great fund of surplus profits, which is
available for higher wages, as it is also amenable
to taxation, and which can be obtained by a sufficiently strong pressure of trade unionism.

In other words, forced gains and differential

---

[1] *Elements of Economics of Industry* (1892), pp. 407-8.
[2] *The State in Relation to Labour*, pp. 105-7.

rents of capital are not permanently necessary payments to the owners of capital who take them, and may be transferred, either to the public by taxation, or to the workers by a rise of wages. It is not difficult to see that differential rents of labour, mental or manual, may be reduced or transferred in similar ways. Primary public education has had a plainly recognised effect in reducing the differential rents of ordinary clerical employments. Technical education, in so far as it extends to larger social areas the opportunity of successfully learning high-skilled and well-paid trades, makes in the same direction. In fact, every enlargement of education, in so far as it makes for greater equality of economic opportunities, tends to reduce differential rents of employment and likewise the marginal specific rents which are seen to depend upon them. If the marginal physician is better paid than the marginal cornporter, it is not because of any greater inherent skill in the former calling which gives its services a higher marginal value. We pay the marginal physician a relatively high fee because the present distribution of economic and educational opportunities is such that only a small proportion of the population can equip their sons for competition in that market, hence the competitors, by fairly close organisation, can maintain a high rate of piece wages. The high rate does not depend on a natural scarcity of high skill. When it is

made as easy to any lad who has the desire to pre-
pare himself for medicine as it is to become a dock
labourer, the piece wage for the former work will
be as low and probably lower than the piece wage
for the latter, so far as the marginal labourer is
concerned. Even those high fees which professional talent of a distinguished rank can draw
will be greatly cut down when every career is
open to natural talent from any social or economic
grade. A distinguished specialist in surgery may
now take a fee of £1000 for a single delicate operation. He will not now do it for less because he
can actually get this sum. But his ability to get
it depends on two facts, one relating to supply,
the other to demand, neither of which is a permanent necessity. The first fact consists in the
limitation of supply of finest surgical talent by
reason of the exclusion of most children from any
opportunity to discover such a talent, to educate
it, and to enter upon a medical career. Destroy
this artificial limitation of supply, and instead of
one surgeon able and willing to do this job we
should have three or four upon a fairly equal level
of skill and reputation, whose competition direct
or indirect, would bring down the fee from £1000
to say £20. On the other side, there is the fact
of the existence of a certain number of very wealthy
people who, drawing large elements of unearned
income from various rents, can afford to pay
£1000. Every equalisation of economic oppor-

tunities, each application of sound principles of • progressive taxation, will reduce this number, and reduce the effective demand for work at such a price.

Thus it is seen that there is nothing inherent or immutable in these differential rents of ability which are sometimes regarded as a necessary reward for superior skill which cannot be refused or materially reduced.

§ 11. I have for convenience reserved for a special, separate consideration those payments to which Professor Marshall gives the name "quasi-rents." He has done more than any other economic writer to break down the barrier which has separated land from other factors of production, and to extend the name and the application of the Law of Rent. The rent of land is to him "no unique fact, but simply the chief species of a large genus of economic phenomena," and he recognises "that there is a continuous gradation from the true rent of those free gifts which have been appropriated by man, through the income derived from permanent improvements of the soil, to those yielded by farm and factory buildings, steam engines, and less durable goods." [1]

A careful consideration of the chapters in which the theory of quasi-rents receives full treatment,[2] shows that the quasi-rents are analogous, not to

[1] Bk. VI, Ch. IX.
[2] (Bk. V, Chs. VIII, IX, and Bk. VI, Ch. IX.)

differential rents of land, but to scarcity rents.
First to illustrate his meaning he takes the cases
of a find of meteoric stones and of the ownership
of the pictures of a dead artist.   Here we have
an absolute monopoly selling at a monopoly price
and yielding what Marshall terms a "true rent."
A tax upon such articles falls entirely on their
owners.   If, however, by labourers' search other
meteoric stones could be found, or if we were dealing with the pictures of a living artist who still
continued to produce, the monopoly price or rent
would only last for a short season, since it would
serve to stimulate such exertion and would equate
supply and demand at ordinary expenses of production.   But while the higher price lasted, the
stones or pictures might be regarded as yielding a
quasi-rent.   In other words, a quasi-rent or monopoly element would figure in short period or
market-price, and would gradually disappear as
the period was lengthened and what is commonly
termed a normal price was reached.   Any supply
of highly specialised capital, ability, or labour,
which cannot be quickly and widely replenished,
may for a season stand in the position of being
able to take, in addition to ordinary rate of profit,
a quasi-rent which must, however, disappear when
the lapse of time brings into the market a sufficient number of new forms of specialised capital
and labour.

Now it is evident that these quasi-rents marking

short-time monopolies are nothing else than the more variable forms of monopoly or scarcity rents of capital and labour, and it is not easy to understand why the disparaging epithet "quasi" should be appended to them. So long as they exist they are as true rents as any land-rents, nor are they necessarily of brief duration : highly specialised labour and capital are frequently able, by checking investments of outside capital and labour, to hold up market-prices above "marginal expenses of production" for long periods. Some of these monopolies may be as stable and as strong as the monopolies of natural resources which are admitted to draw true rents.

It appears that these quasi-rents are simply less enduring forms of monopoly rent. The test of rent commonly accepted is this, Will it bear a tax? Marshall asserts in one passage that wealth drawing quasi-rents is taxable. "A tax on any set of things that are already produced falls exclusively on the owners of those things, if it is not accompanied by a tax, or the expectation of a tax, on the production of, or bringing into use of, similar or rival things. If it falls also on all rival things, and the supply of them is not absolutely fixed, its incidence will be gradually transferred to the consumers. . . . For a shorter period in which the tax falls mainly on the owners, the income may be regarded as more or less of the nature of rent."[1]

[1] Bk. V, Ch. VIII, par. 2.

Under the class "quasi-rent" come the earnings of improvements of land,[1] buildings, machinery, etc.,[2] nearly all the profits of business institutions,[3] and in one passage it is suggested that all "skill, material capital, and business connections" when and in so far as they are specialised, "cease to exert a direct influence on the value of the products due to them; and, on the other hand, the value of these products . . . determines the income which can be derived from these factors, *i.e.* it determines what we have called their quasi-rent."[4]

§ 12. Now Professor Marshall does not explicitly discuss this theory of Quasi-rents in relation to taxation, though a passage previously quoted seems to signify that they are taxable. But Mr. Cunningham, in a discussion of these quasi-rents, considers that not merely are they directly amenable to taxation, but that a tax upon products into which they enter will lie upon them. According to him, the profit upon capital that is "irrevocably fixed" is "of the nature of rent," and he concludes by saying, "It follows from what has gone before that a tax on production will affect price in so far as it is not paid out of that part of price which is of the nature of rent. And whenever a tax is laid upon production, whenever it can come out of rent, it will do so."[5]

---

[1] pp. 665, 459.   [2] p. 670.   [3] p. 659.   [4] p. 655.
[5] *Economic Journal*, March, 1892.

Now it is certainly true that forms of capital which are "irrevocably fixed" are in the first instance liable, like rent of land, to bear a specific or an *ad valorem* tax upon the products to which they contribute. But it by no means follows that they cannot recoup themselves by causing a rise of prices. Take the case of the interest on capital sunk in houses; houses already built would not be withdrawn from supply if the interest upon the sunk capital fell toward zero, but it is equally certain that a tax upon houses could not and would not be borne by this capital. For there is a constant flow of fluid capital toward houses so long as this capital is able to earn normal interest, which flow would be checked[1] by a tax upon the capital already "irrevocably appropriated" in the form of houses. In one passage Mr. Cunningham does seem to admit that the taxation of quasi-rents might affect price and production, but he urges that it would do so "very slowly after a time." Now this is not correct; in any trade open to investment and vitally sustained by a flow of capital from without, the effect of taxing the quasi-rents of fixed forms of capital would be rapid and immediate. It is only when such "ir-revocably appropriated" capital enjoys a power of

---

[1] This check might operate either by a restriction of saving in case the tax reduced the rate of interest below that required by the marginal saver, or it might divert new capital from building into other forms of investment.

monopoly, derived from checking the flow of out-side capital, that the profits on fixed capital will be unable to resist taxation on production. If the breweries of a district have a corner upon the supply of public houses, so that interests on fixed capital in brewing are 2% higher than normal out-side interests, that 2% is indeed amenable to taxa-tion, but it is so amenable, not because it takes the form of "irrevocably appropriated capital," but because the interest of such capital enjoys a power of restricting the inflow of outside capital and so of earning a special rate of interest. This special interest is what I term "a forced gain or scarcity rent." It may be included in the quasi-rent of Professor Marshall, but it differs vitally from the ordinary interest on fixed capital in being unable to resist taxation by raising prices. In the supposed case, a tax upon beer would fall upon the 2% excess interest and could not be recouped by raising prices ; it could not fall upon any further part of the interest without reducing brewing profit below the normal rate and prevent-ing the fresh influx of capital required to sustain a growing trade, or even to maintain a deprecia-tion fund.

The mere fact, then, that capital or labour is specialised and cannot be withdrawn does not en-title us to regard the earnings of such specialised factors as a surplus, so long as the industry is open to fresh investments of capital and labour.

A tax will not lie upon these specialised forms, but will be transferred to the consumer by enhanced prices to be bore ultimately by such "consumers" only as enjoy some unearned elements of income. Only in cases where some natural or economic power restricts the inflow of capital or labour will the earnings be rightly regarded as a surplus and liable to bear taxation; and in such a case the tax, so far as it falls upon interests or wages which are results of monopoly, and are in excess of "competition rates," will not be confined to the capital which is "specialised." In a word, the specialisation of capital or labour is not really a condition which assimilates its earnings to rent.

§ 13. These quasi-rents, then, in so far as they are rents at all, are monopoly or scarcity rents and are liable to taxation. They also enter into prices, for we have seen that wherever a scarcity rent exists, the marginal portion of supply is able to obtain it, and it will figure in supply prices. Professor Marshall indeed denies that they enter into price, but when the marginal labourer in a class of labour or the marginal mill in a particular industry obtains a higher wage or a higher interest than "free competition" would assign, that marginal wage or interest must figure in expenses of production and in price. It can only be excluded by the fallacious "dosing" application of the Law of Diminishing Returns.

Professor Marshall himself illustrates a "quasi-rent" of labour by the high wages miners drew in 1873. Now it would scarcely be possible for him to affirm that the high piece wages then paid did not "enter into" the price of a ton of coal, for every ton of coal paid this piece wage. If it be admitted that the quasi-rent here "enters into" the price of coal, it may be contended that it does not help to determine the price of coal, but consists in a surplus which remains after the necessary "expenses of production" are defrayed from the price. But even here the denial that the quasi-rent helps to determine the price is a mere verbal quibble. For the quasi-rent is a direct measure of the pressure of scarcity, which is as much, and in the same sense, a determinant of value and of price as the utility measured by demand. The quasi-rent is under the circumstances a necessary payment of marginal labour, it is not a mere surplus in the sense that it takes what remains after expenses are paid out of price, for that implies that price is determined exclusively from the demand side, which, as we have already seen, is not true, even of the closest monopolies. The quasi-rent of the miner not only enters price, but helps to determine price. It is true that it is also determined in its amount by price, but this only means that it is one of a number of mutually determinant factors of price.

If, however, the quasi-rent of miners enters

price and helps to determine price, the same is true of every other quasi-rent of labour, capital, or ability. It is only differential rents, whether "true rents" or quasi-rents, which do not enter into or determine price, because they form no part of the expenses of the marginal supply.

Such, then, of these quasi-rents as deserve to have the term "rent" applied to them should receive it without the timid justification of quasi. They are to all intents as much true rents as the scarcity rent of land, entering price as an addition to marginal expenses and being unable to resist taxation.

§ 14. We have seen that elements of forced gain marking superiority of bargaining power arise in all the processes of exchange, and that an accurate analysis of the payments for finished commodities would disclose a large number of such "gains" payable to owners of factors of production at various stages. Our investigation of the markets for the use of the several factors indicates that, while any of these factors may assume this position of superiority of bargaining, there is no warrant for supposing it to be equally distributed among them, even in the long run.

A closer regard to the actual mechanism of modern industry seems to indicate that an increasing proportion of this power to take "forced" gains adheres to the class called *entrepreneurs*, or undertakers, and is included under the vague title of profits. The undertaker is sometimes the owner of one of the factors of productive capital or business capacity, or both, who buys the use of the other factors, and, organising them for productive purposes, is able to sell the products upon terms which are highly "profitable." These profits, in so far as they exceed necessary interest and necessary wages of management, consist of "forced gains," not necessarily extracted entirely out of bargains with labourers, but partly perhaps by bargains with owners of capital, and partly by restriction of free competition in the markets in which he disposes of the products.

The typical form of private business to-day is one in which the undertaker buys in the cheapest market each of the factors of labour, capital, and land which he requires, and organising their uses for production, sells the product in the dearest market he can command. Our analysis of the relation of buyers and sellers indicated that the buyer was in modern industry normally the stronger bargainer, so that the undertaker may well exert a power to take "forced gains" in his bargains for the use of labour and capital. The real crux lies in the question, "Can he retain for himself these gains when he assumes the position of seller in disposing of his products?" Where competition is said to be free, he cannot, and must hand over to consumers such portions of his "forced gains" as are not swallowed up in ex-

penses of competition. He can only hold these
" forced gains" by restricting freedom of competition in markets where he is seller. Hence,
everywhere he is devoting his energies to one of
two policies. Arranging price-lists by agreement
with competitors, entering into closer agreements
with these competitors, and eventually organising
alliances, syndicates, or trusts, he labours to
strengthen the bargaining power of his " trade "
in these dealings with middlemen or consumers.
Or else he strives, by striking out some slight
novelty in goods or by securing a supremacy over
a particular part of the market, to be able to
evade the superior bargaining power which normally belongs to the buyer.

His success in achieving these results is the
dominant feature of modern industry so far as the
distribution of wealth is concerned. There is
good reason to believe that an increasing proportion of "forced gains" or "unearned income"
continually assumes the form of the business
profits of undertakers.

Even where formally it is capital that takes the
initiative, as where a number of capitalists pool
their capital and form a joint-stock company, capital buying the use of labour and law and management, a closer scrutiny will generally disclose the
fact that the real gains of such an enterprise are
absorbed, often by anticipation, by one or two
business men who as financiers, promoters, or

managing directors, have organised the business in their own interests.

The recognition of these "forced gains" or surplus elements in price involves important consequences in considering methods of social reform.

§ 15. If price contains no surplus beyond necessary payment of money costs, the arguments, by which not merely "old" economists, but so modern an economist as Jevons, proved the futility of trade-union organisation in seeking to achieve a general rise of wages, would be valid. If the profits of the marginal supply of capital are kept at a minimum in all classes of investment, it will be evident that a rise of wages (unless attended by a corresponding increase of efficiency of labour) would be impossible, and any attempt to extort such a rise would be injurious. A similar condemnation must be passed upon the eight hours' movement, or upon any other progressive movements which would raise the wage bill. The portion of the real income of the nation which went as differential rents to owners of land or capital or ability, could not be touched by such a policy. In other words, differential rents do not constitute a surplus value. But marginal rents, which enter into price, do constitute such a surplus.

We have seen that, if a single business in a trade, owing to exceptional advantages, is earning a higher rate of profits than others, it is not pos-

sible, under normal conditions, for the employees
to take this profit in higher wages; if by special
organisation of a group it were possible to take
the whole or part of it, it would only pass from
being a differential rent of capital into a differential rent of labour, *i.e.* a certain group of
workers would have established a sectional monopoly in a labour-market. If, on the other hand,
a whole trade were earning a higher profit than
was necessary to keep the required capital in the
trade, a surplus exists, which can raise the price
of labour for a whole market, provided labour is
sufficiently well organised to take it. If it can be
shown that not merely do certain trades rise for
brief seasons into the condition of earning surplus
profit, but that other trades, by reason of special
limitations upon the field of investment, are permanently in that condition, the existence of a
large element of surplus profit gives to the labour
movement that firm economic basis of support
which otherwise is lacking.

§ 16. Karl Marx was right in his insistence
upon the fundamental importance of recognising
the idea of surplus value. He was wrong in regarding the surplus value as exclusively the product of labour-power taken by capital in the
process of bargaining for the sale of labour-
power. He failed to explain why labour, alone
of the factors, should be conceived as making all
the "value" of material marketable goods. He

failed also to explain what the nature of the power was by which capital took the surplus value made by labour; and, finally, he failed to show how any individual capitalist who took it was not compelled to relinquish it under the stress of competition with his fellow-capitalists.

The surplus value here described issues, not merely from one class of bargains (between capital and labour), but from every class; it represents the economic might of the stronger in every market. The true economic motive of the organisation alike of labour and of capital is to establish such a power of bargain at some point or other in the field of industry as to obtain some of this surplus. Capital, by various processes, limits free competition; price-lists and other trade agreements regarding prices and wage-rates, corners, and other temporary coups, syndicates, amalgamations, trusts, are all endeavours to enable the capital in a given market to obtain a rate of profit above the necessary minimum, by raising prices, reducing wages, or both. So far as capital succeeds, these higher profits are represented in market-prices which exceed the economically necessary money-costs of production.

The organisation of labour must also be considered to be directed, in the main, by a similar motive. So far as trade unionism is confined to protecting a class of labour against specially injurious conditions of low wages, irregular employ-

ment, and other risks imposed by the greed or
carelessness of employers, and in thus securing
a bare maintenance for labour, we are entitled to
discriminate trade unionism from organisation of
capital. But trade organisations in most skilled
trades are evidently devoted, not to a merely protective policy, but to a strengthening of their capacity for bargains by restricting competition in the
labour-market, so that they may obtain in higher
wages or increased leisure a surplus corresponding
in nature to the higher profits of capital.

In every process of production where capital,
labour, and land are employed, one or other,
whether by organised contrivance of its owners,
or else by what may be termed accident, is apt to
be relatively short in supply: in such case the
whole supply of this factor will take a price
containing a "surplus" element.[1] Where many
different sorts of capital or labour or land are
required to contribute directly or indirectly to a
given process, a number of these elements of
surplus will emerge, attached sometimes to one,
sometimes to another factor. So if we followed
the raw material of any commodity from its
earliest extractive stages to the final form it
received as it passed over the retail counter, we
should find it gathering, not only "costs" of pro-

---

[1] *I.e.* the final seller in the market for the use of this factor
of production will be stronger than the final buyer, and will
extract a large element of "forced gain."

duction, but surplus elements at various stages
of its advance, the final price of the commodity
containing the aggregate of these costs and sur-
pluses.

The price of any ordinary material commodity
of a complex order will probably contain scores of
these elements derived from the component prices
of the productive goods and of portions of the
services of land, labour, and capital, which have
contributed to the final result.

In any given condition of industry, land, labour,
and capital will probably all share in this surplus,
but in very different proportions. Our general
analyses of the bargaining powers of owners of
land and of many kinds of capital indicate that
in the bargains for the use of these factors their
owners will normally occupy the stronger position,
whereas in the bargains for the sale of labour-
power, the sellers (save in special cases where
they are aided by monopoly of skill or economic
opportunity) will be weaker than the buyers. If
the large portion of surplus which passes to the
commercial *entrepreneur* and the financial classes
be regarded as wages of management rather than
as interest upon the capital which they operate,
these grades of skilled labour must be regarded
as possessed of a monopoly of business opportunities which assigns high marginal rents of labour
to the work they undertake.

The fact that among these *entrepreneur* classes,

as also among the professional classes, some individuals fail to make a living, while among those who succeed there is the widest variety of success, must not blind us to the inequality of economic and educational opportunities which secures for these and other forms of skilled work marginal rates of remuneration that measure the strength of the protection which is applied to them.

§ 17. Surplus value, then, is not something which emerges in the dealings of capital with labour or of land with labour; it emerges in every competitive bargain and adheres to the stronger bargainer; it is only because in modern industry the owner of capital, land, or business capacity is normally found to be the stronger bargainer, that he obtains most of the surplus. Labour, even manual labour in certain markets and at certain times, shares this surplus, takes in wages what is not essential to the maintenance of labour-power. The fact that the labourer gets so little as compared with the capitalist, landowner, and *entrepreneur*, ought not to lead us to adopt a false or one-sided theory of the origin and nature of surplus value. The amount and the proportion of the surplus which goes to the owners of the several factors will be determined by two general conditions closely related to one another: (1) the character of consumption; (2) the growth of industrial arts in relation to natural conditions of supply. It is needless here to rehearse the chief laws that govern these forces. It must suffice briefly to summarise the influence which these forces exercise upon distribution of the surplus.

(1) In a community where a rapid growth of population, or a low order of individual culture, causes a larger increase of effective demand for common articles of food and other material goods than for intellectual, artistic, and, in general, more qualitative goods, the owners of sources of raw materials and the organisers of manufacture and of transport machinery will find the requisites they own to be ever in larger demand, and the proportion of surplus or "marginal rents" which accrues to them will be larger. Whereas, in a community where the demand for large masses of material goods was subordinated to a growing demand for highly qualitative goods, either material or non-material in character, the demand for land, machinery, and capital in general would be reduced, the demand for skilled manual and mental labour increased, and the surplus would tend to be distributed in accordance with the new conditions.

(2) Changes in the industrial arts will obviously affect distribution of the surplus by giving a greater or a less importance to one or other of the factors. The application of machinery and steam-power is, of course, a most familiar example of a substitution of capital for labour in the production of a given quantity of many classes of

goods. But, as we have seen, the Law of Substitution has countless applications; new materials, new sources of supply of old materials, the opening of new fields of cheap labour, the training of large quantities of skilled labour, new processes or methods of industrial organisation, — all these familiar movements change the balance of power in bargaining among the different classes of owners of capital and labour-power who contribute to the production of a commodity, and so affect the distribution of the surplus.

§ 18. We may briefly sum up our reasoning as follows: Distribution consists in, or is conducted by, the process of fixing market-prices, the price of goods in the various stages of production, and the price of the use of the various forms of land, capital, and labour, which are serviceable in production. The sales of goods, of land-use, capital-use, or labour-power in the various markets, are conducted by a process of bargains which does not even tend to an equal division between each pair of bargainers of the gain of the bargaining, being determined in part by the superior economic strength or cunning of the marginal buyer or seller, in part by the differential estimates of the several buyers or sellers as measured from the margin, which estimates are themselves referable to a complex of unequal needs and economic opportunities in the various bargainers on either side.

In a very large proportion of these bargains one side is notoriously the stronger, forcing a sale upon conditions which give to its members almost the whole gain of the bargain, leaving to the weaker only a minimum inducement. So far from competition being free, it is fettered and impeded everywhere by the growth of innumerable forms and degrees of monopolies and forced gains. The theory that the enlightened self-interest of producers keeps down normal prices to the bare expenses of production, and that in consequence the whole gain of modern industrial improvements filters down to the community in their capacity of consumers, is seen to be quite unwarranted. Indeed, the whole notion of the consumer as residuary legatee is as groundless in theory as in practice. There exists no such fourth party in the working of distribution : the various owners of land, capital, and labour take each according to his strength. Thus emerges the true surplus value, derived not from some vague, unintelligible idea of tyranny, but from the various hindrances to perfect equality of bargaining-power in the owners of the various factors of production and the consequent establishment of different forms and pressures of economic force.

The recognition of this force explains the opposing theories and policies of economics. For the imperfection of equality of competition may be met and overcome by securing equality of economic opportunity for individuals. This is the idea of *laissez-faire* economists, though they have commonly, or perhaps universally, failed to provide or even to advocate equality of opportunity for obtaining possession or 'use of land and capital. Or else, recognising the difficulty or the impossibility of maintaining perfect equality in all departments of economic activity by the free play of individual interests, we may allow such inequality to issue in "forced gains," and afterward attempt to redress this inequality by taxation. If this method of redress prove too difficult or too uncertain, economic progress will demand the substitution of a public monopoly for those private monopolies which inequality of economic opportunity has founded, and to which inequality of bargaining assigns "forced gains."